CATTLEMEN & GHOSTS
OF THE HIGH PLAINS

Published in Australia

This book was designed and produced by
H. H. Stephenson at the Graphic Workshop,
Graphic Books, 14 Railway Avenue, Armadale, Victoria, 3143

NATIONAL LIBRARY OF AUSTRALIA

Index.

Bibliography
ISBN 0 949847 00 3

1. Cattle - Victoria - Mountain Grazing - History
2. Mountain Huts - Victoria - History
1. Title

994.5

CATTLEMEN & HUTS
OF THE HIGH PLAINS

WITH 326 ILLUSTRATIONS

and 34 MAPS & DIAGRAMS

HARRY STEPHENSON

BIBLIOGRAPHY

A Colonial Doctor and His Town - *Joan Gillison*
Across the Hills - *H. H. Stephenson (unpublished)*
Alps at the Crossroads - *Dick Johnson*
Among the Mountains of Gippsland - *John Wilson*
Australia's Alps - *Elyne Mitchell*
Bogong Jack - *Eric Harding*
Bushwalking in Victorian Ranges - *F.W.Halls*
Echoes from the Mountains - *A.M.Pearson*
Final Recommendations, Alpine Area - *Land Conservation Council , Victoria*
First Settlement of the Upper Murray - *Dr Arthur Andrews*
Grazing the High Country (thesis) - *Peter Bryan Cabena*
Is Emu on the Menu? - *Patrica Crooke*
Kiewa Valley - *Esther Temple*
Letters from Victorian Pioneers - *Sir Joseph LaTrobe*
Memoirs of a Stockman - *Harry H. Peck*
Mitta Mitta - *S.A.Colquhoun*
Official History of Avon Shire - *John Wilson*
Pastoral Pioneers of Port Phillip - *R. V.Bills and A.S.Kenyon*
Peaks and Plateaux - *H. H. Stephenson (unpublished)*
Pioneers of the Omeo District - *Jane Vince Pendergast*
Recollections of Early Gippsland Goldfields - *Richard Mackay*
Recollections of a Victorian Police Officer - *John Sadlier*
Report on the Alpine Study Area - *Land Consercation Council, Vic.*
Tales from the Australian Mountains - *Niall Brennan*
The Discovery of the Bogong High Plains - *State Electricity Commn. of Vic.*
The Dog's Grave - *Flora Johns and O.S.Green*
The Open Road - *Robert Henderson Croll*
The Ovens Valley - *Angus and Forster*
The Upper Murray - *Royal M. Miller*
The Victorian Alps - *Thorry Gunnersen*
Walhalla Heyday - *G. F.James and G. C.Lee*

PERIODICALS:

Parkwatch - *The National Parks Association*
Proceedings of the Royal Society of Victoria, Vol 75 Part 2
The Australian and New Zealand Ski Year Books - *Ski Clubs of Australasia*
The Bushwalker - *N.S.W. Federation of Bushwalking Clubs*
The Gap - *Schools of Bairnsdale Inspectorate*
The Melbourne Walker, Vols. 1 - 52 - *Melbourne Amateur Walking Club*
The Sydney Bushwalkers Annual - *Sydney Bushwalkers*
The Victorian Historical Magazine - Vols 1911 - 1980 - *The Royal Historical
        Society of Victoria*
The Victorian Ski Year Book - *Ski Club of Victoria*
Schuss - *Ski Club of Victoria*
Voice of the Mountains, Vols. 1 - 6 *Mountain District Cattlemen's
        Association of Victoria*
Walk, Vols. 1 - 31 - *Melbourne Bushwalkers*

PAPERS:

Collected Papers - *Alan Wilson*
Handwritten Diaries of Patrick Coady Buckley, 1844 - 1876 (2 vols.) -
        Patrick Coady Buckley

NEWSPAPERS:

Age (Melbourne), *Bairnsdale Advertiser* (Bairnsdale), *Bulletin* (Sydney),
Argus (Melbourne), *Alpine Observer* (Bright), *Border Morning Mail* (Albury),
Courier (Corryong), *Courier* (Mansfield), *Constitution and Ovens Mining
Intelligence 1857* (Beechworth), *Herald* (Melbourne), *Leader* (Melbourne),
Ovens and Murray Advertiser (Beechworth), *Spectator* (Maffra),
Spectator (Omeo), *Times* (Myrtleford), *Weekly Times* (Melbourne).

CONTENTS

W.F. "Bill" WATERS
Doyen Bushwalker

THIS BOOK IS DEDICATED TO

BILL WATERS
who showed the way

THE MATES
who came with me

and

THE CATTLEMEN
we met along the track

ALAN

ALBERT

EDDIE

FRANK

HARRY

ROY

ILLUSTRATIONS

DIAGRAMS, SKETCHES, MAPS

FRONTISPIECE

The colour photograph used for the dust jacket and the double frontispiece was kindly supplied by Jack Lovick, who appears on the left of the group. The photograph was taken between The Bluff and Magdala, with Mt Buller in right background.

The snowplains, wildflowers, cattle, cattlemen and mountain scene across the Howqua Valley depicts near perfection in the Alpine region.

ENDPAPERS

The endpapers are two sections reproduced from a remarkable map compiled and drawn by James Stirling when travelling in north-eastern Victoria in the years 1856—60. Stirling, who was then Land Officer at Omeo, later became the Victorian State Government Geologist.

PREFACE

THE "WINDS OF CHANGE" have blown steadily across our mountain
regions, as indeed, they have across the plains and the cities of our
community. The pioneers, cattlemen, explorers, and in many instances, they
were three-in-one, no longer drive their herds from the Monaro across the
indescribably rugged route that took them to Suggan Buggan and the Plains
of Omeo. No longer do they set out with bullock teams, stout waggons and
even stouter hearts on the annual pilgrimage to Port Albert, or Mossiface, or
Twofold Bay, to load and transport home a whole year's provisions. And,
no longer, hopefully, will they be obliged to boil down their prime beasts,
pack the tallow in bags made from the hides of the animals, and sell it for a
mere pittance because the meat market has failed - a heartbreaking reward
for a year's toil.

The bullock teams have given way to modern transport, no longer will the
modern counterparts of "Bung" Harris drove a thousand head from
Queensland across the great divide to Bairnsdale. The pack-horse is now far
less common a sight that a four-wheel drive and the roads that have spider-
webbed across the ranges have provided access to the remotest corners
of what, even in our time, was close to a primordial wilderness, frequented
only by a small number of mountain cattlemen in Spring and Autumn, by an
even smaller number of strong-backed bushwalkers in Summer, and was held
in the icy grip of a mantle of snow throughout the Winter.

The scene has changed, but for the fortunate ones, now few in number,
the memory of the mountain scene and the charisma remains. The wonder-
land could be measured vertically from the magical 4,000 feet mark, that
arbitrary contour line, which, having climbed through the forested slopes
of mountain ash and woollybutt, we reached to enter the zone of snowgums
and flower-bedecked snowplains from which our highest peaks rose to
above 6,ooo feet. Not a great height by world standards, but as Frank
Smythe once wrote, *"The hills of home may be low in stature, but they
reach very nearly to Heaven".* Here, was isolation, undisturbed even by the
mountain cattle which found a place in the total scene, and the cattlemen's
huts, scattered at strategic points across the High Plains.

The scenery, in the main, remains, a little scarred by the ravages of fire, the voracious appetites of the timber-getters, and the organised vandalism that accompanies the creation of ski-villages above the snow-line. Mercifully these intrusions have left much as it was. The cattlemen's huts that we knew however, have largely disappeared, many having succumbed, as we all must, to old age, others consumed by fires, sometimes carelessly and on occasions, regrettably, deliberately lit. Many have been replaced, but the galvanized iron sheds of today are a poor visual substitute for the timber huts with shingle or bark roofs that were once constructed from the most suitable natural materials that were available close at hand.

Nobody can determine just how many huts existed throughout the alpine regions and, indeed, it is sometimes difficuly to determine how many huts have occupied a single site. The author has endeavoured to reproduce in the following pages as many of these old mountain cattlemen's shelters as possible, in some instances illustrating the same hut in various stages of its lifetime. Regrettably, no perfect set of photographs is available and the reproductions from newspapers, magazines, faded snapshots copied from treasured family albums, often copies, and sometimes copies of copies are the best that were available.

No colour photographs of the earliest huts exist, for the simple reason that colour roll film was not marketed in Australia even as recently as the mid 1930s. Alan Wilson was probably the first bushwalker to use colour in the alps, when in the winter of 1936, he 'acquired' a single spool of 35mm 'Dufaycolor' and over a period of 15 days wound and re-wound it into his 'Leica', interchanging with black and white and obtained 32 colour shots of the mountains under snow, between Wellington and Howitt. This is a treasured set and it would require more persuasive powers than I possess to obtain the set for copying or reproduction!

So, all illustrations in this volume are in black and white and if the quality of some is poor, consider that the originals available to the platemaker were of like quality.

In depicting the mountain huts, it would be inappropriate not to record the pioneer cattlemen and their families and to briefly describe the country over which their cattle grazed. However, no attempt has been made to produce a directory of all who participated in mountain grazing and little mention has been made of the 'newcomers' who have entered the scene in the last forty years. It has been deemed sufficient to trace the history of mountain grazing in our alps from the beginning 145 years ago and to recall a number of cattlemen who were representative of the industry in all of the areas in which cattle grazed, many of the families having had a continuing association with their mountain runs for more than a century.

A list of acknowledgments is not included, for the number of people who have assisted me makes a formidable list, and I have no wish to embark on a name-dropping exercise. These people have, I believe, been thanked along the way.

The "Winds of Change" are still blowing across the mountains and they carry a chill that was not present before. The winds are fanned by forces striving to remove the cattle from the lush snowplains and it would be presumptious for me to express an opinion on the validity of their case. A bushwalker is, after all, only an observer, who passes briefly across the mountain scene. And it may well be, that I was a poor observer. The cattlemen I met were friendly people and for this reason alone, I would be sorry to see them go, but the decision should be left to experts, of whom, I believe, there are all too few.

Harry Stephenson
23rd February, 1980

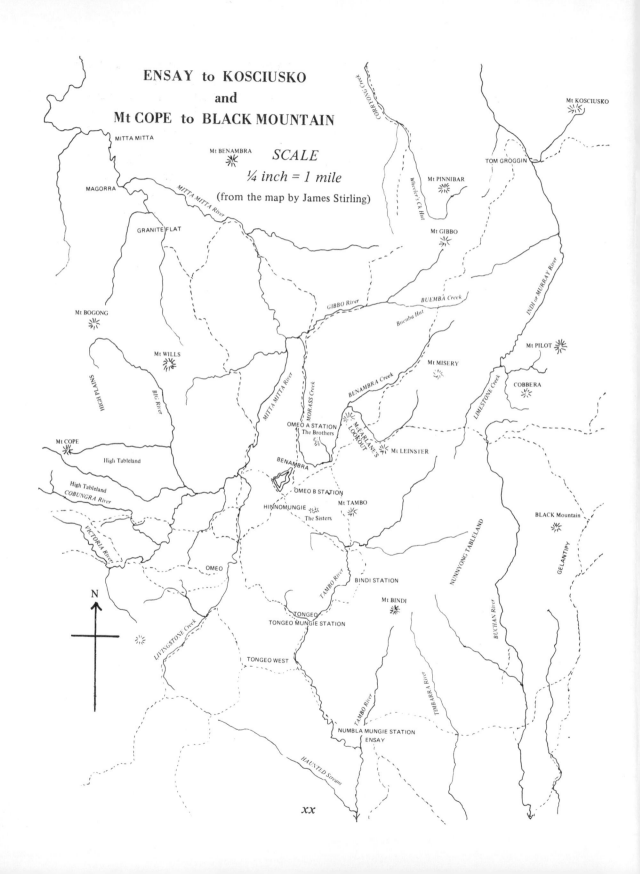

ENSAY to KOSCIUSKO
and
Mt COPE to BLACK MOUNTAIN

Mt BENAMBRA

SCALE
¼ inch = 1 mile
(from the map by James Stirling)

MITTA MITTA

MAGORRA

GRANITE FLAT

MITTA MITTA River

Mt KOSCIUSKO

CORRYONG Creek

Wheeler's Ck Hut

TOM GROGGIN

Mt PINNIBAR

Mt GIBBO

INDI or MURRAY River

Mt BOGONG

GIBBO River

BUEMBA Creek

Buemba Hut

Mt WILLS

HIGH PLAINS

Big River

MITTA MITTA River

MORASS Creek

BENAMBRA Creek

Mt MISERY

Mt PILOT

LIMESTONE Creek

COBBERA

OMEO A STATION
The Brothers

Mt COPE

High Tableland

McFARLANE'S LOOKOUT

Mt LEINSTER

BENAMBRA

High Tableland
COBUNGRA River

OMEO B STATION

HINNOMUNGIE
The Sisters

Mt TAMBO

BLACK Mountain

NUNNYONG TABLELAND

VICTORIA River

GELANTIPY

BUCHAN River

OMEO

BINDI STATION

TAMBO River

Mt BINDI

N

LIVINGSTONE Creek

TONGEO
TONGEO MUNGIE STATION

TONGEO WEST

TAMBO River

TIMBARRA River

NUMBLA MUNGIE STATION
ENSAY

HAUNTED Stream

xx

To the Omeo Plains

Angus McMillan

*T*HE SETTLEMENT OF THE BENAMBRA AREA, known originally as Omeo Plains, commenced about 1834 when cattlemen from the Monaro district in New South Wales began exploring the mountainous country to the south, taking cattle with them as they searched for new pastures.

THE PIONEERS

James Macfarlane was established on a run at Macfarlane Flat, about one mile on the Victorian side of the border in 1835 and while historians claim that Charles Hotson Ebden was the first man responsible for driving cattle into the north east of Victoria, when he sent his stockmen with a mob across the Murray near Albury to form the Bonegilla station in October 1835, it is claimed that Macfarlane's entry may have been as early as 1834.

James Macfarlane, the first to this part of the state played an important part in the opening of the Omeo district. He is described as an overlander but little is known of him prior to his arrival at Goulburn, N.S.W. and his subsequent depasturing of cattle on the Monaro, before moving stock to Macfarlane's Flat and taking up Omeo B (Mt Pleasant Station), and in later years Tongeo Mungie, Bindi and Tom Groggin. Although holder of these runs, Macfarlane never lived on the properties, but kept managers there, amongst whom were John Higgins (known also as Sheean), Matthew MacAllister and Bill Wallace. He ran upwards of 5000 cattle at Mt Pleasant, he had two stockyards of six acres each, a cow paddock enclosed by a nine mile long post and rail fence, and an extensive bull paddock similarly enclosed.

Macfarlane spent the later years of his life in Heyfield, where he died in 1860 after disposing of his Omeo properties to De Graves in 1859.

Edmund Buckley (b.1782 d.1859), travelling alone and probably without cattle, is believed to have penetrated as far as Tongio and Ensay in 1835,

1

while *George Mackillop* and *Livingstone* set out, also in 1835 to seek a land route to Port Phillip Bay. They were joined by *James Macfarlane* of Macfarlane's Flat. The three reached Omeo Plains, named them Strathdownie and from here Macfarlane returned home, leaving Mackillop and Livingstone to continue their journey. Dense scrub around the Livingstone defeated their endeavours and they also returned home. Later, in 1836, Mackillop reached Melbourne as an overlander and took up the Yarra Yarra run. Livingstone, after holding the Livingstone Creek run briefly in 1835 moved on to occupy the Tarcomb run near Longwood.

A few months previously, Lhotsky, after discovering Mt Kosciusko — he preceeded Strezlecki — on his return journey had received hospitality at all the Monaro Stations on his route and had given them all a fair idea of the grazing potential of the country he had visited.

In 1836, *John Pendergast, John Hyland* (or Ryland), *Edmund Buckley* and *James Macfarlane* journeyed as far as Leinster. Macfarlane, feigning illness, returned home, to quickly bring back a large mob of cattle to graze at Strathdownie.

He selected for his homestead a spot on the creek near Mt Pleasant, sheltered from the north by the picturesque Brothers Mountains.

Pendergast, Hyland and Edmund Buckley explored further before returning to Moonbah and the Monaro. Buckley then drove a mob back to Beloka, at that time known as Benambra and also began to graze the Leinster Plains which he named the Benambra Run. None of his holdings were ever registered as leaseholds. In 1837 three *Pendergast brothers,* John, Thomas and William took up the lease for the Homeo run (Omeo A) and John and Thomas brought cattle to the Leinster flats and part of Strathdownie. William, although a partner, never came to Omeo.

John Hyland shortly afterwards took up a run west of Morass Creek. (Kenyon refers to him as Thomas). *Patrick Coady Buckley* (b.1816 d.1872) a son of Edmund Buckley, arrived to settle on Tongeo Mungie, which he registered, and Ensay (Numla Mungee) which he did not register, in 1839 and his Tongeo Mungie cattle spilled over to graze Bindi. P.C.Buckley was a cattleman who had come through the Gap and settled on the banks of the Tambo River where he built a small hut of which all trace has disappeared. He was in the area when Angus McMillan and Strezlecki passed that way in 1839 and 1840 respectively. *Angus McMillan* and *Dr Alex Arbuckle*, acting for *Lachlan Macalister* took up the licence for Numla Mungee (Ensay) and also grazed Bindi. Buckley also held runs at Wulgulmerang (1851—59) and Gelantipy (1864—75) as well as Benambra (1862—75). He took up Coady Vale run, south of Sale, in 1843 and held it until his death in 1872.

All the early pioneers to travel to the Omeo plains came from the Monaro district in New South Wales. The route which they followed is still the main track between the two areas. It commenced at Cottage Creek and went through Moonbah, then via Ingebyra to the head of Jacob's Ladder to descend that steep mountain to the Jacob's River. It followed some very steep sides for six miles above the Snowy River to reach the Pinch River. To negotiate this stretch without the drays overturning, the top-side wheel of each dray had to be removed and was replaced with an iron-rimmed hub to thus enable the dray to maintain some degree of level, so steep were the slopes that were traversed. The Pinch River was followed up for a couple of miles and then a three thousand feet climb up a narrow spur led up the Nine Mile to Ingeegoodbee.

Macfarlane's Flat was reached in a further six miles. A drop down to cross the Berrima Creek, over a spur into Freestone Creek and up the very steep Freestone Hill, some nine miles in length to reach the Playground, a glorious park-like snowplain (if the weary travellers were in a mood to appreciate it), just below the 6,000 ft. Cobberas. Surely, all overlanders must have paused here, thankful that the worst of the climbing was over.

From the Playground, the way led down to Native Dog, through Native Cat, another short climb to the Limestone and then on through Meringo and Leinster to Benambra and the Omeo plains. Undoubtedly, a route for stout hearts.

Dr. A. W. Howitt, 1876

Limestone Creek, Murendal River.

John Rogers, writing in "Voice of the Mountains", says,

We should spare a thought for those early cattlemen who passed this way from the 1830s onwards. Spare a thought for McMillan toiling for days with his bullock dray climbing the Nine Mile from the Pinch River, and dragging for days in deep snow with a broken axle on his dray. Think of "Straighty" Pender's deeds in carrying water in a horse rug to men knocked up while taking a mob up the Nine Mile hill. Mrs William Woodhouse, giving birth to a child in the loneliness at the Pinch River. Then the death of her husband at Ingebyra, when she asked four passers by going to the Omeo Gold Rush in 1860, to bury him for her.

If we terminate the initial pioneering era at 1841 we must include *Edward Crooke,* the son of a successful English businessman. He arrived in Australia in 1838 after service in the Indian Army. He was involved in a disastrous pastoral venture in New South Wales, where his cattle and sheep were lost in a severe pleura epidemic, which was followed by a bank crash. On arrival at Omeo he acquired several large runs, Hyland's, the adjoining Livingstone Creek and Mitta Mitta flats. These he registered as Hinnomunjie in 1841. He also took over Edmund Buckley's previously unregistered Benambra run in the same year. Subsequently he added to his grass empire Holey Plains (1845) which he used as a holding area for horses from Hinnomunjie, then Tongeo Mungie (1853) and Bindi (1853).

After holding the various runs which totalled more than 100,000 acres, Edward Crooke relinquished the last of his leaseholds in 1859.

Of the above men who could rightly be called the pioneers of the Omeo district all but the Pendergasts, came, stayed a while and then moved away.

The Pendergasts, whose family name was originally Pendergrass, were Welshmen who migrated to Ireland from whence the first member of the family to arrive in Australia came. Two of his Australian born sons, John

Dr. A. W. Howitt, 1876

Mt. Tambo from the Omeo Station

the only son of his first marriage, and Tom, the eldest of three boys of the second marriage, had properties at Cottage Creek near Cooma and at Moonbah respectively, and then in 1837 they came to Omeo to found a dynasty. Today, more than 140 years later, a great many descendants of the original Pendergasts still live in the Omeo and surrounding district. The family history deserves a chapter to itself and is dealt with elsewhere in this book.

THE RUNS

Official records, which sometimes lagged behind, and occasionally were unaware of the actual occupiers of the early major leaseholds are as follows:

Omeo B (Omio) or Mt Pleasant Station, 51,200 acres; 1835—1859, James Macfarlane;

Omeo A (Homeo) or Three Brothers, 25,000 acres; January 1837, John Pendergast;

Tongeo Mungie, 36,500 acres; March 1839, P.Coady Buckley; 1845, John Curtis; 1846 James Macfarlane; 1849 Dr.D.E.Wilkie; 1853 Edward Crooke;

Numla Mungee (Ensay), 38,400 acres; 1839, Angus McMillan and Dr Alex Arbuckle for Lachlan Macalister; 1845, Arch Macleod;

Benambra, 2,650 acres; 1841, Edward Crooke; 1858 Wm.Pendergast and Tom Sheean (Edmund Buckley, first occupier in about 1836, never registered).

Hinnomunjie, 36,000 acres; 1841—1859 Edward Crooke. (Earlier occupied in part by Hyland)

Bindi, 12,800 acres (originally grazed by stock from Tongeo Mungie); 1845—6, Wm.Walker and Boyd Alexander Cunninghame; 1846—51, James Macfarlane.

Tom Groggin (Omeo Ranges), 20,000 acres; 1848—53, Wright and Tandy; 1858—60, James Macfarlane.

As shown in the accompanying map, a section of the Pastoral Runs of Port Phillip District 1835—1851, the above runs extended from the New South Wales border to Ensay.

OMEO A STATION

Omeo A was taken up by John Pendergast in 1837 and was never disposed of. It remained in his sons' hands until free selection reduced the area, but the original site has always been in the possession of the family.

OMEO B STATION

Omeo B was taken up by James Macfarlane in 1835, and was probably the first cattle station ever founded in Victoria. Only one other station could dispute the claim; that would be Bonegilla Station. It seems definite that both stations were occupied within a short time of each other. Macfarlane sold to C. and J. De Graves about 1860, and in 1879 they disposed of the property to Wilson, Dougharty, Burt and Company. The station became almost non-existant within a few years of the arrival of the free selectors, but the original pre-emptive right (640 acres) and homestead at Mt. Pleasant was eventually purchased by the late C.H.V. Pendergast and is still in the hands of the family.

BENAMBRA STATION

A small station of only 2560 acres, Benambra was first occupied by Edmund Buckley who drove a mob of cattle on to the Leinster plains in 1836 and named the area Benambra. It was first registered when Edward Crooke moved in, in 1841. Crooke moved several hundred head of cattle on to it, probably from Hinnomunjie, when he converted the latter run to horse-breeding. Crooke sold the run to Tom Sheean who held it for a short time. It passed through several hands before William and John Pendergast bought the land, stock and improvements in 1860. Descendants of William still own the property.

Thus, in due course, the three runs, Omeo A, Omeo B and Benambra were all acquired by the Pendergasts.

HINNOMUNJIE STATION

Edward Crooke founded Hinnomunjie in 1841 by taking over Hyland's Morass Creek run and the adjoining flats of Livingstone Creek and the Mitta Mitta River and stocking the area with 2000 head of cattle.

Crookes main interest, however, was in horses and with the backing of his father, a successful businessman in England, and his knowledge of remounts required by the Indian Army, he turned the Hinnomunjie run over to the breeding of thoroughbreds. He imported stallions from England and also a brood mare named Hinnoomunjie which were walked from Eden after landing there. This was the foundation of one of Australia's largest horse-breeding studs. As a holding property for the horses he shipped from Port Albert, Crooke bought Holey Plains (near Rosedale) in 1845 from the Curlewis brothers.

The homestead, Holey Plains

The discovery of gold in Omeo in 1851 was about 300 yards from the Hinnomunjie station huts. The discoverer was George Day, superintendent for Crooke. This discovery brought many miners into the district who caused much inconvenience for Crooke, who reported that they became resident on nearly every watercourse and kept cattle from the best pastures. They also seemed to consider it their privilege to help themselves to meat and anything else they could lay their hands on. For some years there was no police protection and little law and order. Together with the transport difficulties, it was understandable that Crooke sold his interests in the Omeo district.

After holding the various runs which totalled more that 100,000 acres, Edward Crooke relinquished the last of his leaseholds in 1859.

Hinnomunjie continued as a cattle station with Matthew Hervey in occupation for 1859-1867, after which time it passed into the hands of William, and later Charles and John Degraves.

Mrs Jane Vince Pendergast describes the arrival of selectors at Hinnomunjie in 1875:

When the mountains near Bruthen were reached, the most difficult part of the journey began.

There were no roads, only bush tracks which went up one mountain and came down again on the other side to the foot of the next ridge. In the intervening gully there was generally a stream to be crossed.

At times the track was so tortuous that the same creek had to be crossed and recrossed over and over again. Mr. Weir recalls that, when he came to Omeo with his parents, they had to cross Navigation Creek seventeen times.

During ascents and descents of the mountains, wheels had to be firmly chocked in position, while the horses and bullocks rested. Often on the downward trip branches of trees were dragged behind to act as extra brakes.

McMillan's trail was followed by these hardy selectors. It led from Bruthen over Little Dick, crossed the river at Tambo Crossing, went over Fainting Range and Reedy Flat to Swift's Creek, then up the long steep spurs of the Tongio Gap, and over the tops of the Alps to Omeo, then over McMillan's Look-out and down Sugarloaf to the Omeo Plains.

At Hinnomunjie the selectors pitched their tents on the Mitta side of the ridge, about three hundred yards from a spring, where later a well was put down by Mr. Sloan.

The first undertaking was to hunt out bark for a hut, but, during this quest, they found a saw pit on the side of the Sisters' mountains. The man who had made the pit had been unable to manage it, so Mr. Weir, who had been a sawyer in Edinburgh, was able to make good use of it. Until a temporary hut could be built, Weirs lived under the wagon tilt placed on the ground.

Palings were bought from Mr. Alty, and carried there in half wagon loads, from the Lazarene at the head of Wilson's creek, to his selection.

Here he erected a two roomed hut, 25 ft. by 10 ft. with walls 8 ft. high with a roof made of woollybutt bark. The chimney was a wooden frame filled with stones and plastering; with a paling top. This served well and did not catch fire. Iron camp oven, kettles and saucepans were used for cooking.

Shortly after the hut was built, a shed was made, where the boys slept. The quartering was sawn, and the boards were palings five feet long. Mr. Weir cut timber for W. Spencer and Paddy Whyte. He also helped to build huts for other settlers, before he built his own new home of sawn timber.

Later on he bought an engine and saw mill, setting it up along Hop creek in Murphy's Forest. There he sawed timber for many homes, including 'Forestside', 'Pender's Court', and for Charlie Huggins, the Gill's three homes and many others.

Mr. Weir also owned a bullock team, which was used for hauling logs, fencing etc. The next move was to obtain some sheep. With Mr. Jeffrey, he went across the mountains to Bindi, where Wilson and Dockerty had a big sheep run.

They bought comeback sheep at four shillings per head. Jeffrey took 300 and Mr. Weir obtained 250 for himself and 250 each for Jim Spencer and his son Edwin who had come with him to the Plains.

BINDI STATION

Bindi station, not far from Omeo, is perhaps one of the most distinguished properties of Gippsland. Although now much smaller than in the days when the land was first settled (then 12,800 acres), the property is still renowned for its leadership in the pastoral world.

The property homestead is situated on an arm of the Tambo River formed by the Bindi Creek, and both the homestead and the building around it are very old, dating back to the Omeo gold era of the late 1850s and 1860s.

The earliest buildings date from 1850, the main homestead being of mountain ash, built around 1880. A storehouse of the same period was

Old stone building,
Bindi Station

built from woollybutt slabs brought from Mt Nunniong. Old stone buildings (now stables) have granite walls and hand-made bricks with the inside walls lined with plaster.

Patrick Coady Buckley was the first settler at Bindi but the first registered holders were William Walker and Boyd Alexander Cunninghame in 1845.

James Macfarlane took over both Bindi and Tongeo-Mungie in 1846, selling the latter to D.F.Wilkie in 1849 and Bindi to the same man in 1851. At this time Bindi was one of the largest cattle stations in Victoria. Edward Crooke took over Bindi in 1853 and held it in conjunction with Tongeo-Mungie. It was at this time that the gold rushes began in Omeo and the surrounding areas and Bindi quickly became prosperous. It continued as an important supply centre for Omeo till the early 1880s when selectors had broken up the run.

Thus the inevitable law of the eternal fitness of things went on. The squatters who had played an important part as pioneers of the country found themselves driven back by the march of civilisation and progress.

A reporter for the Omeo Telegraph, writing in 1884, described Bindi as follows: "Of all the charming bits of scenery in the district, Bindi is par excellence - the best. Surrounded by an ampitheatre of hills, whose rugged heights fade into purple hue, the clear, park-like, undulating land, with just sufficient patches of honeysuckle to redeem the aspects from bareness, presents a scene that would gladden the heart."

In 1859 it was sold to Matthew Hervey. In 1865 the Hon.William Degraves became the registered owner. He transferred the property to Chas. Degraves in 1869. Chas.Degraves sold to W.Wilson and J.G.Dougarty and W.Graham Rhind in 1877.

In 1880 W. Wilson and J. G. Dougharty purchased Mr Rhind's interest. Wilson and Dougharty held the place until 1886, when Edmund Phillip Maberlt Margetts took over the property and stock.

The Margetts family carried on the station until about 1913, when Sir Edward Mitchell and Mr.Duke Armit purchased the property and it is still in the possession of Armit's son John.

Bindi had been badly affected by erosion, mainly caused by the rabbit plague of 1900–1920, but under the present owner's management, is fast re-establishing a good cover of grass. The original Bindi Station took in the whole of the Tambo watershed north of Tongeo Station.

TONGEO MUNGIE STATION

Tongeo-Mungie Station was originally held by P.Cody Buckley from 1839–1845, who sold to John Curtis in 1845. James Macfarlane purchased the property in 1846. Dr.Wilkie took over in 1849, and Edward Crooke, of Holey Plains, bought the property in 1853, selling it to Matthew Hervey in 1859. The Hon.Wm.Degraves became the owner in 1867, and in 1869 Chas. and John Degraves took possession. They disposed of the property to Messrs. Wilson and Dougharty and Coy. in 1877. In 1880 it was held by Wilson and Dougharty.

BINDI STATION
Perhaps it doesn't comply with this century's building regulations, but it had a flower garden, curtains at the windows, a wide chimney for the big log fires needed to warm the house in winter and the bark roof well anchored against winter gales, provided excellent insulation. It was undoubtedly a cosy 'Home Sweet Home' for this early Victorian family. The log house was at Bindi in the Station's early days.

NUMLA MUNGEE STATION

The Numla Mungee Station was established in the Tambo River valley on the south side of the Great Australian Divide. The property is generally understood to have included the whole of the Tambo River watershed south and east of Tongio-Mungie to where the river cuts through the Fainting and Angora Ranges. The definition of the boundaries was at one time the subject of a law case resulting in the cancellation of the Chillington station license as an infringement of the Ensay lease.

Lachlan Macalister, Scots born soldier and pioneer, was the proprietor of a station at Picton NSW when another young scot Angus McMillan arrived in January 1838 with letters of introduction. Drought in 1838–9 led to McMillan being sent off to find new pastures in the then unsettled eastern half of Victoria:

Taking with him the chief of the Monaro tribe, Jimmie Gibber, he rode south on 28th May 1839. Five days later he had crossed the Snowy River and was in eastern Victoria; from a mountain in the Buchan district that he

ENSAY STATION
The Shearing Shed, from a painting by John Mather, 1889.

named McLeod (now Haystack) he obtained a view of the sea and of promising country to the south-west. However, his companion was afraid to venture farther into the territory of the Varrigal blacks, and he thought it wise to go west-by-north to an outstation near the site of Omeo. He returned and reported progress to Macalister, who encouraged him to make another attempt.

A few months later McMillan formed a cattle station for Macalister on the Tambo near Ensay, and in January 1840, using this as a base, he set out down the Tambo with a party of five (including two aborigines), and after a most difficult journey reached the lowlands near the coast.

McMillan opened up the way to the coast and from Corner Inlet exported cattle to Tasmania. He himself settled at Bushy Park near Stratford. The first mentioned property near Ensay had been taken up by Angus McMillan and Dr.Arbuckle on behalf of Captain Lachlan McAlister and Thomas McAlister and called Numla Mungee. In spite of such an auspicious beginning the run was abandoned in 1842.

Arbuckle is credited as being the first man to grow potatoes in the Omeo area. This could be so. Arbuckle built a hut for himself on the Tambo River and acted as boundary rider on the border of Numla Mungee and Tongio. The site of the hut is known as Doctor's Flat.

The name of the station was changed to Ensay in 1844 when John Campbell Macleod squatted on the property, and was granted legal possession in 1845. Macleod was accompanied by his brother Norman Roderick Macleod and his father Archibald Macleod. In 1847 and later mortgages over the property were held by various people and in April 1873

11

The Ensay Shearing Shed, 1980.

complete control was obtained by J.S.Horsfall with the brothers Colin Alexander McKenzie and Malcolm McKenzie with Colin as the resident and managing partner.   Colin McKenzie also held a lease for the entire Bogong High Plains station of some 90,000 acres and this became the property of the Ensay Station.   In 1877 control passed to the brothers John and Henry Campbell, the Bogong run was cut up into smaller lots of which Ensay retained 6,000 acres in Pretty Valley and in 1883 the Campbells sold out to Thomas Macknight Hamilton. Hamilton held in addition to Ensay (Numla Mungie), the Bogong High Plains (6,000 acres) and Tongio Mungie and Cassilis Stations.

Following the death of T.M.Hamilton in 1907 the management of Ensay was carried on by his son James Irvine Hamilton on behalf of the family.

In 1914 the Hamiltons sold Ensay Station to Colin Christian McCulloch, Askin Morrison Foster and John Dowbiggin Foster, the Fosters being descendants of John Foster of Glenfalloch, Boisdale, Dargo and Castleburn.

When sold Ensay comprised 16,500 acres freehold and leaseholds in Cassilis and South Nunnyong, including the Tombarra River area extending south to near Bruthen.

In 1920 Ensay was acquired by the Government for Returned Soldier Settlement following which Thomas Ian Hamilton (a brother of James I. Hamilton), acquired the homestead block and he, in partnership with James Lilburn Commins retained the Nunnyong run.   Thomas Ian Hamilton died about 1935 and his widow retained Ensay until about 1950 when she sold it and retired to Metung.

From 1935 onwards James L. Commins alone, retained Nunniyong run. Since his death in 1950, his sons James A. Commins and Charles Commins have been grazing the Nunnyong run in partnership.

12

"OMEO"

There's a wild charm in the mountains that is not met with elsewhere,
    Free as the vagrant winds, and pure as snow,
There are songs in crystal fountains, bubbling in the hills up there,
    That echo in the name of 'Omeo'.
There's a lure in snow fed waters, rippling by sweet Inisfail,
    With Cobungra River singing on it's way;
While Fitzgeralds sons and daughters, in the groves of Shannon Vale,
    Bring memories thronging of a bygone day.

There's the melodies of Ireland, there's minstrelsy up there,
    Like the blackbirds singing in the "Braes o Marr",
From the mountains and the mineland from Limerick to Kildare,
    In the lilting Celtic names — and here they are,
MacNamara, Pender, Cusac, Neddy Gray, and Mick McGrath,
    Kelly, Shelley, Carney, Condon, and Minogue,
They are filled with Irish music while the lilt in Paddy Maher,
    Is dancing to the blarney and the brogues.

There are voices ever calling, in the bushbirds carefree trills,
    And I'm going back up there for old times sake,
Just to watch the snow flakes falling, on the grand Benambra Hills,
    And to see the wildfowl swimming in the Lake.
I want to see the cattle stringing, from the topmost height,
    Their white horns gleaming in the morning sun;
I want to hear the hoofbeats ringing, through the bush at night,
    From brumby mobs on some lone mountain run.

Tis good to live life over, as we near the journeys end,
    When we have roamed the world by many ways;
When a welcome greets the rover, in the handclasp of a friend,
    The friend we knew, back in the golden days,
To recall the years long vanished, with the mingled joys and pain,
    To revel in the old tales newly told;
With the prodigals long banished, who wander back again,
    To live in dreams the halcyon days of old.

                        Wm. Jas. Wye.

Pendergasts of Omeo

*T*HE FIRST PENDERGAST to arrive in Australia from Ireland, after the family had originally emigrated from Wales, had four sons - John, the eldest and Thomas, by his first wife, and William and James, the youngest, born to his second wife. The boys were born at Wollombi, where the pioneer father had settled.

The sons looked to the land for a living. John had a farm at Cottage Creek near Cooma, and a property at Campbelltown. Tom bought a farm at Lower Moonbah and James leased a property near the Moonbah river, and later sold it to Thomas.

After exploring the Omeo area in 1836 with John Hyland, Edmund Buckley and James Macfarlane, John returned in January 1837, with his brother Thomas, bringing 300 Shorthorn cattle. In partnership with brother William, who never visited the area, they took up the Homeo (later Omeo A) run of 25,000 acres on Lake Omeo. The run consisted mainly of plains and tablelands to the north and east of Morass Creek. They built a slab hut at the foot of three mountains, the Three Brothers, near the site of present day "Penders' Court".

For some years the two brothers worked their grazing properties. The first years were hard; they had to pack in their supplies from Eden. As the journey was long and strenuous, only bare necessities of life were packed in.

The journey to Eden was only negotiable to bullock drays part of the way, and only the most essential products were carried. The track travelled was —

Eden to Bombala	52 miles
Bombala to Little Plains	13 ”
Little Plains to Delegate	12 ”
Delegate to Tubbut	17 ”
Tubbut to Deddick	13 ”
Deddick to Snowy River	5 ”
Snowy River to Black Mountain	8 ”
Black Mountain to Bow Yard	13 ”
Bow Yard to Mt. Leinster	18 ”
Mt. Leinster to Omeo B	12 ”
Total distance	163 miles

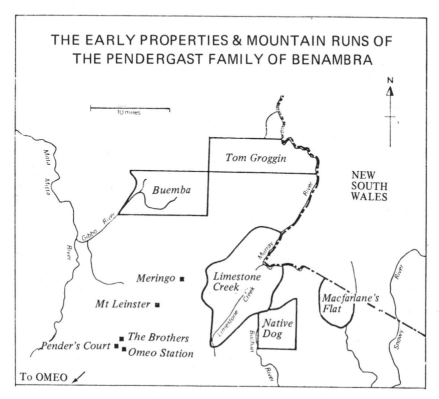

THE EARLY PROPERTIES & MOUNTAIN RUNS OF THE PENDERGAST FAMILY OF BENAMBRA

10 miles

N

Tom Groggin

Buemba

NEW SOUTH WALES

Mitta Mitta River

Gibbo River

River

Murray

Meringo

Limestone Creek

Limestone Creek

Mt Leinster

Macfarlane's Flat

River

Native Dog

Pender's Court

The Brothers

Omeo Station

Buchan River

Snowy River

To OMEO

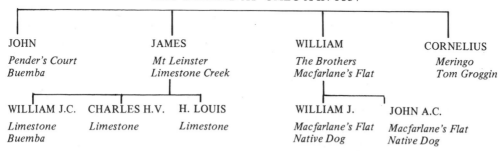

THE FOUR SONS OF JOHN PENDERGAST
WHO SETTLED AT OMEO A IN 1837

JOHN	JAMES	WILLIAM	CORNELIUS
Pender's Court	*Mt Leinster*	*The Brothers*	*Meringo*
Buemba	*Limestone Creek*	*Macfarlane's Flat*	*Tom Groggin*

WILLIAM J.C.	CHARLES H.V.	H. LOUIS		WILLIAM J.	JOHN A.C.
Limestone	*Limestone*	*Limestone*		*Macfarlane's Flat*	*Macfarlane's Flat*
Buemba				*Native Dog*	*Native Dog*

15

The original hut, at rear, was built by John and Tom Pendergast in 1837. Note the surviving bark roof.

The market for stock was extremely limited, their surplus fat cattle being sold to the boiling-sown works at Eden for about £2 per head.

They planted the first wheat in the district. This was only a small plot of about two acres. It was dug with a spade and the crop cut with a sickle, threshed with a flail, and cleaned in the wind. The grain was then ground by hand with a pestle and mortar. It was a lot of work but it saved long trips through the mountains to pack in flour. Their next crop was planted with a wooden plow drawn by two bullocks, and so year by year progress was made.

The first mob of fat cattle to be taken out was driven over the mountains to Sydney in 1883.

By this time, John's three elder sons, William, James and John, born at Campbelltown in 1835, 1837 and 1839 respectively had come to Omeo and they helped with the mob taken to Sydney. The Omeo property was given to these three sons by John senior in 1855.

John jun. made his home on the original site of Omeo A. He later named his homestead Pender's Court, as it is still called today. He married a Miss Parslow, of Cobungra, and reared a large family. The original property passed to the hands of his two daughters, Mary and Ada.

William made his home lower down the creek. He planted a number of poplar trees, and the property was given the name of "The Poplars". This property is still in the hands of his descendants.

James confined his attention to the Mt.Leinster, area and later married Mrs.Sheean, widow of Mr.Sheean, who was the late owner of Benambra Station. Later they settled with their family at Kimberley Park, Benambra.

Cornelius, William, John and James Pendergast, sons of John Pendergast who settled at Omeo A in 1837.

A severe winter in 1865 killed most of their cattle and James left to earn money by packing and catching and breaking wild horses. With the profits he earned James established a new herd and introduced Hereford bulls and Hereford cows, which could withstand the cold better than Shorthorns. Today, Herefords are the generally accepted breed throughout the High Plains in all parts of the Alpine Region.

A further setback was experienced when James Tyson, driving a herd from Queensland, introduced pleuro pneumonia to the district and almost all the Hereford cows were lost. Cornelius, a fourth brother arrived to settle at Meringo in 1869.

All the pioneer cattlemen who came to the Omeo district in the 1830s and 1840s held their leases for a period and eventually left the district. Only the Pendergasts stayed and they must be considered the pioneers of the Omeo-Benambra country. Before the end of the century more Pendergasts and their young families arrived from Campbelltown and settled nearby.

The new and old huts at Limestone Creek.   Left to right: Charles Pendergast, Cornelius Pendergast, Louis Pendergast, Surveyor, J.J. Pendergast and W.J.C.Pendergast.

Among them was Patrick and his son "Big Jack" who was renowned for his bushmanship. To bushwalkers of the 1920s and early 1930s "Big Jack was a popular figure. The late W.F. "Bill" Waters penned this tribute to him.

"Early in 1935, J.T.Pendergast, of Buloka (out back of Omeo), trapper, bushman, cattleman and guide, more familiarly known as "Big Jack", packed his "nap" and rode over the Great Divide on Life's last journey.

In the eighteen-thirties, stockmen from the Maneroo country, in New South Wales, on an exploratory journey, discovered the rich plains around Lake Omeo and, subsequently, drove mobs of cattle across to found a settlement where the Benambra district is now established.

One of these pioneer settlers was a Pendergast, and, to-day, numerous families of his descendants are living in the district. "Big Jack" was one of them and received the appellation "Big" from a custom in the district of adding a distinguishing nickname to those cousins all bearing the same Christian name. Thus, in addition to "Big Jack", there are "Little", "Black", "Omeo", and "Swampy" Jacks.

My first impressions of Jack, in 1922, were those of a kindly face and voice, a ready smile, and a twinkle of humour in his eyes, when his glance first fell on that party of sunburned, young, Collins-street bushmen, clad in khaki shorts, and full of excitement over their first acquaintance with pack-horses. Most ready to pack up, they were likely as not to put the pack-saddles on back to front, and I well remember some of Jack's witticisms at our expense. Incidentally, some of Jack's pack gear was an absorbing study of the important part that fencing wire, gleaned from the nearest source, may perform in holding ancient and modern in close contact, but be it said, I never knew him to have any untoward delays over gear.

He was particularly kind to his animals. Many of us are familiar with the perverse habits of pack-horses and the surprising reactions of the most amiable human, but, though I recall tense situations with a very angry Jack among the nags, abusing them in lurid terms, I never saw him ill-treat them, and, on arrival in camp, his first care was always for his team.

"Big Jack" Pendergast and his dog, January 1929.

On one occasion, when camped on the Ingegoodbe River, just over the New South Wales border, one of our horses became bogged and it took hours to pull it out. Jack was greatly affected by the animal's plight and almost overwhelmed by the time we had the horse on its hoofs.

At meals, he invariably saved portion of his food for old "Bill", his dog, despite assurances that the animal would be fed, and we grew to respect the custom as part of his code.

An excellent cook, he could sense the occasions when the food routine had become monotonous to the party, and, for a change, would cook dampers and pufftaloons that were culinary triumphs.

As a bushman, he had a marvellous knowledge of all the mountain country between Omeo and the Monaro, and had the bushman's prejudice against map and compass. He preferred to travel by ridge and watershed. Every track and spur and landmark seemed to be catalogued in his mind, and only once, and that in thick fog in the trackless Pinch River country, do I remember him puzzled. We camped; and from 7 p.m. he rode in the hills in black darkness, returning at 1 a.m. with the brief comment: "I know now where we are".

In 1924, "Big Jack" led a party to the falls below the Pilot. One of the climbers was seriously injured and Jack rode fifty miles through the night to Benambra for help.

As a companion in the bush, he was genial, reliable, and ready to help. By his death, the fraternity of walkers has lost a warm friend and a picturesque figure, whose presence seemed as essential to complete enjoyment as, say, good weather, camping gear, or the big hills.

Those border mountains will ever remind me of "Big Jack" and our friendship. They are almost everlasting, but one of the most romantic figures who rode their summits has passed."

By the early 1920s, James was the only surviving one of the brothers who came to Omeo in 1853. The following tribute, written by Ed. Alday, appeared in "The Gap" in 1922.

"James Pendergast, of Kimberly Park, Benambra, is the only remaining pioneer who originally came over the Murray from New South Wales. His father and mother were born on the Hawksbury River and Pendergast senior was one of those who followed the lure of the land and pushed right back. He had an interest in three stations at Monaro, but the wanderlust seized him and he came through the mountains about the same time as Macfarlane came through Ingeegoodbie. From the top of what is now Macfarlane's Lookout, he saw the place which is called Little Plain. He returned to Sydney and put in first claim for the land. In 1837, Pendergast took up the station known as "The Three Brothers".

James Pendergast was born at Campbelltown, 20 miles from Sydney, on October 8th 1837 - the year his father took up and named "The Three Brothers". He was one of a family of twelve; eight brothers and three sisters. In 1853, as a lad of sixteen, he made his first trip to Omeo Plains, coming over to help take a mob of fat cattle to Sydney. He spent six days in the mountains, so his first experience of the district was a rough one. In 1859, Pendergast senior gave his interests in the stations to his three sons - James, John and William. John settled down in what in known as "Penders Court"; William at Springvale, further down Morass Creek; James at Mount Leinster

Most of the country from the Tableland to the Limestone was held by the three brothers, but when the Berry Act came into force, the best of the land was selected by others. With the exception of eighteen months, which he spent at Lindenow, James Pendergast lived in the Omeo district. When it is remembered that the three brothers married and all had large families, it will be understood that there is no fear of the name dying out. You may imagine how bewildering it is to a new arrival in the district, for nearly every other person you meet is a Pendergast, or a relation of one.

PAINTER CREEK HUT

> After climbing out of a fairly difficult gorge, a sharp look-out for water
> was kept, and we were rewarded, at about 15 miles from our previous
> night's camp, by sighting (some two or three hundred yards down a
> gully) a tumble-down mustering hut, and what was more important, a
> good soak.
>
> W.R.WHITEHEAD 1936

*. . . from the Limestone Creek crossing follow the track down-stream
along the west bank for 2 miles to Painter's Creek (or Pendergasts)
Hut.   From here the Limestone Caves are downstream ¼ mile on the
East bank and the old homestead a further ¾ mile downstream.*

Their local names are very amusing to a stranger, but one soon comes to
understand how useful they are in sorting out the different ones.   There is
Long Will, Lightwood Bill, Weary Will, Big Jack, Little Jack, Pender Jack
and Young Jack.   There is Old Jim, Young Jim, Kimberly Jim, Jim, Black
Jim, and Courty Jim.   How names are to be found in the rising generation of
Penders, and how they are to be sorted out, is a mystery of the future.

When the original Pendergast, in 1837, took up a station on the farthest
limit, he hardly expected that half the population in a fairly settled district
would be the result.

When James Pendergast first came to the station the bush country was
fairly open, as there had been few bush fires, and no ringbarking (to cause

21

NUNNIONG HUT

Locked in the ranges, surrounded by high hills, the isolation of Nunniong is complete. The central stream of this snow plain down a steep incline at the plain's north-western end, to join a large branch of the Tambo that rises on Mt Bindi away to the south-west. It is upstream of this branch of the Tambo to the Nunniong Hut, eight miles from Bentley's Plain.

Across the plain runs an old fence, a little east of north, at the northern end of which are the remains of an old stockyard, and on a rise above the creek a stone paving and piles of chimney stones mark the site of an old dwelling. This area was selected many years ago and until recently was the property of the Boucher family of Bindi, from whom it was purchased by the Forests Commission.

RAY WHITFORD 1950

suckers) had taken place. Places which are now a wilderness and where it is almost impossible to ride through, were then fine open country not too thickly covered with large trees. In the early days, a two wheeled bullock dray was used to convey goods from one place to another.

When the side of a mountain too steep to go straight up, had to be climbed the wheel on the top side would be taken off and replaced by the spokeless nave, and thus they would go around the sides of the hill to the top. It is easily understood that where mountains are so steep, it mattered not how

MARENGO HUT
We were soon trudging up to the crest of the ridge which separates the
Marengo Creek and the Limestone Creek. Over this ridge and down
the other side, and before long we were walking through lovely
unspoiled river flats down the Limestone Creek.   In the afternoon we
came to an old hut. . .

D.A.GROSS 1951

strong the bullock team, only a light load could be taken; so it was soon
found that pack horses on such tracks could do the work much better.
James remembers that one bullock driver tried to take his dray back by a
short cut used by the pack-horses, but it was so steep and rough that the
dray remained there until bushfires destroyed it!

When a team started on a trip in those days, a bag or two of wheat, a
steel mill and a sieve were always part of the equipment. You were your
own miller and there were certain places on the route where you could fix
up your mill, grind your wheat and sieve out your bran. Then, with salt,
water and an old bag to mix it on, a damper could be made.

In his long experience of these parts, James says that 1865 was the worst
year of all. Not one calf was branded by him that year as he lost all his
breeding cows. From the Tableland to the Limestone only 37 calves were
branded.

23

James Pendergast

With such a bad year and such losses, it was necessary to look around for some other means of livelihood, so he took up packing between Omeo and Bairnsdale. Money could be made at it, and he got as much as £20 per ton for flour, but as soon as he left the horses in charge of others, his profits went. Since then, though there have been many bad and many good seasons high prices and very small prices for stock he managed to keep to the land, and make a living on it. The worst trip in his experience was with a team of pack-horses from Monaro, loaded with provisions for Mount Leinster. It snowed all the afternoon as they climbed the mountain, and was snowing hard when he and his mate pitched camp near the top.

It snowed all night, and the next morning showed from two to six feet of snow, and a twenty-six mile trip lay before them. It was soon found that the shod saddle-horses were worse than useless for riding, as great balls of snow gathered in the shoes, making it very hard for them to keep their feet, so they were turned loose with the pack-horses which were led by an old snow-battler. It was one continuous struggling, tumbling, plunging process, and never has he seen a more welcome sight than the lights of the homestead, as, tired to death, he stumbled up to the door.

James died, at the age of 87, in 1924.

BENTLEY'S HUT

Bentley's Plain is one of those delightfully open spaces that occur among the timbered spurs of those eastern mountains. Hedged in by the ranges and bordered by snow gums, its six acres of open grassland, shaped somewhat like a boomerang, lies at an elevation of nearly 4,000 ft., and is covered in winter by a mantle of snow. In summer it becomes almost wholly a garden and feeding cattle tread a carpet of wild flowers. Clumps of white and purple Alpine Daisies, beds of the Mountain Violet, patches of golden Everlastings, purple Hovea, and the pink of the Trigger Plant add pleasing splashes of colour to the view. On a still day the strong, sweet scent of small flowers among the grasses hangs in the air. Tiny creeks meander through the Plain and unite to feed the Timbarra River and to the north-west, overshadowing all, looms the bulk of Nugong, 4,700 ft. in height.
W.F."Bill"Waters 1933

Bentley's Plain was named in the 1860s for a cattle duffer who was in the habit of rustling cattle out on the Omeo Plains and driving them away into the mountains, to what destination no one could discover. Many years later a party of stockmen discovered on Bentley's Mount (Black Mountain) the site of some old cattle yards. Nose rings picked up there were identified as belonging to prize bulls rustled in the Omeo country years before, and the conclusion reached was that these were Bentley's duffing yards, at which he must have changed the brands of the stolen cattle and driven them over the Snowy River into the Monaro country for sale.

UPPER LIMESTONE CREEK HUT

Suggan Buggan & Black Mountain

IN THE REMOTE wild border country, a few miles from where the Snowy River flowing down from the Australian Alps, crosses the New South Wales — Victorian border, is the fertile valley of Suggan Buggan.

Encircled by rugged mountains, the valley was first settled by the O'Rourkes one hundred and forty years ago. They came from the Monaro and like the pioneers to the plains of Omeo, they travelled down to Jacob's Ladder and on to the Pinch River. Instead of turning west to Benambra, they continued south down the Snowy River for some miles, then climbed over the Monaro Gap to Suggan Buggan. From there they had to climb two thousand feet up an extremely rough spur to Black Mountain. They brought their families with them, the young children riding in baskets slung across the backs of the pack-horses.

In the wake of the explorer-settlers came the stock traffic and the track later became the main west Monaro—Gippsland stock route down which tens of thousands of cattle, sheep and horses were walked to be sold in Bairnsdale and beyond.

There would be no more rugged stock route anywhere than this track, with drovers being stranded for days between the Pinch and Jacobs rivers, or horses crippled when they lost their footing on the steep sides and rolled to the bottom. Many big mobs were to come down this route. "Bung" Harris brought a thousand head from the Gippsland border down through Black Mountain to Bairnsdale. He had four men helping, and thirty pack and spare horses. He lost no cattle and was on the road for 21 weeks.

Later at Willis the protectionist Victorian Government levied duty on cattle crossing the border. Hector McKenzie collected fees at Willis for a time, but later made Black Mountain the "paying-up" centre. He gathered a harvest of sovereigns when big mobs of up to thousands of head went into Victoria, the duty being as high as 30 shillings a head in the 'nineties. Hector married Christopher O'Rourke's daughter and built a new home and out-buildings in 1898.

A much used track was also established from Black Mountain through Rocky Plain to Native Dog and on to the Limestone and Benambra.   This track was used extensively by travelling stock and people going to and from the Omeo gold diggings.

The O'Rourkes were involved with Suggan Buggan, Wulgulmerang and Black Mountain Stations over a period of more than sixty years, the principal members of the family to hold properties being the brothers James and Christopher and their sons, Edward and Christopher jnr, and John and David jnr.

The condensed family tree below and chronological list of involvement with the various properties may be of interest.

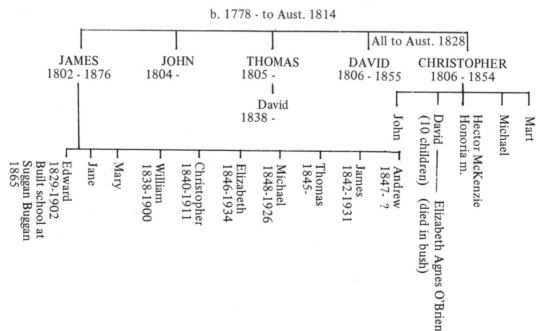

MICHAEL O'ROURKE m. JANE REYNOLDS

b. 1778 - to Aust. 1814

All to Aust. 1828

JAMES 1802 - 1876   JOHN 1804 -   THOMAS 1805 -   DAVID 1806 - 1855   CHRISTOPHER 1806 - 1854

David 1838 -

John   Andrew 1847 - ?   David —— Elizabeth Agnes O'Brien (10 children) (died in bush)   Honoria m. Hector McKenzie   Michael   Mart

Edward 1829-1902 Built school at Suggan Buggan 1865   Jane   Mary   William 1838-1900   Christopher 1840-1911   Elizabeth 1846-1934   Michael 1848-1926   Thomas 1845-   James 1842-1931

JAMES

1838 Suggan Buggan and Wulgulmerang
1840 Black Mountain
1845 Wulmulgerang
1852 Yarram

CHRISTOPHER

1838 Suggan Buggan and Wulgulmerang
1845 Black Mountain
1854 Died

DAVID

Lived at Wulgulmerang for some time.
1855 Died at Appin.

EDWARD

1848 Suggan Buggan (Forest Paddock) Managed Little River (Black Mountain)
1858 Suggan Buggan lease granted
1884 Benambra, but continued to run cattle on Suggan Buggan
1902 Died in Forest Paddock on Suggan Buggan (aged 73 years)

CHRISTOPHER Jnr.

1859 Wulgulmerang

JOHN

1845 Occupied Little River (Black Mountain)
1859 Little River (Black Mountain) lease granted.
1868 Wulgulmerang
1904 Retired from Wulgulmerang

DAVID Jnr.

Had home on Wulgulmerang until 1867
1867 Little River (Black Mountain)
1879 Bruthen

The O'Rourke's involvement in the three stations may be summarised as follows:

SUGGAN BUGGAN
(Jingalala Creek and Snowy River.)

1838 James, Christopher
1848 Edward (occupied)
1858—84 Edward (lease granted)
Continued to run cattle till death in 1902

Suggan Buggan was also known as Deddick, Mt Deddick or Tongimbooka and in the period 1842—1858 when the lease was granted to Edward O'Rourke, licensed holders of the property were 1842 Ben Boyd, 1848 Alexander Boyd Cunninghame, 1850 S.Browning and H. Kesterton, 1855 J.S.Hensleigh and 1856 Jas McGuffie.

BLACK MOUNTAIN

1840 James
1845 Christopher, John, Edward
1859—68 John (lease granted)
1867—79 David jnr.

WULGULMERANG
(11500 acres on Snowy River opposite Suggan Buggan,)

1838 James, Christopher
1845—52 James, David
1852 P.Coady Buckley
1859—65 Christopher snr, David jnr.
1868—1904 John

Between 1865 and John's later occupancy the property was held by Marshalls, Turnbill, Howden and P.C. Buckley for brief periods.

Little River Hut

THE O'ROURKES

In 1814 Michael O'Rourke, born in 1778 arrived from Tipperary in the sailing ship *Three Bees,* to become overseer of all properties owned by the Australian Agricultural Company. He settled at Appin, near Campbelltown. In 1828 his five Irish born sons followed their father to Australia. They were James (b.1802), John (b.1804), Thomas (b.1805), David (b.1806) and Christopher (b. 1806). Their ship was the "Morley".

JAMES

On arrival James engaged in farming pursuits and after marrying in 1832, he bought Maloon Station on the Murrumbidgee, later selling it to purchase two Monaro properties. In 1840 James sold his Monaro holdings and came to Black Mountain where he established his home. He built the first house in the district, situated on the river flat, a quarter of a mile south east of where the McKenzies were later to build their house on a rise.

Black Mountain had first been settled by Richard Brooks in 1834. He, however, found the country too difficult, and vacated.

James later bought Wulgulmerang and built another house there. When he was ready to move in there, in 1844, Christopher came down from Appin and took over the Black Mountain Station and the first homestead.

When the Wulgulmerang grazing lease was first granted it was specified that "the river should be one of the boundaries of the run." This referred actually to the Tooginbooka or Suggan Buggan River, but the settlers interpreted it as the Snowy, and Edward built his dwelling on land to which he had no official right!

The pine timber for the house was cut in the local "Sawpit Creek" from logs obtained in the immediate vicinity. In the Suggan Buggan—Deddick area one finds forests of native Murray Pine that belongs rightly to the inland and not the coastal side of the Dividing Range.

The old homestead weathered the elements until 1955 when one of the settlers of that time "cleaned up" the remains of it!

In 1851 tragedy struck when James' four year old son Andrew was burnt while standing in front of a fire, and died twenty hours later. James and his brother were away mustering at the time, which meant that their wives were alone at their respective homes, with the children. Eliza (James' wife) sent one of the children to Black Mountain with a message for Elizabeth (Christopher's wife). She came immediately, bringing her children with her. Together the sisters-in-law dug the grave and buried Andrew, while all the children stood around and said prayers. It was a terrible shock for James to return a week later and learn of the tragedy. He decided to leave Wulgulmerang and the property was sold to Patrick Coady Buckley. James bought two properties, Reedy Creek near Yarram and Bruthen Station. The family first lived in a slab and shingle house on the banks of Bruthen Creek.

In 1875 Eliza passed away and was buried across the creek from the site of the old slab home. James health failed rapidly and he died from pneumonia in 1876.

Edward O'Rourke

William O'Rourke

Christopher O'Rourke

Thomas O'Rourke

Michael O'Rourke

David O'Rourke

CHRISTOPHER

Christopher O'Rourke remained at Black Mountain from 1844 until his early death from pneumonia in 1854, at the age of 44 years. The Stone on his grave at Black Mountain was carved in Bairnsdale and figures were transposed to incorrectly read "death in 1844 at the age of 54 years".

DAVID

Michael O'Rourke's third son, David, came with Christopher to Black Mountain and then moved over to Wulgulmerang with James. After living at Wulgulmerang for some time he bought a property at Gelantipy. He died in 1855 at Appin.

EDWARD

Of the sons, Edward, then aged 19 years, started improvements to the 'Forest Paddock' on the Wulgulmerang plateau (although not in the Suggan Buggan valley it was part of the Suggan Buggan run) in 1848.

Following Christopher's death, James eldest son Edward and his brother Christopher jnr. went to manage Black Mountain until Christopher snr's sons were able to carry on. Edward remained until 1858, when he bought Suggan Buggan from McGuffie.

Although the O'Rourkes had been at Suggan Buggan for brief periods, the first license was issued to William Woodhouse in April 1843, although he had been there since the previous year. Then followed Ben Boyd, William Boyd, Kesterton and McGuffie for brief periods before Edward took over. It was Edward, who in 1865, built the Suggan Buggan schoolhouse and engaged a schoolteacher to enable his thirteen children to receive an education.

(Some years ago a party of Melbourne Bushwalkers replaced the shingles on the old schoolhouse to save it from total decay. In 1972 the Gelantipy Historical Society completed the restoration.)

Edward moved from Suggan Buggan to Black Mountain in 1883 and in 1884 bought Mt Pleasant Station, Omeo from a member of the Pendergast family. The family moved there to live, but Edward retained Suggan Buggan and he and his two sons ran cattle on both properties. He rode back and forth frequently and while staying at the Forest Paddock in 1902 with his sons, Edward died of heart failure. He was 73 years of age.

CHRISTOPHER jnr.

Christopher jnr. (brother of Edward) took up Wulgulmerang, his father's old property, in February 1859 after P.Coady Buckley and a Capt.Jones had held the property for 7 years.

JOHN

John (son of Christopher snr.) first occupied Little River (Black Mountain) in 1845 and was granted the license fourteen years later. He moved to Wulgulmerang in 1868 and held it until his retirement in 1904.

DAVID jnr.

David jnr. (John's brother) had a home on Wulgulmerang until 1867 when he took up Little River (Black Mountain) and held it until he moved to Bruthen in 1879.

ELIZABETH ANN

The death of Andrew, James' four year old son, was not the only tragedy to strike the O'Rourkes. Elizabeth Ann the eldest child of Christopher's son David, lived with her parents at Wulgulmerang on a hill near Blue Bullock Creek. When little Elizabeth was about eighteen months old in March, 1866, her mother was sick in bed, and her father's sister, Honoria O'Rourke was minding the children. David O'Rourke, Elizabeth's father, got on his horse one day after lunch, and rode away from his house, and it is thought that, unknown to him Elizabeth followed him. Honoria thought that her brother had taken the child for a ride, as he sometimes did, and did not become alarmed at her absence until some time elapsed, and she realised that he would not have taken the child so far without telling them. Everyone in the district searched for the child, but she was not found until about a year later, when some blacks found her body. Elizabeth had wandered about a mile, and fallen over a cliff near the creek. Before she was found her parents continued to look for her every day, and her mother used to ask the blacks who passed if they knew of any blacks who had a little white girl, and were looking after her. About a year later a party of blacks came to the house and asked for David O'Rourke, who was away taking cattle to Port Albert. Mrs O'Rourke was uneasy at the presence of the blacks and talked to them through an opening in the door. They went and camped down by the creek below the house, and waited three days until David O'Rourke returned from Port Albert. They told him that they had found the body of his child and took him to the place. The pink dress that she had been wearing was proof that it was her, and the position of the body indicated that she had probably died instantly of a broken neck, after falling over the cliff. Many years afterwards when Mary O'Rourke was an old lady she told one of her grand-children how grateful she was to the blacks and said she would never be frightened of them again. Little Elizabeth was buried at Black Mountain family cemetery near her grandfather, Christopher O'Rourke. Her mother could not bear to continue living at Wulgulmerang, and David O'Rourke moved the house to Black Mountain and re-erected it on a rise on the south side of the river.

MICHAEL

Michael (brother of John and David), a bachelor, lived in a hut south of Pack Bullock Lake, not far from where his brother David had lived.

SUGGAN BUGGAN HOMESTEAD
*In the tranquil valley of the Tonginbooka River is the old settlement
of Suggan Buggan. Only two dilapidated buildings in an extensive
clearing now remain as evidence that, in this remote spot, man lived and
laboured to carve out a home in the bush.*

A.M.CORBETT 1950

35

SUGGAN BUGGAN SCHOOLHOUSE
Originally selected by Edward O'Rourke in the 1830s, Suggan Buggan became in later years the centre of a small community, and it was in the schoolhouse, still used occasionally by stockmen as a shelter, that the descendants of the original O'Rourke received their schooling. The river valley is broad and flat here and, seen under a summer sun with hillsides clothed with gums and Murray pines, captivated the imagination.

A.M.CORBETT 1950

A merchant-adventurer, Ben Boyd of Twofold Bay sent stockmen to try their fortunes with cattle in the valley of Suggan Buggan and Snowy River. The men employed by Boyd were the Kiss brothers, who in turn employed William Woodhouse. Later came the Williams and next generation of Woodhouses. The Williams and Woodhouses used Mount Trooper across the Snowy Plains for a mustering paddock and many unbranded wild cattle were mustered into it at the turn of the century and driven to Gippsland.

The O'Rourke dynasty in the Black Mountain — Suggan Buggan — Wulgulmerang country ended between 1902 when the patriarch's grandson Edward died and John retired from Wulgulmerang. So ended the family's 66 years occupancy. The MacKenzies and others had been there, of course, but, predominantly it had been O'Rourke territory.

ROGERS

John Churchill Rogers purchased Black Mountain Station in 1902 and moved up, with his family, from the Warragul area in March 1903. One of the children died during the journey.

The name 'Churchill' derived from Churchill Island in Western Port, with which the family had earlier been involved.

John stocked Black Mountain and the runs with drought affected bullocks from Queensland. It was a successful venture and their eventual sale enabled him to buy Wulgulmerang — in about 1910.

The Rogers ran about 400 — 500 breeding cows, raised their own bullocks and sold them, generally at about 3½ years, droving them to Maffra where they brought about £3.10.0 each.

Black Mountain consisted of only about 600 acres freehold in 1902, much of it not cleared. Leaseholds, however, amounted to about 4000 acres fenced with logs and about 100,000 acres of open runs, most of which are still held by the Rogers family today.

Prior to World War I, John Churchill Rogers brought in his supplies once a year from Mossiface on the Tambo River, a distance of some 80 miles from Black Mountain, using his own bullock waggon. Anything that was forgotten had to wait until next years trip.

By the late 1920s Black Mountain consisted of about 4000 acres freehold, most of it cleared and enclosed by rabbit-proof netting fences. Rogers had acquired another property on the Murray (now submerged by the Hume Dam) and used it to fatten cattle from Queensland.

Half the original Black Mountain property was sold to Dr. Hayden in 1933, the portion retained by Rogers being known as "Rockbank". In due course, J.C.'s three sons Keith, Richard and John shared in the management and to-day John's two sons, David and John and daughter, Mrs Joan Moon are carrying on the family tradition.

continued on page 45.

Edward O'Rourke's old home at Suggan Buggan

John Churchill Rogers and son, Keith Churchill Rogers. Photo, 1920s, was taken by Rev. John Flynn, then local pastor, later to become well known as 'Flynn of the Inland'.

John Churchill Rogers at Black Mountain.

Mrs J. C. Rogers and baby son David at Black Mountain homestead, 1928.

Suggan Buggan Homestead and a party of surveyors - pre 1939.

John and June Rogers at Ingeegoodbie, 1930.

A pack-horse unsuccessfully attempts a narrow opening between two trees.

Black Mountain Homestead. The front portion is new and behind a courtyard at rear, is McKenzie's old home.

A Rogers party at historic Macfarlane's Flat

David O'Rourke, the third of the O'Rourke boys who came across to Black Mountain with his brother Christopher in 1843, introduced a fine breed of horses to the area and ran them near Turnback.

When David died at Appin in 1855, many of the horses were never mustered. They spread into the surrounding country and soon built up into vast numbers. They were the forerunners of the "brumbies" of North Gippsland and through to Koscuisko.

Black Mountain Brumbies

J. M. MacKenzie.

I WENT UP TO NORTH GIPPSLAND over 35 years ago to join my brother who owned, in partnership with the O'Rourke Bros., a big tract of country stretching from the head of the Murray (which there went under the name of the Limestone) to the Snowy River at a place called Willis, on the N.S.W. border.

The O'Rourkes, three brothers, owned, with my brother, this country, which was called the Black Mountain Run. The Black Mountain was, I think, taken up by my father and uncle of these brothers.

At the time I write of, there were only two fences between Bruthen and the Snowy River, one at the Buchan boundary — Buchan was then owned by Ricketson — and the other at the top of Turnback Mountain, the boundary between Black Mountain and Suggan Buggan. The latter place was owned by Ned O'Rourke, a cousin of the Black Mountain O'Rourkes. Good old Ned, of Suggan Buggan was a real white man, and a character in his way. He has passed in his checks a good many years, but I can see him now riding after cattle and handling a mob of touchy ones, born to the game, as cunning as a fox, and as keen as mustard.

Soon, this wild, and rugged country and the surrounding districts became the home of a community of wonderful bushmen and wonderful horsemen and horses. Every man's living depended on his ability to ride and track and steer a pathway by the sun and stars.

At that time North Gippsland was full of wild horses right up to Kosciusko and all through the Black Mountain country. As boys the O'Rourkes used to run them, but they had not been molested for years. The O'Rourkes and my brother decided to see if they could make anything out of them. They were all comparatively young men at the time — probably not over 35 years.

David O'Rourke was a fine stamp of bushman, over six feet and wiry, a good steady rider, not dashing, but generally in the right place after a mob of brumbies or cattle.   John O'Rourke was one of the best horsemen I have ever seen, and a regular fire-eater after stock.   I can see him now after a hard run, his flashing, and his horse pretty well all out.   He could let some language   fly about if his mob was not kept in the tailers when he had brought them in sight.   He was always right on the tail of a mob, sending them through the thickest scrub as hard as his horse could pelt, giving a mob of brumbies no time to swerve or turn.   Michael O'Rourke rode well over 18 stone.   Good old Michael!   He had the best judgment in the bush after stock of any man I have ever seen.   He was never bustled or at a loss, and was always in the right place, and generally about at the finish.   It took a good beast to get away from Michael if he was riding old Darkie, a cranky devil of a black horse, which was as powerful as a bull, and would follow a beast like a dog.

What a company gathered for those old "Brumby" runs (they were "wild horses" in those days.   "Brumby" was a much later word.)

Hector, mounted on old "Phil"; his brother Farquhar, a wild and reckless horseman with all the dash but lacking the cool judgment of his elder brother; George Johnstone of Tubbut Station, a hard riding Englishman; Fred and Ned Smith, Billy Cobyam one of the full-blooded aborigines, with judgment and horsemanship combined.

Perhaps Bob Moon from Buchan might be one of the party.   The wonder man who seldom seemed to do more than trot or canter and still was always just where he was wanted and riding a fresh horse when the others had bellows to mend, Bob was probably the best white tracker that Australia ever knew.   His keen eyes never spoiled by reading small print or any other kind of print for that matter.

Bob Moon has long since been gathered to his fathers and surely, if horses are over the divide, Bob is mounted on a prancing steed stamped with an RTC (The brand was that of Ricketson, who held a large area of the land in the Buchan district in the early days).

Through the haze of years, I can see Dave and Billy Kiss in charge of a wild-eyed mob of Monaro cattle; Barry passing through with a mob of stores for the Gippsland market; Barry haggard from long night watches and wild rides with mobs that rushed till they would jump when a leaf falls.

A long procession of the boys who took places, rides past.

I can see young Farquhar MacKenzie on 'Ora', Sam Gilbert on a Buchan grey that would have delighted the heart of a Desert Arab; young Charlie Gilbert on 'Bluey'; George Harrison from the Murray; Charlie Woodhouse from Monaro; Joker Johnstone on 'Sea Spray'; Harry Biggs from Glenmore, the furthest outpost of the Buchan, on a raw-boned bay that was miles better than he looked; Charlie Biggs on old 'Stumpy', a horse without a single hair in his tail; Andrew Davidson, Jimmy Dixon, young Bob Moon, Tom Connors in the days when his beard was black, Ted and Tom Cox; one

Jim O'Keefe, Frank Welby with a team of fiery R.T.C.s and Tom Hamilton from Ensay with his four greys.

H. Mackenzie came from the Billabong with the reputation of a crack horseman, which I think he gained partly by sweating Willie and Ned Kennedy's horses, they having a good many more in those days than they could handle. He kept his reputation up well in the mountains, and was a hard man to beat in any country. For dash at a critical time and for judgment he had few equals. He could ride any sort of horse and knock good quarters out of him. Hector was perhaps the dandiest horseman of them all. Six feet two inches of wire and whipcord, hands gentle as a womans and as strong as steel, he had an easy graceful seat that drew old horsemen's eyes when he rode into Moree from his N.S.W. property forty years later.

I have ridden behind all these men, and it is not easy to say which was the hardest to follow. I think for real dash and smashing through John O'Rourke took the cake. For myself, I didn't feel altogether out of the running as I was able to follow them.

We had a good deal of hard work putting up trap yards with long, light wings, we prepared for the first run. Horses were got in and shod, every man doing his own shoeing in those days. The horses were of the good old sort — like cats on their feet and game as pebbles. I shall never forget the first run we had, and wish I could describe the country as I can see it now. There was a patch of fairly level ground called Wulgulmerang Forest, which sloped off in almost perpendicular spurs to the lower country on the Buchan River and Farm Creek. I had some adventures on that same Farm Creek in later years, which, however, do not belong to this yarn.

Down these spurs the brumbies went for water. If they were disturbed they always kept to the sidelines, never going straight down if they could avoid it.

We built our yard on one side, and ran wings just under the brow on each side nearly to the top.

On this particular run D. O'Rourke went out to start the job. He knew almost to a mile where every mob ran, and which way they would make. Michael was on Darkie and F. Mackenzie on a fine bay horse called Phil, a very hot-headed horse with the reputation of being a bolter if he was in a bad humor. These two were to take the mob from Davie and bring them along towards the wings where John O'Rourke and I were waiting, one on each wing, about half a mile from each point, and well hidden in scrub. Our job was to take the mob from the other two and send them down the spur towards the yards as hard as we could pelt.

I must say while I was waiting for my turn to come I had great doubts as to how I was going to do my part. The spur was as steep as the side of a house, and timber and undergrowth as thick as it could stick. I remember I was riding a horse called The Toad — a sweater, by-the-by — named from a habit he had of swelling himself out when first mouthed, and giving three or four flying bounds before settling down. I had many a good ride on him afterwards.

My instructions were: "As soon as the mob passes you, after them like blazes, and don't give them a chance to turn on the wing".

I looked at the spur, which seemed steeper and steeper, and at the timber which seemed much thicker than the day before, and had many doubts.

Brumby Trap on Limestone Creek

John O'Rourke was riding a little bay horse called The Arrow, and he took some riding through scrub or down hill. The least bit of humbugging with him and up would go his head, and he would race through the scrub straight on end — no doubt thus getting his name.

After waiting what seemed a very long time, well hidden in the scrub, we heard the thud of galloping horses — there is no other sound like it, and once heard it is never forgotten. On they came, nearer and nearer. The Toad, beginning to jump about with excitement, and my feet jingling in the stirrups with fright. Now scrub is smashing and stones rattling as the mob gets nearer, galloping so close that you could cover them with a table-cloth. The king of the mob is now in the lead — early in the run he was at the tail of his mob keeping his mares together. He is a jealous fellow, the King of the Harem, and keeps good watch on his mares to see that none single off. But now that the matter is serious he is taking the lead for he sees a man on each side of his mob riding hard and quietly. There is no shouting or cracking of whips at this game; one shout, and the whole mob would probably wheel short round on its tracks, and the run would be spoilt. The old king is not very much alarmed yet; he has often before been sent for a spin, and he looks for safety round the side of the spur as usual. The mob is beginning to waver a bit just as they come abreast of my stand, but they flash past at top speed and I take up the running. I just see

my mate on the other flank, and know I will have to ride as I have never ridden before to keep my end up, but the old Toad was full of go, and I had lost my fright, and found no difficulty in keeping well on the mob's tails.

They were now mad with fright, and fairly threw themselves down the wings, smashing many a sapling on the way. I glanced across and could see my mate well abreast of me and riding hard. The Arrow head up and going for his life. The mob made a wheel towards my side, and I thought it was all up, but I put on an extra spurt and straightened them up again. I could now see the wings closing in, and down went the mob straight into the big yard and through into the smaller yard beyond. We had a temporary gate up before they turned again, and there they were, securely yarded — a big chestnut stallion, eight mares and a couple of foals. More foals started with the mob, but the pace was too hot and they dropped out.

The mob was in the pink of condition — fat, with coats like satin. Some of the old mares had manes to their knees. We were all together again now, and rode the run over again. Someone asked me "How did you get on through the timber?" I said: "I never saw a darned tree" which was absolutely true. I had no recollection of pulling my horse off a single tree — he did it all himself. Later on I found that the secret of success in riding in rough country is summed up in the words "Let your horse alone". I asked H. Mackenzie if Phil had bolted. He said: "The beggar hadn't time".

The horses were in the yard but they had to be branded and taken home, all of which is another story.

"Pastoral Review", September 16, 1919.

44

I wish I could go back forty years and hide in the corner of a big stone fireplace and listen, ears tingling, to the tales of the cattle camps and gold rushes, the trapping of big mobs of brumbies at the Points yard or hear again the tale of how the wild bull pinned John O'Rourke against the big corner post with a horn each side, with points driven into the hard wood and not a scratch on John.   Or the tale of the same John (a noted athlete) who cleared the six foot fence with a man-eater two strides behind.

Never have tales of Rider Haggard or Ballantyne stirred me like those old years.   Never has the finish of the Melbourne Cup made my heart play tricks like the thunder of a mob of galloping wild horses as I watched out of the wings of a trapyard.   Never has music sounded as sweet as the bell bird's note or the tinkle of real bells round the camp in the Snowy River valley. Never will wild horses look so handsome as the old comrades that carried on fast and far; and never will men seem as staunch as those comrades of the mountains of Croajingalong.

SUGGAN BUGGAN AND BLACK MOUNTAIN
continued from page 37.

The one-time isolation is gone, the highway linking Buchan with Ingeebyra, Moonbah and Jindabyne allows cars and stock transports to cover in a few hours the distance that once required weeks on the droving track. The area over which the cattle graze extends westwards to the divide between the Tambo and Mitta Mitta headwaters, and of the Buchan heads, thus making the Rogers and Pendergasts run neighbours, and northwards to the Border, including the historic Macfarlane Flat.

With the exception of the "Playground" below the Cobberas, and a few small pockets, the area is devoid of snowplains and much of the grazing is in forested grasslands.

After mustering the Roger's cattle are driven into Bairnsdale and forwarded by road transport to Melbourne.   Rail transport is more economical but the unreliability of the service from here and other railheads persuade the Cattlemen to favour road transport.

The country that for 66 years was O'Rourke territory has now been in Rogers' hands for 78.

These recollections of Edward J. O'Rourke appeared originally in the 'Bairnsdale Advertiser', and due acknowledgment is made. (c. 1930s)

Recollections

Edward O'Rourke,
grandson of James

*I*N THE YEAR 1840, my grandfather James O'Rourke, sold his property at "County Guinea", in Monaro, then known as the New Country, and headed for Victoria. His household goods and other equipment were transported in a bullock dray, driven by John Spriggs and John Carpenter, head stockman. A man named Goodwin also accompanied this small party of pioneers, who had set out to explore Victorian Pasture lands.

Black Mountain at that time was green country, and had been forfeited by Richard Brooks, of Gejedric Station, New South Wales, now owned and occupied by Woodhouse Bros.

When the climb from Suggan Buggan to Black Mountain was being negotiated the family flour mill fell from the bullock dray. As it was badly damaged the mill was not reloaded on the dray. Though ninety-six years have since passed, this relic of that historic journey has been retained, the parts having been "packed" into the homestead by the present owner.

A better grade out of Suggan Buggan was subsequently found at the head of Buchan Creek — always called the Old Mountain.

My grandfather also acquired Wulgulmerang, to where he shifted after residing at Black Mountain for some time. It was at Wulgulmerang he lost his youngest son in an accident, and he sleeps in a lonely grave near the site of one of the earliest mountain homes.

In 1843 his two brothers Christy and Davey O'Rourke joined my grandfather at Black Mountain. Subsequently Christy O'Rourke lived at Black Mountain with his wife and family. He died at an early age. He was buried near his mountain home.

The first wheat crop grown at Black Mountain was planted by James O'Rourke, the seed being obtained at Omeo Station, to reach which place involved a difficult journey. James O'Rourke, his eldest son (Edward), and Tom Dillon, a friend, rode across the mountains to Omeo Station, to obtain the wheat seed. They had to walk on the return journey, leading their horses, on which they packed across their riding saddles three bushells of

46

wheat.   The horses used on that occasion were Black Billy, Flash and Hardtimes.   A new mill was obtained and flour was made the following year from wheat grown at Black Mountain.

In 1843 Davey O'Rourke brought 70 horses and two sires to Black Mountain.   The latter were a black stallion called Peacock, and Gander, a grey.   They were of the Steeltrap breed, and were turned on to portion of the Black Mountain afterwards known as Turnback, where the bridge across the Snowy River was recently built.   These were the first horses brought into this portion of Gippsland and from them originated the brumbies which became so numerous in later years.

Davey O'Rourke, a tall, powerful man of eccentric habits, though a great lover of horses, seldom rode.   He would walk through the mountains for many miles carrying with him a small supply of food, camping for a night or so near his horses and then move on.   Sometimes he would walk from Appin, near Sydney.   One morning he started out from the station and stated he would not return until the following evening.   However, he made his appearance the same night — a very weary man.   He then related to his brother Jim, the story of how he tried to take a short cut to reach his "caboose".   "But, by gob," he said, "I never got there.   I got into a place where the hills are kissing one another.   Never go there, Jim.   I turned back, I did, twenty times or more."   Ever after that incident, the historic crossing over the Snowy River retained the name of Turnback.   Davey O'Rourke, who gave the name to this crossing was unmarried.   He died intestate at Appin, near Sydney, and as horses were then valueless, his were never mustered.   They roamed the mountains of East Gippsland and multiplied in a few years.   And so commenced in this part of Gippsland the wild horses which have been made famous in Australian literature.   Wild horses, or brumbies, as they were termed amongst horsedealers, were in later years mustered in large numbers.   It was a familiar sight at the early horse sales in Gippsland to see strings of them being driven in to offer at auction sales, which in those days occupied at least three full days.

Davey O'Rourke had a penchant for naming landmarks, their ruggedness and strange contour reminding him of familiar places in the Emerald Isle. So on the descent of Turnback Mountain is found Beaver Castle.   Other landmarks named by him are Hanging Rock.   Farther north, on the Suggan Buggan fall, and nearby, aptly designated, is World's End Creek.   Turnback Crossing, subsequently became known as McKellar's Crossing, taking this name from the residents who had charge of the ferry.

Since the second steel bridge has been erected over the Snowy River at this point it has been officially called McKellar's Crossing.

My grandfather, being of a roving nature, turned his attention to southern parts of Gippsland and sold out his interests in Gippsland East to Captain Jones.   Later, my granduncle, Christy O'Rourke, purchased the properties from Captain Jones, and lived for the rest of his life at Black Mountain.

My grandfather and father often discussed their trek from Black Mountain to Port Albert, in a bullock dray in which all their journeys were made. They travelled until they reached the sea, at Port Albert, and then turned back. They acquired two properties in Southern Gippsland, Bruthen Flat and Reedy Creek. At the latter place my grandfather made his home and was laid to rest at the age of 74. His grandchildren still own and occupy the properties.

Referring to the death of the late James O'Rourke, *The Gippsland Standard,* of July 1876 stated:— The late James O'Rourke was a native of County Kildare, Ireland, where he was born in 1802, and from thence he emigrated in 1828, being then unmarried, making Sydney, N.S.W., his destination. His father had already come out to the same colony some years previously, and had settled down to farming and grazing, the locality being Appin, near Campbelltown, and where he also held the responsible office of manager or overseer over stations and live stock on behalf of the company, many of these squatting associations being then in existence in New South Wales, the principals, in many instances, residing in the old country. Deceased came out with his four brothers, all of which have since passed away, with the exception of one, who is still enjoying a green old age on his father's estate at Appin. After engaging in farming pursuits for a few years, during which he married a Miss Slate, a native of Dublin, the marriage ceremony being performed by the Rev. Father Terry, deceased took up a tract of country known as Maloon Station, this was his first enterprise in the way of squatting, which he successfully carried on for several years. He then disposed of the station, and removed up into what was then known as the New Country, but now as Monaro, N.S.W. He bought two stations in that district, the one being known as the Tight Little Island, and the other County Guinea, both of which he held for a number of years. Eventually he sold his interest in these properties, and came over to Victoria, where he chose North Gippsland for the scene of his future labors, and bought a station known as Wulgulmerang, on the Monaro road. He lived in the north until the year 1854, when he turned his attention to South Gippsland, and purchased two properties known as Bruthen and Reedy Creek stations. Deceased lived on Reedy Creek property from the year 1854 until within a few months of his death, which took place on the 28th of June, 1876, at the house of an old friend at Emerald Hill, viz., Mr. Matthew Mackay, proprietor of the O'Connell Centenary Hotel, to which place he had removed for the benefit of change of scene on the advice of his friends and relatives. The deceased gentleman enjoyed sound bodily health until a few years previous to his death, but after the loss of his wife, on the 15th of October, 1874, his health slowly showed signs of breaking, and he frequently complained of those ailments which are, after all, but natural to man when he has passed the golden meridian of his days, and is slowly sinking down towards that distant horizon where it is ordained for man to arrive sooner or later. Up to the last he enjoyed his mental facilities, and died at a ripe old age, being in his 74th year. Deceased had a large family, viz., seven sons and three daughters, the surviving being five sons and three daughters.

Deceased, as will be gathered from the foregoing narrative, was a very old colonist. He was a man of indomitable energy and keen foresight, and on that account he met with none of those reverses which too frequently attend the life of the more adventurous. His hospitality and genial spirit were well known and appreciated by a large circle of friends, who will long remember the name of James O'Rourke as that of an old pioneer, a good neighbour and strictly upright man. His remains were brought down from Melbourne in the steamer Avon, on the 5th inst., and interred in the family cemetery at Reedy Creek Station, on the 6th, the last sad offices being administered by Mr. John Verling, in the absence of Rev. Father Hayes, who was prevented by illness from attending the funeral. The body was consigned to the grave in the presence of a large number of sorrowing relatives and friends. And thus closes the scene in the life of one who knew the trials and struggles of early squatting life in the colonies and who died at a good old age, as already recorded."

In later years Black Mountain Station was carried on by a son-in-law of Christy O'Rourke, the late H.R.Mackenzie, who lived there for many years and subsequently sold out through A.McLean & Co. to the late Mr.C.C.Kerr, of Denison.

The late Edward O'Rourke, my father, of Suggan Buggan, was the eldest son of James. He acquired Suggan Buggan by public tender. Hugden was the first occupier of Suggan Buggan, and next it fell into the hands of Woodhouse Bros. His grandson is now residing at this locality.

Suggan Buggan homestead is situated on the river on the main Jindabyne-Monaro road, five miles from Black Mountain, 11 miles from the border of New South Wales and 100 miles from Cooma.

For many years Edward O'Rourke and his Lake Tyers man, Jamby, made two annual trips with 12 pack horses, each bearing two hundredweight of provisions on the return journey. A 220-lb bag of flour then cost £12, which was packed 100 miles from Cooma. Cooma is my native town. When I was five weeks old, my mother and her favorite horse, Chester, carried me to Suggan Buggan, where some of my sisters and brothers were born. After living there for many years they were obliged to leave owing to my mother's failing health. My father acquired Omeo Station over 50 years ago, and so the old homestead was deserted and has now become bachelor's quarters.

This country, like many other tracts of land taken up in the early days, has deteriorated, but it has a good future. When provided with good roads men who understand the nature of the land will develop it. My father branded up to 628 head of cattle in a year — to use his own words — from four years to four days old. That was before my time. Those days have gone, but so have the difficulties of transport by pack horses, over bush tracks. In a new era modern transport and good roads will play a big part towards achieving success.

Whittakers of Tubbut

AMONGST THE EARLY SETTLERS to the Snowy River area were the Whittakers. Born in Chester, England, on February 19th 1814, William Whittakers decided to seek his fortune in the Colonies and several years after completing his boarding-school education at Aston-under-Lynne, he sailed for Australia in the "Mellish" and arrived in Sydney on 5th June 1839.

Shortly after his arrival, William purchased "Snowy River Run" from one, W. Ross - 102 head of cattle at £4 per head, 3 horses at £35 each, improvements £60, cart and other items £30. After his marriage in 1841 William set out for the Monaro and in 1843 purchased "Tombong" from Thos. Moore, selling "Snowy River" station to pay for the new property.

An early drawing of the Tombong homestead depicts slab walls, squared with a broadaxe, enclosing two rooms and a skillion. The residence was bark-roofed, its window spaces were glassless and its floors hard rammed earth. Depression hit New South Wales in the 1840s and stock sales barely kept creditors at bay.

In 1848, William Whittakers decided to move into Victoria - to "Tubbutt" and although settlement was effected on 7th July 1849, the official transfer was dated 1852. Tubbut was in use as an out-station of Thomas Moore's Burnima Station in the Monaro, as early as 1838, and would thus have been the first cattle run in the area.

Whittakers' family apparently returned to an earlier home at Burnima leaving William to establish their new Victorian holding which consisted of 790 acres Freehold, 672 acres Leasehold, and 97,950 acres Pastoral Occupation Licence. Whittakers had 3,300 head of cattle and 50 horses.

It was not until 5th January 1851 that Mrs Whittakers and family rejoined William at "Tubbutt", the children being carried in boxes slung across pack-horses.

"Tubbutt" was on the track to Gippsland between the Black Tableland and the wild gorges of the Snowy River. The sun rose over Monaro, behind the peak of Tingy-Ringy and set behind the black and bold bastions of Mount Deddick and Bowen. It was in the land of "Croajingalong", the native word for "looking east", aptly named because it is impossible to be in these parts without being conscious of the tableland lying towards the sunrise.

The run was on the Jingelalla River which flows into the Deddick and about 12 miles from the Snowy. The homestead had glass windows and a wooden floor in the parlour. The clay for the chimney, the slabs for the walls and the bark for the roof all came from the property.

Across the Snowy, Gippsland was nine years old. On its fertile pastures, too, many bullocks were fattened until there was a glut on the Hobart market. Squatters boiled down their "fats" in 50 gallon cauldrons and shipped the tallow to England or India.

At last William's first mob of cattle was ready for the road. The first night was spent at Deddick - an anxious night with the cattle, too close to home, fretting and uneasy. McKellar's Crossing had claimed several lives but next morning men and horses faced it, forcing the cattle in and across the Snowy. The puntman's boat made many dangerous crossings before the gear and towed horses were all safely over. (An old map shows this crossing to be near the present McKillop's Bridge. The map bears the notation, McKellar's Ferry, Accommodation.)

Up they went over stiff country to Wulgulmerang, helping to beat out the old Monaro cattle-track up Mount Turnback where today the trail is still ungrassed and unhealed in many places. Butcher's Ridge was the next camp. The cattle steadied before they came to Buchan; and so on to the low country, where they were sold to fatteners. Trying not to show his disappointment, William rode home; the venture was a failure - bullocks selling for £3 a head, cows for 37/6; all sold on a six month's bill.

Jimmy Hill of the bushranging partnership of Jones and Hill worked at "Tubbut" for some time. Later, while on the way back to plunder the homestead, he was arrested.

Billy Coe, who came as a boy, grew up and died at the age of ninety not far from "Tubbut". It is on record that Billy Coe, with eight inches of snow on the ground, swam a flooded river with rations for hungry men.

In 1867 Hannah married J.G.W.Wilmot. It is a family legend that, while journeying to "Tubbut" for the wedding, Wilmot fell out of the punt and was ably retrieved by the puntman's wife who seized her drowning passenger by his long silky beard!

In December 1868 on his return from leading the rescue party to the ill-fated Burke and Wills Expedition, Dr. A.W.Howitt visited the station. It was the first time a buggy had been driven to Gelantipy. Dr Howitt had with him his wife and children and they continued the journey to "Tubbut" on horseback. Following are extracts from a letter Dr Howitt wrote to his mother in England:

"For eight miles we followed a winding track amongst grassy hills and every rise showing glorious distant views of the blue mountains around us till in the sunset we climbed the long ridge above "Tubbutt" and the promised land was before us. The ridge we were on was, I think, about 500 feet above the river and low grassy hills fill the valley gradually rising at three of four miles distance to the heights of Ringy-Tingy Mountains.

Down below us we could see the "Tubbutt" huts clustered on a narrow point of land round which runs the river, with the huts and yards and gardens and fencing laid out as if on a map. . .

I must tell you about the "Tubbutt" station, so that you will have an idea of the place. Like most Australian stations it consists of several huts, in this instance, built in a row because the tongue of land is very narrow. First, the kitchen, then a hut containing the dining room and four bedrooms. Then a hut containing one large room which was our bedroom — a dairy, a store room and a saddle room. Then two huts built of slabs and roofed with bark, white-washed inside and out and very clean. . . . Besides these huts, there are huts for the men and the usual stockyards - besides a stable over the river. . "

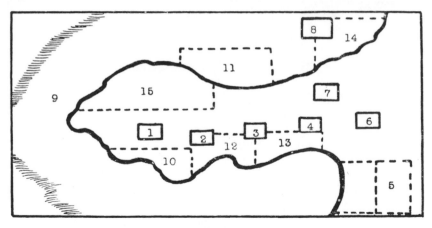

Dr HOWITT'S PLAN
of "the Tubbutt Huts clustered in a narrow point of land,
round which runs the river".
(1) Miss Moore's House. (2) Our bedroom, etc. (3) Dining
Room (4) Kitchen (5) Stockyards (6) & (7) Men's Huts
(8) Stables (9) Croquet Ground (10) - (15) Gardens

On 19th October, 1870 the eldest daughter, Minnie, was married to Eyre Louis Bruce. The couple lived at Bairnsdale, where their daughter, Mary Grant Bruce, authoress of the "Billabong" books, was born.

May 1871 brought a change to the life of the Whittakers. The sheep were giving trouble and the licence rents were to be raised. In a letter to his Aunt William explained his problems and concluded, " . . there is no way of getting out of it. Therefore I shall abide by my first plan — give up the run".

They left in March 1872 to take up their new property "Loy Yang" at Traralgon. Billy Coe, when an old man of 90 spoke of the departure —

"The Snowy river was high and dangerous. In case of accident, the boss would let only one woman at a time go in the boat, so the job was a slow one. After the passengers were over, we piled in the pack saddles with all their belongings and then saddled up again and headed for The Turnback. I rode with them to the top," the old man said, "I watched them go. When my best friends rode out of sight, I cried. I tell you I cried. Then I rode back to "Tubbutt" alone."

THE WHITTAKERS

The group includes William Whittakers, his wife Louisa, and her Aunt Martha·Moore. Two of the family, a son and daughter, were absent.

A Droving Epic

ONE OF THE MOST IMPORTANT of the historic stock routes between the north-east of Victoria and the Monaro plains of New South Wales was the Ingeegoodbie track leading from Suggan Buggan, over a 4000 ft range and along the Snowy River to Jacob's River and Jindabyne.

Ingeegoodbie was on the route taken by the first overlanders to cross the Snowy and enter the Gippsland area one hundred and forty years ago and in the 1940s, a hundred years later it was still the stockmen's link between the cattle breeding grounds on the Monaro highlands and the great Bairnsdale market. The great droving traditions of the pioneer stockmen were carried on then by men such as Tom Goldby and Henry "Bung" Harris of Yaouk.

"Bung" Harris achieved a great droving feat in 1947 when he brought a thousand head of Herefords from Tabulam, on the Queensland border to the Bairnsdale market. The 1300 mile drive took five months, but it was not just the length of the journey which was noteworthy, but the achievement of coaxing the big mob through the 26 miles of rugged country between Jacob's River and Suggan Buggan was a masterly piece of droving.

Approaching Jacob's River. the cattle traversed a precipitious siding and along the Snowy the track winds between boulders or follows a narrow ledge high above the river. After crossing a stream the track rises steeply for 2000 ft over the Pinch.

Beyond Freebody's old run on the Ingeegoodbie River, the Razorback is reached, falling away to a gorge on either side. Finally the track drops 2400 ft in a mile and a half down through loose scree of the mountainside to Suggan Buggan.

Along this track Harris brought 1000 head without the loss of a beast. Four young drovers were his only assistants. They shared 23 horses on the trip. A thousand head of cattle is a big mob anywhere and it has not been surpassed in the veterans' long memories of mountain droving.

On the Ingeegoodbie stock route near Jacob's River;
horsemen pause to admire the Snowy River flowing towards
the Victorian border.

Veteran stockman Tom Goldby rests his horse on a steep
traverse near The Pinch.

Stockmen who travelled the Ingeegoodbie track owed their lives to riding skill and the sure-footedness of their mountain horses. Stampedes were rare, but frequently the rider took his life in his hands to race down mountain sides littered with boulders, scrub and logs to turn back cattle that had strayed from the mob.

The crossing of this mountain frontier was part of the pastoral expansion, prompted by a severe drought in N.S.W. and the need to seek new pastures, which pressed Southwards in the 1830s as cattlemen, their wives and families, with bullock drays, their worldly possessions, their flocks and herds moved in Australia's parallel to America's covered waggon age.

There have, of course, been many memorable droving feats over the years. In 1914, Tom Goldby brought through 800 head and other cattlemen have big tallies to their credit. Goldby achieved another memorable drive in the 1920s with a flock of 7000 sheep — not a big flock by plainsmen's standards, but almost incredible for the mountains.

The opening of the Buchan—Jindabyne road in 1961 heralded the end of the notorious Ingeegoodbee track and we may never again see the great droving feats of Harris, Goldby and the other great stockmen who used the route for 125 years.

Leaders of "Bung" Harris's big mob of Hereford lined up at Gelantipy awaiting examination by the Victorian stock inspector.

Wonnangatta Cattle Station

IN 1861, AN AMERICAN, OLIVER SMITH, attracted by the gold rushes in Australia, arrived in Grant and tried his hand at tobacco growing and gold mining at Matheson's Flat, some 17 - 18 miles above Dargo. He later moved to the junction of the Crooked and Wonnangatta Rivers and with a plough of his own making, turned the first sod at Crooked River. In his prospecting, he found his way up to the rich flats of the Wonnangatta valley, first entered by A.W. Howitt in his search for gold.

Sensing its great possibilities as a cattle run, Smith moved in with his wife Ellen and her son, Harry, and built the first section of the Wonnangatta homestead.

There is reason to believe that Ellen, whose son Harry was born in Melbourne in 1867, had first been married to a man named Hayes, and after separating from him, took her son to Gippsland. Harry worked on the Bairnsdale wharves and in street construction in Bairnsdale at the age of thirteen years, in 1860, before moving with his mother to Dargo, where she met and married Oliver Smith. Subsequently, they all moved out to Wonnangatta.

The homestead was at the junction of Conglomerate Creek and the Wonnangatta River, the confluence of two valleys which provided a wide sweep of green fertile pasture. The structure was of slab construction with a roof of shingles split at the site. The interior walls of the three rooms were lined with hessian over which was pasted newspapers.

About this period John William Pender Bryce, an Edinburgh university man who had studied engineering there, arrived in Wandiligong. He met and married a widowed governess, Elizabeth Cantani, who had one child, William

57

John William Pender Bryce.

Mrs William Bryce (nee Elizabeth Catani) in 1895 on a bridge over Conglomerate Creek built by her sons.

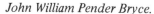

After prospecting for gold, Bryce commenced packing stores between the goldfields of Bright, Harrietville and Grant, by way of the road to Mt St Bernard and the Dargo High Plains track. When snow closed this route in winter, he sought an all-weather track and pioneered the Myrtleford - Dargo way, 100 miles up the Buffalo River, across the Divide at a low saddle between The Razor and Blue Hill and thence down into the Wonnangatta valley. On this route he passed the Smiths at their Wonnangatta station and in addition to packing in their stores, he took on to his friend, storekeeper Harrison at Grant, cheeses made by Mrs Smith.

Smith and Bryce became friends and Bryce was invited to join Smith in partnership. To increase the herd, Bryce brought a mob of cattle from

New South Wales to Wonnangatta. Unfortunately they were infected with the dreaded pleuro-pneumonia and it spread to Smith's cattle, killing many. Ellen Smith died with twins in 1866, at the age of 36 and after her death, and disheartened by the loss of his cattle, Oliver Smith sold the remainder of his herd to Saley of Tabberabbera and left the station to Bryce.

The Bryces had arrived at the station with one of their pack-horses carrying two gin cases, each containing a baby, and the remainder of their worldly possessions on a further string of pack-horses.

On leaving the Wonnangatta station, Oliver Smith bought a hotel from Denis Connolly, but after the lease expired he returned to America, it is said, to rejoin the wife he had left behind when he came to Australia.

The hotel building had originally been McMillan's Smoke-house, when he had the Dargo cattle run.

The son, Harry Smith, moved down the river and built a home, a comfortable two-roomed log hut with bark roof and a split paling chimney, adjacent to the Holmes brothers' Eaglevale station. Over the years, Harry Smith, who rarely left the valley, acquired a total of 1500 acres freehold and his home became a welcome staging point for travellers up and down the valley. He was a superb horseman and on one occasion when a member of the Bryce family took ill, Harry Smith rode to Stratford, well over 100 miles away, for medical aid. He changed horses on the way and accomplished the

Harry Smith outside his Eaglevale home in 1934. The building is now Bruce Dungey's shearing shed.

journey in one day, then returned the following day. On another occasion when Harry was working as a stockman for the Bryces, he took a mob of Wonnangatta horses into the stock market at Sale. Entering the town, the mob was startled by a train whistle, stampeded and headed back along the road towards Stratford.

Harry wheeled his mount and set off after the mob. Realising that he had to head them off, he left the road and riding through the adjacent properties, jumped every fence for nine miles, before catching the leaders and, single-handed, turning the mob back torwards Sale.

The peace of his valley was disturbed in 1917 - 18 by the Wonnangatta murders, and Harry played a prominent part in the subsequent events. Harry enjoyed splendid health throughout his long life, and when well into his 90s rode 22 miles to meet a visitor and then returned with him the same day.

The first wheeled vehicle to enter the valley was the one that took Harry away for the last time. He became very ill and had to be taken to Sale hospital. A rough way had to be hewn to widen the horse track through the bush to enable the vehicle to enter. Harry was not to return, and he died at the age of 98 years.

The Wonnangatta Station Homestead (above)
Jack Bryce of the historic Bryce family (right).

The Bryces, assisted by Thomas Nesbitt (a relative of Mrs Bryce) made substantial additions to the homestead, adding eight rooms to make it an eleven room dwelling. Thomas Nesbitt was a carpenter, who, following the death of his wife in Scotland, came to Australia and went directly to Wonnangatta. He was responsible for making most of the furniture using blackwood from a grove of trees in the valley, pit sawing the timber near the homestead. Apart from the locally hewn timber for both house and

A glimpse of Wonnangatta valley with the station cemetery in the foreground.

Alan Bryce in 1880s.

A corner of Wonnangatta Cemetery.

furniture, all materials and equipment for the homestead were packed in on horseback over the tortuous mountain track from Dargo.

The Bryces made their living by selling cattle in Gippsland and their excess farm produce (cheese, butter, bacon, etc.) to the miners at Crooked River.

Mrs Bryce had ten children, losing only two, a baby Ellen dying at three and Jessie, of appendicitis at twenty-two. Both are buried in the little family cemetery. The two eldest children were born at Myrtleford, two at Grant, and five at Wonnangatta. Each child was taken for christening to Grant, a day's ride each way, and all were educated at home by their parents. The girls were tall and graceful and sought after at social functions.

William, Mrs Bryce's son by a former marriage was the first to leave home. Dave Bryce, after a disagreement with his family, moved from the main home-stead and built himself a hut on the flat known as Dave's Flat, across the Dry River. The remains of this hut still stand. Elizabeth married and went to live interstate, Annie married a Morgan from Omeo and went to live in that district. She called herself Annie Bryce Morgan when her poetry was published. Maggie lived at home with her parents and the

Wonnangatta Station Yards.

Wonnangatta Homestead.

62

Wonnangatta stockmen.   Note illustrated papers lining hessian covered walls.

Wonnangatta interior, with open fire and hand-made furniture

BRYCE'S HUT

A substantial bark roofed log hut built by the Bryces, the hut survived for 60 years.

Located on the Snowy Plains a short distance from Bryce's Lookout and the Conglomerate Falls, the one-time substantial structure was in a parlous condition when this photo was taken and was close to ruins when visited in the mid-winter of 1936.

HOWITT PLAINS HUT
Two of William Bryce's sons, from Wonnangatta Station, outside Howitt Plains Hut in early 1900s. The hut, relatively new at that time, was slab sided and shingle roofed, a form it was to retain for another 35 years before being covered with galvanised iron.

— Elliot, Arthur Guy, Jack Guy and — Elliot outside Wonnangatta Station in early 1950s. The Elliot Brothers' father was manager of the station before the Guy's purchased it in 1934.

four boys, David, Alan, Jack and Cornelius all settled in Stratford. Annie and Jack Bryce were twins and were the two brought by pack-horse in gin cases to the station when infants. Jack served in the 1914-18 war. The last of the Bryce family to die was Alan Calder Bryce who is buried in the Stratford cemetery. Born in 1867, he died on November 18th, 1946.

William Bryce pre-deceased his wife and was killed on the road to Bairnsdale and is buried in the Lindenow cemetery. The grave is marked - William Bryce - Died 26th May, 1902, aged 67 years.

Mrs Bryce died in 1914 aged 78 years and is buried in the Wonnangatta station cemetery with her two daughters. Alan Calder and Ellen Smith are also buried there.

This tribute has been paid to the Bryces:

> This remarkable adventure in land settlement, marked by courage, endurance and success, stirs the imagination and compels admiration for these great people. After negotiating the hazardous tracks leading to the Station, one marvels at the indomitable spirit and determination in face of great difficulties of the family who lived and grew up together in the heart of these roadless mountains. In the annals of the history of Victoria's early land settlement, the pioneering work and the lives of the Bryce family of Wonnangatta, will always be an adornment to its pages."

Shortly after Mrs Bryce's death the station was sold to Messrs Arthur Phillips and Geoff Ritchie of Mansfield. They embarked on a large scale dealing enterprise. The station manager was James Barclay who bought several hundred head of cattle after the spring thaw had cleared the snow from the Snowy and Howitt Plains. The cattle were usually bought at Wodonga and were then walked to Wonnangatta. From Myrtleford they followed the old Bryce track up the Buffalo and Catherine Rivers and across a low saddle on the divide to the Wonnangatta valley, where they were grazed on the high Plains through summer and on the Wonnangatta valley flats during the winter. When the market was right they were generally sold in Mansfield or Alexandra.

It was during Phillip's and Ritchie's ownership that the Wonnangatta murders took place. For some years afterwards the homestead was unoccupied except for overnight shelter for stockmen and passing wayfarers and the fine old place began to show signs of neglect.

In May 1934, Alex Guy purchased Wonnangatta Station from a syndicate based at Alexandra whose members included Messrs Ritchie, Hogan and a doctor. The station was purchased for £9,000 walk in/walk out. The stock included 400-500 head of cattle, nearly half Friesans, and about 40 horses. The freehold of the Station was 1,100 acres and Snowy (or Bryce's) Plains freehold, 320 acres. Leasehold amounts to 100,000 acres and is used in conjunction with the station. This extends up and on to the Snowy Plains and Howitt Plains, where Guy's Snowy Plains Hut, built in 1940, and the Howitt Plains Hut, built in early 1900s are used at mustering times.

*All that remained after the accidental fire which destroyed the
Wonnangatta homestead in May 1957.*

Alex Guy died in 1949 and his sons Jack and Arthur carried on the station under the name of A. Guy and Sons.

In May 1957 the homestead was burnt, it is thought by walkers who lit a big fire in the fireplace. The chimney caught fire and the old homestead was completely destroyed. Arthur and Jack Guy went to Wonnangatta to muster and found the place in ashes. Arthur tracked two walkers, leading out of the station.

Years later, Arthur spoke to me about it. "Two bushwalkers," he said. Then remembering my old status, he corrected himself. "It was two tourists, on foot", he said.

The Guy family sold Wonnangatta to Bob Gilder of Glenfalloch in 1970.

In the tiny Wonnangatta homestead cemetery are five graves. Four bear headstones which were brought into the valley by pack-horse. 'Mother's' (Mrs E. Bryce) memorial is in the form of an open book. The inscriptions read as follows:

In Memory of	*In Memory of*	*Sacred to the Memory of*
ELLEN MARY BRYCE	*ALLAN CALDER*	*JESSIE BRYCE*
died 5th January, 1878	*Died 27 Dec. 1885*	*Died Dec 8th 1891*
Aged 3 yrs	*Lord Remember Me*	*At Rest*
Thy Will Be Done		

In Memory of Our Mother	*On a large piece of local slate*
Died April 23rd 1914	*and roughly hand carved*
Aged 78 years	*is the inscription*
At Rest	*ELLEN SMITH*
	(The date is no longer decipherable)

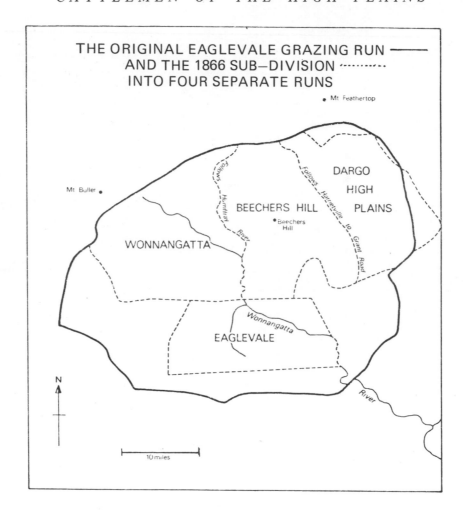

THE ORIGINAL EAGLEVALE GRAZING RUN ——
AND THE 1866 SUB–DIVISION ···········
INTO FOUR SEPARATE RUNS

The area occupied by the Wonnangatta run was originally known as Eaglevale as may be seen in the Lands Department Maps of Runs, Victoria 1863. The first reference to Wonnangatta appears in the Victorian Gazette 1866 which states: "13 July 1866 — District of North Gippsland — Sale of New Runs. Wonnangatta, Annual Rental £50. Estimated area 163,000 acres. Period of occupancy 31 Dec. 1870."

The earliest run holders were:

1866 Walter Wilson Duke	1869 Hugh Nixon
1867 forfeited	1870 Apparently forfeited
1868 No lease gazetted	1870 (July) J.P.W. Bryce

Lands Department information, however, indicates that Bryce had occupied Wonnangatta since 1865. As Oliver Smith's name does not appear in official records it may be assumed that he was an unlicenced occupier, probably from 1861 till after the death of his wife in 1866.

Eaglevale, along with other runs, was, in part, occupied by Angus McMillan prior to 1861, and the Bennison Plains section was grazed by Richard Bennison 1861–1868.

We reached the outpost of remote cattle-stations in this State, the historic, beautifully situated Wonnangatta Station. Although the name, paradoxically enough, is perhaps more famed for tragedy than beauty, an atmosphere of peace and loveliness pervades this romantic and historically interesting homestead and environs. The Wonnangatta Station is one of those places that prompt the determination to "come back again", for Wonnangatta is the most interesting and beautifully situated station property that I have encountered.

P.W.CERUTTY 1946

Wonnangatta
Murders

ONNANGATTA CATTLE STATION is probably the most isolated homestead in Victoria. Situated about 20 miles from the old mining town of Talbotville, itself isolated from Dargo, it is still only accessible by pack-horse over cattle pads winding and twisting around the steep mountain sides and crossing icy cold streams.

In spite of these hardships, an American, Oliver Smith settled here in 1861 and built the first section of a homestead, three rooms of logs and daub with shingle roof, located on Conglomerate Creek, a tributory of the Wonnangatta River. A few years later, he entered into a partnership with William Bryce, a Scot. Following the death of Mrs Smith, in 1866, and an outbreak of cattle disease, believed to have been introduced by an additional mob of cattle purchased by Bryce, Smith withdrew from the partnership and the Bryce family took over the property, subsequently selling out in 1913 to Messrs Phillips and Ritchie, of Mansfield.

Surely a more peaceful and isolated spot could not be visualised, yet even here the grim hand of the murderer was to cast a shadow on the quiet old homestead of the Bryce family.

In 1917, James Barclay had been manager for the last few years, during most of which he lived alone in the homestead, with only his dogs as companions. Frequently he went for long periods without seeing a human being, as his nearest neighbour was Harry Smith, step-son of the original owner. who lived at Eaglevale, about 20 miles down the Wonnangatta River.

James Barclay was acknowledged as being a hardy and competent bushman. He was a contented man, of simple tastes, and at peace up there among the pastures framed by eucalypts and snowgums that clothed the mountain spurs of the surrounding valley.

Having been without a station cook for some time, Barclay, on December 14th, 1917, engaged John Bamford to cook and do odd jobs. Bamford, who came from Black Snake Creek, 12 miles from Talbotville, was a man of 57. He had a bushy, greying beard and a stealthy look. His manner was surly, he was inclined to argue with great intensity, and his anger was fierce. A friend of Barclay, Albert Stout, a storekeeper of Talbotville, warned Barclay not to be drawn into arguments with Bamford.

Mr Phillips, of Mansfield, co-owner of Wonnangatta Cattle Station (left).

James Barclay, manager of Wonnangatta Station. (above).

The old village of Talbotville (1947).
(The late Arthur Stout in the foreground).

On December 17th Albert King of Mansfield visited Wonnangatta Station and stayed overnight. He noticed peculiarities in Bamford's demeanour. While the new cook seemed quite friendly towards Barclay, he was nervy and looked worried. King said that Bamford was very restless and several times paced back and forth across the sitting room of the homestead.

On 20th December, both manager and cook rode down to Talbotville in order to record their votes on the Conscription Referendum. They stopped the night at Albert Stout's home and the next morning they left to return to the station; both were sober, friendly and had no drink with them. That was the last time either man was seen alive.

Wonnangatta Homestead.

James Barclay on his way to the Talbotville polling booth to vote on the Conscription Referendum on December 29th, 1917. The photo was taken on the old horse track on the Mt Baldy — Wombat Range.

Alec. Trahair and Harry Smith outside Smith's home at Eaglevale.

Taking the body of James Barclay down the Howitt Spur to the Howqua River track, en route to Mansfield. The party includes Det. McKerrall (with axe, right background) and Bill Hearn (right foreground). Jim Fry was also in the party. (extreme left)

On 22nd December, Harry Smith rode to the homestead with mail, but found no one there, while on the kitchen door was chalked the words "Home tonight". This message, however may have been written on the day they rode into Talbotville. Harry Smith remained there till Christmas eve, when he returned to Eaglevale.

On 28th December, two bushwalkers, Tom Gould and his brother called at the station while on a walk from Howitt to Dargo, but they noticed nothing amiss.

Harry Smith rode in again with the mail on 14th January and to his surprise, he found the place deserted as on his previous visit.* Becoming suspicious, he returned to Dargo and telegraphed the owners. Eleven days later Messrs Phillips and Ritchie arrived via the Howqua River and Howitt Plains and after a prolonged search noticed that a small paddock near the house bore the impression of some heavy body having been dragged through the crop; an outer gate was open, while the barbed wire fence leading to the creek was cut to make a track to the creek. Following this trail, the searchers came upon the manager Barclay. His head had been severed from his body which had been buried beneath the sands of the creek. The body was clothed and partly decomposed. Dingoes had eaten most of the flesh.. One boot was on and the other was lying on a blanket which presumably had been used to drag the body from the house.

A detective was summoned from Melbourne and Detective Alex. McKerral duly arrived after a long ride up the Howqua and over Mt Howitt. He was escorted by two police troopers and guided by cattlemen Bill Hearn and Jim Fry.

A shotgun in Barclay's room had recently been discharged, and his bed was in a state of disorder, yet there were no blood stains nor shot marks in the room. There was no trace of Bamford; some clothes had been hastily thrown down in his room, while the horse he usually rode was missing, with saddle and bridle. Also missing was a cattle dog, a revolver, his blade razor and a suit of clothes belonging to the dead manager.

Barclay's remains were carried by pack horse over Mt Howitt and thence to Mansfield, where the Government pathologist, Mr Mollison pronounced that he had been shot in the back with a shot gun, from a distance of about 15 feet. A verdict of murder against a person or persons unknown was recorded, and a search was made for Bamford, but without success, although the missing horse was found wandering near Mt Howitt, where it had been bred, without saddle or bridle.

The remarks of the detective at the inquest were: "I am of the opinion that Barclay and Bamford had an argument over working matters and that Bamford loaded the gun and shot Barclay. He then removed his working clothes, and dressed himself in Barclay's suit, which is missing, saddled his horse, and after dragging deceased to the creek, rode the horse away. There was no trace of blood on the clothes Bamford had discarded."

* It seems incredible that on three visits nobody entered the old homestead.

With the onset of winter, the mountains surrounding the station were covered with snow and Howitt and the Howitt Plains were impassable to horsemen for many months.

Then, with the coming of spring, the cattlemen came back and on 11th November, 1918 (Armistice Day), it was reported that Constable Hayes, of Dargo, with Harry Smith, Bill Hearn and Jim Fry, had found the body of Bamford on Howitt plains, about 12 miles from Wonnangatta homestead. They had been searching near the edge of Terrible Hollow, and when returning to the Howitt Plains Hut had accidentally found the body of Bamford, buried under a pile of logs and stones. The body, which had been covered with snow during the winter, was taken to Dargo by pack horse.

At the inquest it was ascertained that Bamford had been shot in the left temple, the bullet being still in the skull, and had been fired from a distance of 15 feet. And he was not wearing the missing suit of Barclay, but was clad in clothes recognised as his own. The revolver was still missing.

Again, the verdict was murder against a person or persons unknown.

Then conjecture commenced. Up till now it had been taken for granted that Bamford was the murdered of Barclay, but the question now arose, if this was so, who had shot Bamford? Cattle duffers were suggested and some still hold this theory. By all who knew him, Bamford was described as a bad-tempered man who would stop at nothing when the mood came over him, and again to quote the papers - "the opinion of the Detective is that

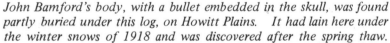

John Bamford's body, with a bullet embedded in the skull, was found partly buried under this log, on Howitt Plains. It had lain here under the winter snows of 1918 and was discovered after the spring thaw.

Bamford shot Barclay and afterwards Bamford was shot by some friend of the manager, in revenge, in the good old wild west manner."

In the years that followed, bushwalkers who called in on old Harry Smith at Eaglevale were always given a warm welcome, but the usually loquacious Harry would 'freeze up' at the mention of the Wonnangatta mystery, and even today, the elder statesmen among the cattlemen, who although only boys at the time, are reluctant to voice an opinion as to the possible motives for the two killings. Many were of the opinion that old Harry Smith might have the answer to the mystery, but if he did, it died with him when he passed away at the age of 98 in 1945.

Bamford's body being transported from Howitt Plains by pack-horse. Jim Lucas, Harry Smith, Jim Fry and Bill Hearn (right centre) were in the party. It was Bill Hearn who discovered the body of Bamford.

The most likely theories are that Barclay was shot by Bamford, and a friend of Barclay, unexpectedly visiting the station, surprised Bamford after he had buried the body but before he effected his escape on the already saddled horse. Bamford, the theory goes, avoided the easier route down the valley past Eaglevale to Dargo and attempted to escape across the Howitt Plains to Mansfield. The second and more likely theory is that Barclay surprised cattle rustlers who to hide their identity, shot the station manager. Bamford, managing to escape, mounted Barclay's saddled horse and rode for his life.

In either event, it appears likely that Bamford's pursuer or pursuers caught and shot him where his body was eventually found - on Howitt Plains, some twelve miles from the Wonnangatta Station.

Those who know the country can only wonder at the fury of the chase. From Wonnangatta the likely route would follow the valley of Conglomerate or Dry Creek, thence up the cattle track that climbs steeply through the shadows of Bryce's Gorge to reach the old Bryce's Hut on Snowy Plains. Then turning to cross the narrow ridge (the Bastard's Neck) the fugutive would enter Howitt Plains near Howitt Plains Hut and head across the snow-plains towards Mt Howitt. Riding in a desperate but vain effort to save his life, one wonders what 'Banjo' Patterson could have made of the story. Having raised John Riley's name to immortality as "The Man From Snowy River", after listening to the telling of Riley's short, sharp ride in pursuit of a run-away stallion, Patterson could surely have made an epic of Bamford and his pursuers 12 mile break-neck chase and the shot, fired in vengeance or to preserve the pursuers identy.

The old Wonnangatta homestead is no more, having, through carelessness, been burnt in 1957; Talbotville, like many another mining town has also disappeared from the scene, and roads have penetrated the isolation and solitude of the Wonnangatta Valley, but the mystery surrounding the double murder, unsolved by the investigators of the day, is likely, more than 60 years later, to remain that way.

BRYCE'S HUT
A substantial bark roofed log hut built by the Bryces, the hut survived
for sixty years.

HOWITT PLAINS HUT

Here shown as originally constructed in the early 1900s, with split slab
sides and shingle roof, the hut is located close to the spot where
Bamford's body was found, when the winter snows had melted.

The Guys of Crooked River

*E*DWARD REMINGTON GUY was born at Leeds, Yorkshire in 1836 and came to Australia at the age of seventeen, in the "Marco Polo", arriving on May 28th 1853. His county of origin earned him the nick-name of "Yorky". He met and married Elizabeth Wilson, a Scottish lass, at Port Albert in 1860.

"Yorky" Guy operated a restaurant at Talbotville, and was once 'booked' for operating a sly grog shop. "Yorky" and Elizabeth had eleven children, including twins. One child died at birth, another, Mary lived only eight days - her mother left her on a bed in front of an open window on a hot day while she visited a neighbor. There was a sudden change in the weather, Mary caught a chill and died of pneumonia. Edward was killed at the age of twelve years when a tree fell on him and Patrick died at Talbotville after contracting T.B. while mining in New Zealand. William Guy, another son of "Yorky" was badly hurt - his back was broken - when a limb from a tree he was felling struck him. He was taken by horse and cart to Grant and then to Sale hospital, where he died six months later. William's widow, Martha, later married Albert Stout the well-known storekeeper at Talbotville.

"Yorky" died in 1910, at the age of seventy-four years and his widow ran a boarding house at Talbotville after his death.

Alexander Guy, one of the sons, was born at Talbotville in 1870. He mined for gold at Grant at the age of fourteen and later possibly as far away as Omeo. Returning to Dargo, he bought a team of pack-horses and took up mail contracting for more than fifty miles from Stratford. While thus employed, he met and married the Dargo postmistress, a widow Catherine Armstrong (nee Connolly). They had eight children, five sons and three daughters, the youngest son Ernie dying of diphtheria when only four or five years old.

Edward Remington "Yorky" Guy, husband of Elizabeth Jane, father of Alexander and William, grandfather of Arthur and Jack.

Elizabeth Jane Guy, grandmother of Arthur, Jack, Nellie (Gibbs), Margaret (Randell), Alice (Traill) and "Ginty" Guy.

Alex turned to cattle raising on the High Plains and eventually became the owner of four properties, totalling about 2,000 acres, in the district.. In 1900 Alex's first run was on the Upper Moroka, and in later years he took over runs at Ti-tree and on the Basalt Tableland. In 1934, Alex Guy bought the freehold of the famous Wonnangatta Cattle Station from the Alexandra syndicate, and took over the adjoining leaseholds of about 100,000 acres, which extended across the Snowy (or Bryce's) Plains and Howitt Plains. In the management of this property, he was assisted by his sons Arthur and Jack.

Alexander Guy died at Waterford in 1949 and the following newspaper report of his funeral is an indication of the respect in which he was held.

Stockmen all over the Dargo High Plains yesterday headed their mountain ponies down the valleys, through the rough Alpine country to the little settlement of Dargo, at the foot of the Australian Alps.

They gathered to pay their last respects to Alexander Guy, 76 year old cattleman, who died at the week-end and was buried yesterday in Dargo's old cemetery.

The lean, hard stockmen formed a cattleman's "guard of honour" outside the wooden church during the funeral service.

Paying their last respects to Alexander Guy

Alexander Guy — "The Man from Crooked River" — was one of Gippsland's best known graziers. The son of a family of pioneers of the district, he was born at Crooked River in the foothills of the Great Divide.

Old timers said Alex Guy was "in the saddle" by the time he was four. "He didn't have much schooling, but he was a good, wise man" said Alec Traill, 88-year-old cattleman. At the funeral was Jack Kelly of Bairnsdale, who, two years ago, was carried, injured, from the High Plains to hospital by Alex Guy. He had fallen from his horse, broken a leg, and knocked unconscious. He said yesterday, "I wasn't the only man Alex Guy rescued from the mountains. There were scores of others who probably owe their lives to his kindness and knowledge of the mountains. Four or five times a year he led searchers into the snows to find parties of lost hikers. Three years ago he and other cattlemen from Dargo found an injured horseman on Mount Wellington. They guided a small aircraft on to a short, clear space, and the plane took the injured man to hospital".

"Sandy" Traill, who found Alex Guy's two sons, Jack and Arthur, after a 13-hour, 50-mile ride across the Alps on Monday, said Alex was one of the strongest of the district's rough-riders. He was "in the saddle" until a fortnight before his death.

Alex Guy's four sons, three daughters, and six grand-children almost filled the small church at yesterday's service. His one great-grandchild was at home, asleep in his cot.

While clouds gathered over the Alps, Gippsland's cattlemen stood bareheaded in the cemetery above the town, paying their tribute.

There was sorrow in the ranges when the rapid tidings spread

That the man from Crooked River, Alexander Guy was dead

Mustering ceas'd upon the uplands,& the stockmen head'd down

On their sturdy mountain ponies to the quiet little town

To pay a final tribute, and to say a last good-bye

To the man from Crooked River, brave old Alexander Guy.

He was born at Crooked River just below the Great Divide.

And was famous as a horseman in that rugged countryside.

As a boy he rode the ranges thro' the gullies and the creeks,

And he learned to love the mountains from foothills to the peaks.

As a rider: as a stockman, as a bushman, few could vie

With the man from Crooked River, brave old Alexander Guy.

ORIAM

r Guy

Many times he struggled upward to the realms of snow & frost
Thro' the dark ravines and valleys on the track of someone lost,
He would follow till he found them in some cold and silent place,
And bear them back to safety from the Snow Queen's cold embrace
There are many mountain stockmen who were saved in days gone by
By the man from Crooked River, brave old Alexander Guy...

As the stockmen stood bareheaded by the grave above the town,
Silence fell upon the ranges & the mists came creeping down
Through the dark defiles & gorges, and all nature seemed to mourn
The passing of the stockman in the place where he was born...
Darkness fell on Dargo township & the night wind sobbed "Good-bye"
To the man from Crooked River, brave old Alexander Guy.

EDWARD HARRINGTON

Arthur and Jack continued to operate the station and leases until their retirement in 1970, when they sold out to Bob Gilder. In their thirty-six years at Wonnangatta and the High Plains, the Guys became one of the best known and respected cattle families in Victoria. Alex and Arthur both led and packed for bush-walking parties on numerous occasions, and an appreciation of their services appeared in "The Melbourne Walker" in 1954.

It was in the multiple role of guide, packer, philosopher and friend on the famous Barry Mountains Christmas tour in 1935 that most Club members will remember Arthur Guy, of Crooked River.

Although nearly twenty years have elapsed since that trip, it does not require any great stretch of imagination to again "see" Arthur, mounted on his favourite steed, leading the team of heavily-laden packhorses over those rough mountain ranges, and the long string of walkers following behind.

The Barry Mountains tour was one of the most successful ever conducted by the Club, and a good deal of the success was attributed to Arthur's untiring efforts and his genial companionship throughout the walk.

Since that time, contact has been maintained with Arthur Guy through the many Club members who, in the course of their ramblings, have visited the Crooked River and Wonnangatta country, where he carries out his grazing activities.

Arthur's father, the late Cr. Alex. Guy, was well known to the Melbourne Walking Club, and because of his intimate knowledge of the Wellington and his long experience with packhorses, he was prevailed upon to make his services available for an extended tour arranged by the Club in that area.

The Guy family has been associated with the Crooked River district for over 80 years, and this part of Victoria could almost be called the "Guy country." Alex. Guy used to tell many interesting stories of the early days on the Crooked River diggings and in the township of Grant (now entirely disappeared), where he worked as a boy.

Arthur and his brother Jack, are now the owners of the historic Wonnangatta Station, and they lease about 100,000 acres of country, some of which extends across to the Howitt Plains and the Bluff, both well known to walkers.

Arthur was born at "Glen Lea", Crooked River, in 1906, where he has resided continuously until recently. A few months ago he purchased a home in Maffra, in order to provide Mrs. Guy (a well-known walker in her single days) and their daughter with some of the amenities of town life. Although he says the old family home at the Crooked River has "had it", it is his intention to continue with his grazing interests, and no doubt much of his time will be spent at "Glen Lea".

There are few families left at the Crooked River, and with the loss of the bridge over the Wonnangatta River in recent floods, access by vehicle is possible only by fording the stream. A swing bridge caters for pedestrians.

Arthur Guy knows the ways of walkers very well, and in addition to the Barrys' tour of 1935, he has escorted parties to Wonnangatta, Mt. Wellington and Mt. Howitt. The Club hopes that some day it may be possible to persuade him to again pack and guide a party over this part of the State, with which he is so intinately acquainted.

These high plains are rich basaltic caps, five miles long by one mile wide, tied in the middle by a short scrubby ridge. The first half tilts into the Macalister River. The other nurtures the head of the Caledonia River and is probably the richest pasture in our uplands. At the southern end, sheltered by tall snowgums, the Howitt Plains Hut still survives.

C.W.GRANT 1960

HOWITT PLAINS HUT
Now roofed and clad in galvanised iron, the Howitt Plains Hut, built by the Bryces in early 1900s was originally slab sided and shingle roofed.

Jack Guy at Guy's Snowy Plains Hut.

Arthur and Jack Guy at Wonnangatta in early 1950s.

Arthur Guy in two horse waggon crossing the swirling waters of the Wonnangatta River at ford below the bend where bridge was washed away.

Alexander Guy.

William and Martha Guy. 'Bill' died after a tree fell on him at Crooked River. Martha later married Albert Stout, well-known storekeeper of Talbotville.

Jack Guy and Denny Connolly building Guy's Hut on Bryce's (or Snowy) Plains in March 1940.

GUY'S HUT in a charming park like setting on a freehold block on the Snowy Plains, has now, along with the Wonnangatta Station freehold and leasehold, passed into the hands of Bob Gilder, of Glenfalloch Station.

GUY'S HUT on Snowy Plains, built in 1940, replaced the original Snowy Plains Hut, built by the Bryces during their occupancy of Wonnangatta Station 1870–1914.

Mr & Mrs Alan Bennie at "Rivermount".

Bennies of Rose River

COBBLER IS NOT THE GREATEST PEAK of our Alpine system, but it is one of the most remarkable and probably the most easily identified — the hunchback of Cobbler — this is a natural feature which makes for remembrance. The distinctive note is struck by a massive projection, like the horn of a rhinoceros, which is almost cut off from the main hill and towers well above it. It breaks the orderly outline of the mount, as seen from below, and gives it character . . . From it, or near it, springs the waters of three pleasant rivers, the Buffalo, the Rose, and that last, whose name is like "the mellow lin - lan - lone of evening bells" — the Dandongadale."

So wrote pioneer bushwalker 'Bob' Croll, who visited the Cobbler Plateau in the first decade of the century, going via the Rose and Dandongadale valleys. He wrote also of the hospitality of Victor Tiernan, of Mt Typo station, one of the first to graze cattle on the plateau

Victor Tiernan employed for a few years, a teen-aged stockman who left his service to enlist in the first A.I.F. and serve in France and Belgium. He was born at Whitfield and baptised James Alan Bennie in 1895. The 'James Alan' was something of a superfluity, as for most of his life he was known simply as "Bennie". "Bennie's" maternal grandparents, the Tyrrells were amongst the pioneers of the isolated King valley settlement of Whitfield having conducted the Whitfield Hotel since it was first licenced, and even before that, conducted the establishment as a boarding house.

Family and friends of the Bennies who had ridden up from Whitfield to the approximate site of the Cobbler Hut on Cobbler Plateau for a picnic lunch in about the year 1900.

Group includes W.H.Swinburn, Rev. Geo. Martin, John Tyrell (in helmet), and Mrs Martin.

Group includes Mrs Jack Tyrell, Mrs Susan Bennie, (Alan's mother), Harry Thomas, Bill Pipers, Harry Tyrell (Whitfield Hotel), Charlie Tyrell, Tom Beauman

"They were tough years", Bennie recalled, referring to his war service, "the senseless killing was enough to drive me from the cities and people and bitterness and cruelty." And so, when Bennie came home he bought from the Government, 2454 acres of hilly scrub country at the head of the Rose river, which included half of Mt Typo, for less than 5/- an acre.

He set out with a horse, a dog and no money, but unlimited enthusiasm, to carve a farm out of virgin bush. The Whitfieldites predicted he would soon be back. "It wasn't easy", he recalled, "clearing, fencing, cutting trees and building a home". But Bennie made it and the boys at the Whitfield pub lost their bets.

He was joined by a wife, and Mr and Mrs Bennie of "Rivermount", as they called their home, became known for their hospitality to fishermen who sought the elusive trout in the upper reaches of the King, Rose, Dandongadale and Catherine Rivers, to which remote spots Bennie packed them, and to bushwalkers who chose the northern approach to the Cobbler Plateau. Their mail had to be collected from Chestnut, 16 miles away, and the nearest township for stores, Whitfield, was three miles further on.

Their only neighbours were their good friends the Tiernan brothers during their residence at Mt Typo Cattle Station. Bennie's main interest was in cattle raising, but he never held a grazing lease for the nearby snow-plains on Cobbler. He had an intimate knowledge of the high country, however, and frequently supplied pack-horses; not only to bring in the fishermen to the little cabins he built for their use, but for riding and walking parties, who, on occasions, he accompanied as far afield as Holmes Plain and Mt Wellington. He knew the mountain country like he knew his home paddock.

In 1937, appreciative bushwalkers gave the Bennies a Visitors' Book and in the years that followed, more than a thousand bushwalkers, fishermen, foresters and cattlemen wrote their names and appreciation of the Bennies hospitality on more than forty of the pages. (The book is now a treasured possession of Bennie's younger brother Leslie.)

A friend recalls arriving one New Year's Eve unexpectedly at Bennies', with a party of a dozen hungry bush-walkers. They were welcomed, and after enquiring if they could be provided with a meal, were duly served a fine three course New Year's Eve dinner and then entertained until the early hours. Bennie had built his own home, but had never quite got around to completing it. There was only an earth floor for most of the dining room though the table was set on a timber section supported by stumps in the centre of the room, and a piano was likewise supported in similar manner against one wall. It in no way detracted from the Bennies'

"Bennie" whose first thought was for the welfare of his dogs.

91

James Alan Bennie at the doorway of the home he built at Rose River.

The cabins that "Bennie" built at Rose River, to accommodate the trout fishermen he packed in to the upper reaches of the stream.

friendly hospitality. As they bade good-bye, around 2 a.m., the bush-walkers asked for the bill. Mrs Bennie seemed a little reluctant to name a price and finally said, "Would 7/6 be alright?" And she meant 7/6 for the whole party! Of course, a 'whip-around' realised a satisfactory amount. But, that was the Bennies. They were rich in everything except money. And that didn't seem to matter to them.

In the 1939 fires, Bennie fought to prevent the flames spreading down the valley. He was badly burned, lost most of his stock and had his timber destroyed. But he fought back to again drive his Circle B brand cattle down the eighteen miles to the junction of the Rose and Buffalo and thence to the saleyards at Myrtleford, where in 1980 the name of Bennie is still remembered and respected.

John Sorell went looking for a story in 1960 and followed a dotted line on Broadbent's Road Map to "Bennie's", for by now, the home in the wilderness had earned a place on the map. Sorell recalls that the house was deserted and returning to Whitfield, he came upon Bennie, who was returning from Wangaratta, forty-five miles from his home, after visiting his wife, then eighty-one years old, who was in hospital. It had been a five day trip, for Bennie had walked both ways!

Mrs Bennie died on 4th May 1962, aged eighty-three years and Bennie remained alone in his mountain valley. "The farm is nothing to look at, it's rough and the house chimney will collapse one day", he said, "but I love these hills and just living here gives me satisfaction in life."

James Alan Bennie died on 15th July, 1968, at the age of seventy-three years, and the valley will never know his like again. Ten years later, visitors arrived whose presence would have stretched old Bennie's friendly hospitality beyond its limits. They burnt the old homestead to the ground and others returned more recently to ensure that Bennie's cabins suffered a like fate!

Mists blanket the 'new' Cobbler Hut in this mid-winter scene.

Snow covered the 'old' Cobbler Hut which had a useful life of about forty-five years.

The Man from Snowy River

*A*N *ALMOST LEGENDARY FIGURE* of the Upper Murray, better known by the pseudenom bestowed on him by 'Banjo' Patterson, "The Man from Snowy River" than by his baptismal name, is John Riley.

After migrating to Sydney from Castlebar, Co. Mayo, Ireland, in 1851, John Riley went to live with his widowed sister, Mrs Joseph Jones, in Omeo. He opened a tailoring business in Day Street, but before long the comings and goings of the mountain cattlemen began to interest him more than tailoring. Riley's sister remarried a man named Rawson in 1860, and Riley being relieved of the obligation of assisting to support her then left the tailoring.

It is believed he was one of the earliest gold seekers, and in 1860 was in the Kiandra Rush. He then worked for many years as a stockman on the Monaro. He quickly acquired a reputation as a bushman, brumby hunter and horse breaker and became well known amongst the Gippsland and Snowy mountain riders.

Mrs M.J.Carmody, in her book "The Pioneering Spirit" (unpublished), relates that John Riley assisted his sister's second husband in droving mobs of horses from Black Mountain area to Sydney for sale. On one such droving trip, the brother-in-law, suspecting possible trouble, asked John to take the horses on to Dalgety alone. Not knowing that the horses were stolen, John agreed, and when police picked him up, he - because of a strict sense of loyalty to his sister - remained silent when questioned. His refusal to implicate his sister's husband cost him a seven year gaol sentence, of which he served five years.

* A second source suggests that John Riley was born in 1827, in Michaelstown, County Cork, Ireland, and that he decided to migrate to Australia in 1843, at the age of fifteen. .

However, when later employed by Mr John Pierce, his reputation as an honest stockman was never questioned. It is known that Mr Pierce had complete confidence in Riley's integrity.

The episode (unpublished and unknown outside the Corryong area) is recorded here, not to disclose Riley's criminal record, but to emphasise his sense of loyalty - even if misplaced - and to record the esteem in which he was held by Mr Pierce.

This photo taken during a walking tour to the Tom Groggin area in 1904 shows Jack Riley at the door of his hut.

In 1884 he was appointed manager of 'Tom Groggin', an Upper Murray pastoral run with an area of 20,000 acres, first leased in 1853 by the successful tenderers, William Wright and Michael Tandy, who built the first huts on the Victorian side of the river in that year. Some two years later, it is believed that a John Barry built a hut on the New South Wales side (the 'Tom Groggin' run was located on both sides of the river) and it was here that John Riley twenty-nine years later made his home and for thirty years managed the property for his employer, Mr John Pierce of 'Greg Greg', near Corryong. There is no evidence to indicate whether Riley occupied the original Barry hut or built one for himself.

His task was to drove cattle out to 'Tom Groggin' in the summer for grazing on the high country, and to bring them back as two year olds to 'Greg Greg' station. The arduous task of droving and mustering cattle was successfully accomplished by Riley and many trips involved guiding them over precipitous slopes such as the Geehi Wall.

In the mid '80s Riley featured in an epic ride that was eventually to bring immortality to his name. He joined a party of stockmen who were attempting to re-capture a thoroughbred stallion that had escaped and was running with a mob of wild horses, near Mt. Leatherhead. A stockyard was built along a creek at the foot of Mt. Leatherhead and the mob was located, as Riley had predicted, on a high ridge. A report of the incident relates, "when the riders closed in on the mob, the stallion broke away and galloped down a fearsome slope with Riley alone in hot pursuit. The mountainside was pitted with wombat holes, strewn with loose shale and covered with low scrub. The stallion and Riley's pony literally tobogganed down to the bottom, where the stallion blundered into the stockyard and Riley, with sliprails up and the stallion secured, was waiting when the rest of the riders, having taken an easier route down, arrived.

In 1890, 'Banjo' Paterson, who was a frequent visitor to the Mitchell's of 'Bringenbrong', probably the most noteworthy family in the Upper Murray region, spent a night with Walter Mitchell in John Riley's hut. During the course of the night's conversation around the fireside, Riley was persuaded to tell the story of his ride and the successful capture of the stallion.

Paterson, a great admirer of the mountain riders, was extremely impressed by the account and shortly afterwards he wrote the now famous poem "The Man from Snowy River" which was first published in "The Bulletin" in 1890 and was reprinted in the Centenary Issue of the same journal in January 1980.

There have, over the years, been numerous claimants to the title of "The Man from Snowy River". However, Mr John Pierce, Mr Walter Mitchell and A.B.Paterson himself all confirmed that John Riley was the man whose ride inspired 'Banjo' Paterson to write the poem, "The Man from Snowy River", and, after all, the 'Banjo' should know!

RILEY'S HUT
Photographed in December 1935 "The Man from Snowy River's Hut"
on the N.S.W. side of the Murray River at Tom Groggin, deserted for
twenty-one years, was then in an advanced state of decay.   It was
burnt in the 1939 bushfires.

A contributor to 'The Melbourne Walker' of 1949, continues the story: Advancing years and the rough bush life eventually began to tell on Riley but he refused to leave 'Tom Groggin', except for occasional brief visits to Corryong. He had no relatives in the district, his only companion being Fred Jervis, who was employed by Mr Pierce to look after John. In 1914 word reached Corryong that Riley was ill, and a party of five men, led by Mr W.H.Findlay, set out immediately to bring him into hospital. Early morning of 14th July 1914 found the party setting out to transport the stricken man 43 miles to Corryong. Riley was carried for the first few miles by stretcher, but when steep climbing, 2,000 feet through scrub and rocks, over the shoulder of Hermit's Hill became necessary, Riley was lifted into the saddle of a stockman's pony and Butler, the lightest rider in the party, mounted behind him. A rider on each side supported the half-conscious man.

The party encountered intense cold, and snow began to fall as they rode on past Hermit's Creek to Surveyors' Creek, where a deserted miners' hut provided shelter for the night. Next day the party remained at the hut and Riley was made as comfortable as possible before the fire, but that evening he passed away. John Riley, 'The Man from Snowy River' had made his last ride.

97

"The flanks of Kosiusko
Loomed vast and veiled and grey,
And the dark vale of Groggin
Was darker than the day
When the Man from Snowy River went away."

He was buried in the Corryong Cemetery on 16th July 1914 and in 1946 a rough granite headstone was erected to his memory:

JACK RILEY
"The Man from Snowy River"
Died
July 16th, 1914

Far, far from Kosciusco
He slumbers deep and long,
While the wild vale of Groggin
Is bursting into song.
And strange winds croon above him
'Corryong' . . . . 'Corryong'.

Due acknowledgment is made to
'The Bulletin', in whose pages
'The Man From Snowy River'
by 'Banjo' Paterson, first appeared.

The man from Snowy River

There was movement at the station, for the
    word had passed around
  That the colt from old Regret had got
    away
And had joined the wild bush horses — he
    was worth a thousand pound —
So all the cracks had gathered to the fray.
All the tried and noted riders from the
    stations near and far
  Had mustered at the homestead over-
    night,
For the bushmen love hard-riding where the
    fleet wild horses are,
  And the stockhorse snuffs the battle with
    delight.

There was Harrison, who made his pile
    when Pardon won the Cup,
  The old man with his hair as white as
    snow,
But few could ride beside him when his
    blood was fairly up —
  He would go wherever horse and man
    could go.
And Clancy of "The Overflow" came down
    to lend a hand —
  No better rider ever held the reins;
For never horse could throw him while the
    saddle-girths would stand,
  He learnt to ride while droving on the
    plains.

And one was there, a stripling on a small
    and graceful beast;
  He was something like a racehorse
    undersized,
With a touch of Timor pony, three parts
    thoroughbred at least,
  The sort that are by mountain horsemen
    prized.

He was hard and tough and wiry — just the
    kind that won't say die;
  There was courage in his quick, im-
    patient tread,
And he bore the badge of gameness in his
    bright and fiery eye
  And the proud and lofty carriage of his
    head.

But still so slight and weedy one would
    doubt his power to stay,
  And the old man said: "That horse will
    never do
For a long and tiring gallop — lad, you'd
    better stop away.
  The hills are far too rough for such as
    you."
So he waited sad and wistful, only Clancy
    stood his friend.
  "I think we ought to let him come," he
    said;
"I warrant he'll be with us when he's
    wanted at the end,
  For both his horse and he are
    mountain-bred.

"He hails from Snowy River, up by
    Kosciusko's side,
  Where the hills are twice as steep and
    twice as rough —
Where a horse's hoofs strike firelight from
    the flintstones every stride.
  The man that holds his own is good
    enough,
And the Snowy River riders on the
    mountains make their home,
  Where the Snowy flows those giant hills
    between.
I have seen full many horsemen since I first
    commenced to roam,
  But never yet such riders have I seen."

So he went; they found the horses near the
    big Mimosa clump;
  They raced away towards the mountain's
    brow,
And the old man gave his orders: "Boys, go
    at them from the jump;
  No use to go for fancy-riding now;
And, Clancy, you must wheel them — try
    and wheel them to the right.
  Ride boldly, lad, and never fear the spills,
For never yet was rider that could keep the
    mob in sight
  If once they gain the shelter of those
    hills."

So Clancy rode to wheel them — he was
    racing on the wing
  Where the best and boldest riders take
    their place —
And he raced his stock-horse past them, and
    he made the ranges ring
  With the stockwhip as he met them face
    to face,
And they wavered for a moment while he
    swung the dreaded lash,
  But they saw their well-loved mountain
    full in view,
And they charged beneath the stockwhip
    with a sharp and sudden dash,
  And off into the mountain-scrub they
    flew.

Then fast the horsemen followed where the
    gorges deep and black
  Resounded to the thunder of their tread,
And the stockwhips woke the echoes and
    they fiercely answered back
  From cliffs and crags that beetled
    overhead;
And upward, upward ever, the wild horses
    held their way
  Where mountain-ash and kurrajong grew
    wide.
And the old man muttered fiercely: "We
    may bid the mob good-day,
  No man can hold them down the other
    side."

When they reached the mountain's summit
    even Clancy took a pull —
  It well might make the boldest hold their
    breath,
The wild hop-scrub grew thickly and the
    hidden ground was full
  Of wombat-holes, and any slip was death;
But the man from Snowy River let his pony
    have his head,
  And swung his stockwhip round and gave
    a cheer,
And raced him down the mountain like a
    torrent down its bed,
  While the others stood and watched in
    very fear.

He sent the flintstones flying, but the pony
    kept his feet;
  He cleared the fallen timber in his stride,
And the man from Snowy River never
    shifted in his seat —
It was grand to see that mountain
    horseman ride

Through stringy-barks and saplings on the
    rough and broken ground,
  Down the hillside at a racing-pace he
    went,
And he never drew the bridle till he landed
    safe and sound
  At the bottom of that terrible descent.

He was right among the horses as they
    climbed the further hill,
  And the watchers, on the mountain
    standing mute,
Saw him ply the stockwhip fiercely — he
    was right among them still
  As he raced across the clearing in pursuit;
Then they lost him for a moment where the
    mountain gullies met
  In the ranges — but a final glimpse reveals
On a dim and distant hillside the wild horses
    racing yet
  With the man from Snowy River at their
    heels.

And he ran them single-handed till their
    sides were white with foam,
  He followed like a bloodhound on their
    track
Till they halted, cowed and beaten — then
    he turned their heads for home,
  And alone and unassisted brought them
    back;
And his hardy mountain pony — he could
    scarcely raise a trot —
  He was blood from hip to shoulder from
    the spur,
But his pluck was still undaunted and his
    courage fiery hot,
  For never yet was mountain horse a cur.

And down by Araluen where the stony
    ridges raise
  Their torn and rugged battlements on
    high,
Where the air is clear as crystal and the
    white stars fairly blaze
  At midnight in the cold and frosty sky,
And where, around "The Overflow," the
    reed-beds sweep and sway
  To the breezes and the rolling plains are
    wide,
The man from Snowy River is a household
    word to-day,
  And the stockmen tell the story of his
    ride.

THE BANJO
(A. B. PATERSON), 1890

100

The Frys of Howqua Hills

*T*HE HOWQUA HILLS area was first opened up by a Mansfield doctor named Steele, in the late 1860s, when he founded a cattle station on the river flats and surrounding hills. Then in the 1870s gold was discovered in small quantities over a wide area. The old-time prospectors were optimistic people, however, and diggers flocked in a mild 'rush', by pack-horse, bullock-team, and on foot, and in a short time claims were pegged, a hotel built and an area subdivided into quarter acre blocks.

The best known mines were the Mountain Chief and the Great Rand. The rush was short-lived however, and after the first few mine crushings there was talk of a swindle. A bank manager who had advanced money to the promoters of the Mountain Chief Mine Company committed suicide and the populace quickly 'folded their tents and stole away.'

The licensee of the hotel was William Mitchell Lovick who had also taken out a licence for the Hunt Club Hotel at Merrijig in 1873, a hostelry that was to remain in the Lovick family for more than seventy five years.

A house which had been moved from Martin's Gap by bullock team, and rebuilt for the Mountain Chief Mine manager, was acquired, when all but he had fled, by Jim Fry, who exclaimed, "It's mine" and lived there for the next 54 years.

Jim, originally came from Darlingford, where Fry's Bridge was a well known landmark until submerged by the Eildon Weir. He married Mary Ann Thompson, a Darlingford girl, and sister of Ralph Thompson, a Mansfield storekeeper. They had two children, Fred and Molly.

Jim worked as a teamster for Ross Brothers whose waggons carted goods in the district and to the mines of Jamieson and as far away as Woods Point and Matlock. With the decline in mining, Jim Fry became a stockman and, a born horseman, he soon acquired a reputation for his skill with stock and unrivalled knowledge of the surrounding mountains. He was a great friend of Bill Hearn and they rode the hills together. They both featured in the search following the Wonnangatta murders and the subsequent discovery of Bamford's body on Howitt Plains.

Jim was a great fisherman and one of his accomplishments was fly-fishing, taking trout from the Howqua while casting from the back of his grey mare which, on sensing a 'strike' would take a quick pace or two backwards and 'grass' the fish on the bank.

Jim, a man of the mountains, never visited Melbourne nor rode on a train. Rejecting offers of both he is reported to have said, "When I go to Melbourne, I'll ride — on a horse". But he never did, and he lived into his eighties, finally passing away in 1927.

JIM FRY

From a bend in the river, the house of Mr and Mrs Jim Fry was visible. Many a walker has pleasant memories of hospitable welcomes received at that home in the hills. To the deep regret of many of us who knew him from passing calls, old Jim passed away early this year, but, in the years to come, those who have the good fortune to revisit Howqua Hills will always have a kindly memory for the white bearded, hospitable old man and his lady who were always so friendly to the passing walker. Old Jim was a very keen trout fisherman and could catch them. The story goes that in his declining years, he angled from the back of his horse, which knew the game so well that, when the fish was hooked, it would back out of the stream to enable the catch to be grassed.

W.F.("Bill") WATERS 1927

The Frys of Howqua Hills

After Jim's death, his nephew Fred, born in 1895, moved in, and followed the pattern of solitary life enjoyed by old Jim, until joined by an older brother Steve (sometimes referred to as a cousin), who, after a short stint in Melbourne retreated to the solitude of Old Howqua.

> . . . *Howqua Hills, also known as Fry's, on the banks of the Howqua River 22 miles from Mansfield, via Merrijig. The old road ends at the water's edge, at a notable bend of the river, the turning point, in fact, of the Howqua's career, as the stream flowing west from its source on Mt Howitt, here swings sharply to the south-west, to set a course direct for the Goulburn.*
> *When Banjo wrote:*
> > *"and the bush has friends to meet him;*
> > *And their kindly voices greet him . . . "*
> *he must surely have been mindful of the charming locality which, ringed by friendly foothills, like a family circle in conclave, has an air of tranquility and the fragrance of the forest to welcome the wayfarer.*
>
> C.W.GRANT 1954

Fred Fry, fishing for trout in the Howqua River

In their spare time they did a little prospecting and their optimism never left them. During a visit in the 1930s, they assured the writer that only the lack of a grant from the Mines Department to enable them to instal much needed machinery was delaying them from "Striking it rich". Sadly, neither the grant nor the 'Strike' ever eventuated.

Neither of the brothers (or was it cousins) were garrulous and days would elapse without either speaking a word. "We don't have many 'blues' ", Steve claimed.

The ravages of time and the voracious appetites of white ants spelt doom to the old house and in the late 1940s Fred built a new one. A superb

Fred and Steve Fry at Howqua Hills.

The Frys of Howqua Hills

The original Fry Homestead on a river flat at Howqua Hills. Originally a mine manager's home it was abandoned about 1874 and then occupied by Mr and Mrs Jim Fry and later their nephew Fred Fry, until it succumbed to old age and white ants.

axeman, he cut and split the timber, as he had done for a number of huts in the Howqua valley.

Fred died after a long illness in 1971, and Steve having pre-deceased him there was for the first time in 100 years, no one to remain at the little river flat which had always been better known as "Frys" than by its given name, Howqua Hills.

"The Mansfield Courier" had this to say:

"A man must be in the possession of many rare qualities if he can live alone in comparitive isolation for a great part of his life and yet enjoy the love and respect of a circle of friends in every walk of life numbering far above the ordinary.

Such a man was Mr Fred Fry, of Howqua Hills. The late Fred Fry was the youngest son in the large family of the late George and Mary Ann Fry and was born in Mansfield just before the turn of the century. His father originally came from Darlingford, where Fry's Bridge was a well known landmark until submerged by the Eildon Weir.

From an early age young Fred was a great lover of horses and was dominated by the pioneering spirit. In the gold boom years he drove a waggon team for Allen Bros and later for John Ross carrying supplies to Gaffney's Creek and Woods Point over roads that were often boggy and always hazardous. Eventually he

The home which Fred Fry constructed at Howqua Hills to replace the old galvanised iron home which had been occupied by Mr and Mrs Jim Fry since its acquisition after the gold rush of 1873.

acquired a team of his own and carried on until a decline in mining and the advent of modern transport rendered the slower horse-drawn vehicles obsolete.

He worked as a stockman at Wonnangatta and later settled at Howqua Hills in the home at Fry's Crossing on the banks of the upper Howqua River. Howqua Hills had lost the glamour and activity of the gold boom days and reverted more or less back to nature, with the only outlet a steep and rugged road over Mt Timbertop. Mr Fry played a prominent part in opening up the area for the Forests Commission and packing in salt for the destruction of noxious weeds for the Lands Department.

In those days only the most venturesome anglers went into the upper Howqua regions and these were largely dependent on Mr Fry for guidance and packing in supplies. As a bushman he was without peer and as such was self dependant and undaunted by difficulties.

With his own hands and with a personal style of workmanship, he split timber and erected many huts which stand as monuments to his memory in the area he loved. amongst these being Ritchie's Hut, Gardiner's Hut, Fry's Hut, Upper Jamieson Hut and Schusters."

The Treasures of Dargo

*T*HE DARGO HIGH PLAINS. These very words sound a note of mystery, in the minds of the uninitiated they conjure up pictures of solitude, soaring eagles or perhaps a newer and stranger Shangri-la. Whatever the case may be the following extracts taken from notes written by the late Mr Harry Lewis Treasure breathe a warmth and homeliness not altogether expected of the difficult pioneering days in the higher altitudes

The Dargo High Plains were known to only a few stockmen in the early 1850s but exploration and development by miners spread to the area soon afterwards. The first cattle run was taken up by Pierce J. Williams and by 1872-3 it had passed to Jones, who built the first home there. In 1878, George Emanuel Treasure, one of the earliest miners in the Harrietville district took up a selection of land on the Dargo High Plains.

Harry Treasure, George Emanuel's fourth son, recorded the family's early history in a diary, still preserved, written from his early notes. "My father arranged with Mr Richard King of Mayford to take sufficient horses to Harrietville to switch his wife and family and all his worldly belongings to King's Spur on the eastern slopes of the Dargo High Plains. My father fitted up two armchairs, with legs removed - one on either side of a pack-horse for my sister Nell and second eldest boy George to ride in. At the time I was nine months old, and my mother carried me in front of her as she rode.

The track from Harrietville, where we set out in April 1878 was not like what it is today. It was a case of following the tops of the ridges. The progress must have been slow and tiresome. The party reached the hollow on the south side of Mt St Bernard where Mother Morrell's was situated, and here a halt was called to boil up a billy and have a cup of tea and some lunch. Again we were on the road climbing up and over one bump and down the other side in readiness to start up the next one over Mt Freezeout. What a climb. Then on further to Blue Rag and Lanky's Plain where mother begged to be left behind even though she might have to lie out all night.

GOW'S HOTEL
The ruins of Gow's Hotel, Dargo High Plains, once a thriving hostelry on the track from St Bernard to the Crooked River Diggings.

But, after a short rest, she was persuaded to continue. Another five or six miles to go and every mile seemed like ten, but there was nothing else for it but to go on. It would be very hard to make a camp and of course, hard to keep the horses. On and on the outfit went, now in the dark and still another mile to go downhill with the horses floundering over logs and boulders until at last the destination was reached. The place of abode could best be described as a two roomed log hut with a bark roof and a verandah over the entrance door to the living room. The chimney was built of slabs and timber on the outside and stoned up to a height of 7-8 feet on the inside. The fireplace had very wide hobs and a colonial oven built on one side. The furniture, except for the two arm chairs we had brought, was mostly home made from bush timber and very rough.

The mountain on which this house was built was of basaltic formation with an altitude of about 4,500 feet. On the top it is as level as a billiard table with a coat of grass to cushion the feet as you walk over it.

The Treasures commenced their farming with a few dairy cattle, and sold milk, butter and cheese to the miners who were crossing the Dargos to Grant and the Crooked River diggings. Soon a store was added and the house became a licenced hotel. A small Hereford herd was established, vegetables grown and sold, and Harry Treasure killed wallabies for skins and meat. The family grew to nine boys and two girls.

"I remember the cold winters which seemed like an eternity", Harry wrote. "In rough weather the wind could be heard to roar through the trees in the distance and then the snow would commence falling. Perhaps only a few inches for a start, but as the winter advanced it would get more

Treasure homestead, Dargo High Plains.

severe. Ofter a depth of 12-20 inches would be lying on the ground. It was a pretty sight to see, all the trees loaded down with snow and when an exceptionally heavy fall came one could hear the limbs on the trees breaking and see them falling all around. Before the winter a huge heap of firewood was built. The wood was hauled by harnessing up a horse and taking him out in the bush to drag in logs and limbs of fallen trees, or any other pieces that could be picked up. After several days of hauling, the wood was then chopped and stacked on end at a convenient place near the house.

"At this stage, Dick Gow also had a run on the High Plains, and owned a hotel, "Noons", about three miles south of Treasures. It was known as the half-way house.

About the year 1886, when I was nine years old, a mail contract was let to a Thomas Gallagher, who carried the mail one trip per week from Harrietville to Grant and back to Harrietville. The route was from Harrietville to Bousteads' on Mt St Bernard and then down along the Dargo river to Stayford, then up the Kings Spur, across the Dargo High Plains and on to Grant by way of the Half Way Hotel. During the winter months Thomas Gallagher would walk, carrying the mail and ofter the greater part of the distance was done in snow shoes. Gallagher was a very strong walker and had wonderful endurance. It was amazing to see the heavy load he could carry on his back through the snow.

Jim Treasure, Carl Wraith, Harry Treasure and Jack Treasure at Gow's old yard, Dargo High Plains, 1938.

Mining had almost ceased by 1900 and the Dargos saw less travellers passing through. The Treasures closed the store and relied entirely on their Hereford herd for a living, grazing the summer pastures on the Dargos and wintering them on the lower slopes at the heads of the valleys. Harry Treasure remained at the old home but the others left.

Rabbits arrived about this time and soon the winter grazing areas were eaten out. The snowplains survived better as conditions were less favourable to the rabbits.

Harry Treasure married in 1904, and later selected "Castleburn" and bought other properties around to establish new winter pastures for the herds that grazed the high country in summer.

This ended the continuous habitation of the old home thirty miles up from Dargo which the family had called home for forty years. The last season spent in the snow was 1913, when on the 13th June, Harry's son Jack Treasure was born. Jack recounts that 12 inches of snow delayed the arrival of the bush nurse, summoned from Dargo, and he arrived a day before she did!

Harry Lewis Treasure died at his summer residence on the High Plains on December 28th, 1961, but his family continued to run 'Castleburn' and the top leases.

Not long ago, Mrs Harry Treasure (then active at 82 years) rode down alone from the homestead on the High Plains to 'Castleburn', 45 miles away.

At 30 miles, she called at the home of her son Jack, had a cup of tea, chatted a while and then rode on.

Jack Treasure, Mack the dog, and Brownie the pack horse.   (Photo mid 1930s)

Jack Treasure and Graham Webb yarding cattle at Webbsdale

Vernon H. Mattingley called at "Rockalpine" the Treasure homestead on the High Plains, in 1936. He wrote of Mrs Harry Treasure, 'The Little Lady of the Alps', "I found her in the fine old kitchen, methodically rolling out the dough and cutting it with a knife as she has done for the afternoon batch of scones thousands of times.

Outside, the fog crept close about the homestead, cattle bellowing through the moss-covered timber; in the next room the menfolk were seated at the cribbage board near the great log fire, while the bread rose in the dish on the hearth.

As I sat at the edge of the table watching the nimble fingers at their work and the quick, deft movements of the little person in the trim frock, I thought to myself that Harry Treasure was a lucky man, and that Jim, Jack and Don were lucky sons, as indeed, all sons are.

Little Lady of the Alps I call her - Mrs Harry Treasure, housewife in probably the highest homestead in Victoria's Alps, on the Dargo High Plains, 4650 feet above sea level.

It was a dismal day on "the roof of the State" yet here beside her glowing oven, with the men about the place so early in the afternoon and a job for her at hand, she was a happy ray of sunshine and a busy little soul. As she popped her scone trays into the oven and reached for the flour again in preparation for a man-sized apple pie, I said: 'Surely, you get lonely up here Mrs Treasure, so far away from town and other people.'

Her eyes twinkled, and I felt that she had been waiting for it. 'Never,' she laughed. 'While I am not with them, they don't get the proper meals -

112

Jack Treasure and Graham Webb branding calves at "Webbsdale".

anything will do, they say - and there is a lot of darning and mending to be done.'

This is typical of the spirit and the personality that have made Mrs Treasure one of the happiest housewives in Victoria, although wireless and an occasional mail, sometimes weeks delayed, are her only contact with civilisation for about six months in the year.

When the snow is approaching and the cattle must be moved to lower levels toward the end of April, she waits to look after the menfolk until the last couple of weeks, and then returns by horseback to her other home at 'Castleburn', on the Stratford side of Dargo.

There she waits till the great Alpine plateau is again almost clear of snow in the spring, and when the big drive of cattle to the heights begins, she follows them up.

Mrs Treasure has two homes to keep in order. Even her dresses are left at either place while she is away, awaiting her return, for she must travel light, and when the time comes for her to leave the Dargo High Plains homestead, "Rockalpine", she literally closes the door on everything and walks out.

Born at Beechworth in 1884, Mrs Treasure was a private school teacher in that town for several years before she went to the mining settlement (now vanished) on the High Plains at the age of 18. Two years later, she married Harry Treasure and they built the fine, big homestead in which they now live for six months of the year. For their first ten years they used to spend the winters there, too.

The homestead is a monument to pioneering endeavour. With the cartage of sufficient sawn timber from lower levels a practical impossibility, Harry Treasure and his helpers built the house completely from wollybutt or mountain ash. For months they worked with a pit saw, one man on top, one underneath, cutting the boards and beams for the home. The finished job took 16,000 super feet of timber, all hand-sawn.

Later additions to the homestead of six big rooms are verandah posts sawn from snow gum which grows on the High Plains, as hard as jarrah. And

The Pied Piper of Dargo. Jack Treasure, in sheep's clothing leads the Herefords into town.

Using a stone as a hammer, Freda Treasure fixes a nail in the shoe of Bluey the pack horse. Brought up in cattle country, where her family have been established for 70 years, she is a competent horsewoman. She is also capable with her needle and, after the day's work on the trail, she sat (left) on her chicken wire cot to catch up with her knitting by the light of the candle in a jar.

(Freda Treasure is now
Mrs Wal Ryder. Ed.)

MT EWAN HUT
A party of riders led by Freda Treasure, outside the Mt Ewan Hut,
Dargo High Plains.

when I met 60-year -old Harry Treasure, he was in the thick of building a new bathroom.

This is the home where Mrs Treasure keeps house on the Dargo High Plains with her husband and her sons - Jack, 23; Jim, 25; Don, 30 - all strong, upright lads who muster on the wildest mountain-bred ponies and think nothing of throwing a three-year-old steer single handed.

Don has 'gone mining' below the High Plains and Freda, the only daughter, who was given her earliest school lessons by her mother, is now boarding at a ladies college in Melbourne.

It is a united and happy family, living on the flat top of the Alps where the summer temperature averages only 60 degrees and where the recreation for all is the work of all - "horses, cattle and horses again, with sometimes a little ski-running, to rescue snowed-in cattle".

Reared and living among cattlemen, cattle and horses all her life, Mrs Treasure follows the out-of-door affairs with expert knowledge. She revels in the household duties, but to race across a rock-strewn flat on the High Plains on the back of a smart, sure-footed pony after break-away steers is for her a pleasure which she insists on sharing with the men-folk.

I should think that no horse could frighten our 'Little Lady of the Alps'. At least once a week she is out with the lads mustering some of their 2,000 or more head of Hereford cattle, for she likes to have a hand in everything, and she does it for the fun of it.

116

I had dropped in on this happy, hospitable family on a cold, foggy day, as an unexpected visitor, yet no close friend could have been given a more real and spontaneous welcome. A chair was offered to me in front of the great, roaring fire before I had dropped my coat in a sodden heap on the verandah.

With their axes the boys came in from a gully half a mile away for a talk. Dry shoes and socks were produced for me; Mrs Treasure had the dinner in the oven. Dinner passed, afternoon tea passed, tea was served, and still the yarns were spinning and still Mrs Treasure urged my two companions and me to stay on.

While Harry Treasure, who has lived on the High Plains, practically all his life, was running into good form with his stories, the boys went out, rounded up 100 or so sheep and slaughtered one for the next week's meat. The stories of the High Plains were many and varied. From what Harry Treasure told me, the weather can get very cold up there, for there was a man there once who went to a spring for water. The spring was frozen, so he returned to his hut for a pick. He drove the pick hard into the spring and it held fast. Throwing all his weight on to the handle, he succeeded in lifting the whole frozen spring out of the ground and carried it back to his hut. It kept him in fresh water for a month!

There was another identity of the High Plains (again according to Harry Treasure) who dropped his hat down a mine shaft one frosty morning. His mate down below was about to bring it up for him when he shouted, "Never mind, Bill, I'll pour a billy of boiling water down". He did, and he pulled his hat up, which was stuck fast to the bottom of an icicle of solid ice. Then, (again according to Harry Treasure), there was a cattleman who had trouble in handling his dogs on the High Plains, because his commands always froze and fell stiff in the snow before they reached the dogs. One day, he found some frozen words lying in the snow. He took them home to his hut, warmed them in a frying pan and soon some cattleman's frightful language was shouted from the frying pan!

Finally Harry had a snake story. He told of one terrifying experience when a billy fire was lit against a beautiful, black log and the cattlemen were sitting around in the comfortable warmth, smoking and yarning, when the billies were suddenly hurled in all directions and the 'black log' wriggled away!

After that, it was time to say good-bye."

The following is a list of early leaseholders of the Dargo High Plains:

1866 Pierce Jones Williams
1867 John Ettershank
1869 William Gray Bailey
1869 William Plummer
1870 William Henry Sweetapple, Henry Sweetapple, Fred Gibb
1872 Alf Jones
1882 William H. Morgan

GOW'S HUTS
Two of Gow's huts on Lankey's Plain, Dargos, 1937.

Yarding cattle on Lankey's Plain, Dargos, 1937.

GOW'S HUTS
Old and new huts on Gow's Lankey Plain leasehold, Dargo High Plains, 1937.

Treasures' cattle on the stock route to St Bernard

Cart Wraith and Tom Bibby on Lankey's Plain, 1937.

GOW'S HUT
One of Gow's huts on Lankey's plain on the Dargos.   (c 1937)

Tom Bibby on Lankey's Plain on Dargos.   (c. 1937)

Treasures mustering Herefords on Lankey's Plain, Dargo High Plains in autumn 1937.

Stockman Jim Kinley, with snow falling over the Dargos, early winter, 1937.

Ruins of a Hut on Lankey's Plain in 1937.

THE GOWS

Whilst the Dargo High Plains are now, and have been for a considerable time, the domain of the Treasure family, others played a part in the early development of the area.

Earliest, if we are to accept the legendary tales of 'Bogong' Jack's sporadic incursions, he is credited with having a hut and holding yard on the Dargos about the end of the 1850s, but evidence of this is very tenuous.

Alfred Jones held a Lands Department lease for ten years (1872 - 82) and built the original high plains homestead prior to 1878, at which time it was taken over by George Emanuel Treasure and his family. W.H.Morgan, who was an early run-holder in the Upper Buckland Valley also had a Dargo run from 1882 - 87. This would have been within easy distance of his Buckland run, being just across the Divide.

Speculators made a brief appearance in the '60s and '70s, as indeed, they did in other areas, but the Gows had a more permanent occupancy.

In the mid-1880s, the Gow family from Harrietville took up a portion of the Dargo High Plains and the old Beecher's Hill run, and with their dependence on mining activities, they diversified their interests.

Richard Gow took over Noone's "Halfway House", a rough, substantial accommodation house for miners on the Harrietville - Dargo track, about 20 miles from Grant and 30 from Harrietville (and about a mile south of the old Jones homestead, occupied by the Treasures). It was converted into an hotel, with a general store, butchery and bakery attached. It was to remain until about 1908, by which time the mining activity had almost ceased.

Members of the Gow family who held Dargo High Plains leases included David Gow (1886 - 1889), Donald Gow Snr. (1886 - early 1900s), Donald Gow Jnr. (1886 - 1911), Richard Gow (1886 - 1889) and Ernest Gow (1902 - 1911). However, like many other families engaged in pioneer grazing, it is likely that they were involved before the dates indicated in Lands Department records.

The Gows grazed their cattle on the extensive Lankey's Plain and it was not until some time later that the Treasures took out their first licence, George Treasure became a registered run-holder in the early 1890s and in later years his family acquired the remainder of the High Plains from the Gows, whose last licences were surrendered in January 1911.

The Gows' influence on the development of the Dargo High Plains was significant and their name is remembered by a number of huts (in some cases regrettably, now only hut sites), Gows' Plain, and, of course, the long abandoned Gows' Hotel.

*The story of the dog's grave is set in the period
when George Gray held the lease of the
Cobungra Station in 1851-60. All the men
concerned in the story were Cobungra Station
men. (All related.) This was the beginning
of the Gold Era, 1851-59.
It relates to the life of the pioneers in this
rugged mountain country, and tremendous
hardships and effort in making a livelihood
from raising cattle.
The story is dedicated to the memory
of their dogs and horses for without them
the life and living of the cattlemen
would not have been possible.*

The Dog's Grave

WITHOUT THE ASSISTANCE OF DOGS Australia's cattle and sheep industry would have been severely retarded. One would have to say that much of the outer and upper regions may not have been developed at all. This story concerns the upper areas of East Gippsland, the winding droving track that links Cobungra Station Omeo to Dargo and down to Stratford. An old saying that "a man's dog is a man's living" holds true today.

Says Don Richardson - Manager of Omeo's Cobungra Station - "Dogs! We just couldn't live without them. We estimate that when we have a big day's work our dogs would travel 100 miles criss crossing in say a 20 mile drive."

On Cobungra, the stockmen generally have four or five dogs predominantly of Kelpie blood but with an infusion of Heeler or Border Collie.

A drover, named Semmens, who some say was the first to breed the Heeler, took mobs of three hundred cattle for hundreds of miles with the help of a couple of dogs.

With a good working dog up the sides, a mob of cattle will move freely and steadily. The cattle know that should they break or stray, the dog will stick with them until they return to the mob. Judith Wright vividly portrays the intelligence of the dog over the beast with her lines -

> *His thunder powerless
> The red storm of his body shrunk with fear
> Runs the great bull, the dog upon his heels.*

Collected poems 1942 - 1970 by Judith Wright.

One lesson is generally enough for cow or bull.

The intelligent, well-trained drover's dog can be depended on (sometimes working out of sight and sound of his master) to work the tail or wings of the mob and can block or wheel. The drover knows his dog will protect his property and remain faithful even until death.

Robert Kaleski writing about the present breeds of cattle dog in *Walkabout* 1949 stated that the first dog used in Australia was the bobtailed Smithfield butchers dog. Then came the 'merle' Scotch Collie, smooth haired and mottled, and crossed with the dingo and Dalmation, all of which have resulted in the production of the Blue Heeler and the Kelpie, an amazingly intelligent and hardy breed.

The link between drovers and their dogs is steel strong so that although the animals may appear to be treated with indifference, they are in fact jealously guarded and in the main well looked after. An unwritten law of the bush is that one never endeavours to make friends with a drover's dog.

An extraordinary illustration of the relationship between dog and man occurred in 1966 when Newmarket drovers sent thirty five dogs out on strike while they themselves remained at work. The point at issue was a compensation claim centered about a dog that had been killed at work.

Surprisingly it's curious but true that although drovers and their dogs have always been an essential item in the pattern of Australian life and have frequently been the subject of a ballad, poem, or story, very few dogs have been specifically named. When cattlemen gather around the camp fires or congregate in 'pubs', 'that dog of Bills' or 'my old Rover' inevitably become topics of conversation or cause of argument. The exploit of 'Nellie' who would never leave a beast that broke from the mob, or of 'Buck' who would stand on his hind legs in the long grass to see if any beast had been left behind, or 'Bluey' who followed his dying master to hospital and remained there awaiting his return until he became too old and had to be destroyed, are related. Henry Lawson's 'Rover' who accompanied the old pack-horse as it struggled up the bank of the flooded stream to take home 'dumb' tidings of the death of young Harry Dale the drover is remembered. Probably the best known dog is that teamster's notorious animal which spoiled the record and became the hero of Jack O'Hagan's rollicking rendering "Road to Gundagi" when it sat on the tucker box, thereby completing the misery of the rain sodden Bullocky Bill with his bogged team. This dog and 'Boney' of our story appear to be the only two Australian dogs to have been immortalised in stone.

Frank Ruscome was commissioned to build the Gundagi monument and John Giannarelli was responsible for the monument to 'Boney'. Both monuments also serve as a tribute to the pioneers as well as the drovers and their dogs.

And this is Jack Treasure's version of the story:

Six miles north of Mt Birrigun, as the crow flies is a speck marker on the map, eerily dubbed "Dog's Grave". Once upon the mountain time it was the site of the first camp out from the Cobungra Station on the cattle run to

Dargo but since the last mob went through in 1937 it has been enclosed by the wilderness and left as a speck on the map.

The story from the hills on how this isolated location got its name is folklore. In the 1860s a portion of the Cobungra Station was owned by the Gray family and their grazing rights extended far over The Divide as far as the headwaters of the Wentworth River.

Bushman Peter Meehan was employed by the Grays to mind the cattle on the Wentworth side. In his lonely vigil he got to know every creek and gully in the watershed, from Mt Birrigun to Mt Badland. His knowledge of stock and the high wild country made him something of a legend in his own time.

Meehan had only two companions. A horse which he called "Skinny" and a dog with a cross-matched name, "Boney". When the trio were camped at the little slab hut in the bush, "Boney" found a poisoned bait which was supposed to be a meal for a dingo. The dog died soon after and his master was so stricken by the loss that he made a small grave of stone slabs and erected a picket fence around the site. Years after Peter Meehan had passed on the grave remained intact.

In 1888, a railway construction gang surveying the area for a proposed rail link between Stratford and Omeo camped in the Dog's Grave clearing. The camp cook, noticing the dilapidated state of the plot rebuilt the little fence in his spare time. But later bushfires ravaged the area, burning the fence and the hut. All but the name was lost.

In 1964, prodded by his famous curiosity for mountain history, Jack Treasure of Dargo set out, in company with Department of Mines Geologist, John Neilson to find the grave. The pair located the clearing and after further exploration, Treasure discovered a heap of rocks that was once a hearth and a chimney.

"Then rebuilding an imaginary doorway and placing myself by the door, I tried to imagine what site I would choose to bury my friend the dog, if I had been Peter Meehan.

"A south-westerly direction seemed appropriate and I walked that way for some 20 paces. And there it was, almost covered from view, a setting about three feet by two feet and another pile of tumbled down rocks."

Treasure and Neilson erected a third fence around the grave of "Boney".

Peter Meehan's dog was most likely an Australian Kelpie, which is still the popular breed for the high country. They have the blood of the Dingo in their veins. Described by Mr McNamara of Omeo - "They are forceful workers, bark well, are equally good with sheep or cattle, their feet are more able to stand up to the rugged terrain than most.

When John Giannarelli, a first generation Italian member of the Australian firm of monumental masons founded by his father, was prospecting in the Omeo district, his companion Jack Treasure, a cattleman and grandson of the pioneer family that founded Castleburn, told him the story of the Dog's Grave as he knew it. In a moment of perception, John Giannarelli determined that the pioneers and their dogs should be memorialised in stone. Accordingly, on his return to Fitzroy, he caused a block of Harcourt granite to be shaped, engraved and lettered as a tribute to the men and women of the past, and their dogs.

Fortunately at that time, he was able to engage the services of an overseas artist whose name he is unable to recall and who has since returned to Yugoslavia. Using a diamond pointed engraving tool, the unknown artist has beautifully engraved the portrait of a Kelpie dog and underneath that has depicted a lonely bushman boiling his billy while sorrowing for his dog.

The picture was appropriately suggested by Frederick McCubbin's well known painting "Down on his luck", the original of which is in the Western Australian State Library. The two engravings are set into the granite. The monument stands some four feet high on its base and was conveyed to the site via Dargo and in May 1975 it was unveiled. Attending the ceremony were Avon and Omeo Shire Council members, members of Stratford and Omeo Historical Societies, together with groups of cattlemen and their families, 45 people in all.

The Dog's Grave with fence erected by
Jack Treasure and John Neilson in 1964

With the assistance of the Forestery Commission staff, most were driven in four wheel drive vehicles across the Dargo River (no bridge), past the old Dargo Cemetery where Peter Meehan was buried and past the famous walnut tree which covers a quarter of an acre and along a forestry road only accessible to four wheel drive vehicles to the site and to the brief unveiling ceremony

The unveiling was performed jointly by the Avon President, Mr Gordon Hughes and Mr Louis Pendergast, President of Omeo Shire. At the time of the unveiling it was not certain in which shire the monument actually stood; however, it was confirmed later to be in the Avon Shire, almost on the border of Avon and Omeo.

On the left of the monument, is a small slab of granite carrying a verse as a tributy to "Boney":

> *He served none else but Peter Meehan*
> *His master and his friend:*
> *A comradeship wove of the bush*
> *To last until the end.*
> *Mute faith in one: a friendship born*
> *In rugged ranges where*
> *A loneliness prevailed the scene -*
> *Just man and dog to share.*
>
> *They shared each others humble way,*
> *The ways of bush lore treading*
> *From dawn to dusk, through wilderness*
> *Where cattle pads went treading*
> *Beneath Australia's sunny skies,*
> *Beneath the tree ferns bending*
> *Along the ranges, by the stream -*
> *A way of life transcending.*
>
> *Until the end, the bitter end,*
> *Though dumb, in canine way*
> *He wove a story of the bush*
> *That we respect today*
> *He served to mould a history —*
> *Though little was he known*
> *He restes beside the mountain stream*
> *Beneath these slabs of stone.*

S. J. Treasure
Dargo 1969

To the right is the original dog's grave. A concave growth of Black Sally makes a fitting backdrop to the group and a short distance away, a mountain stream flows over its rocky bed.

The Dog's Grave

The story as told at the unveiling was that Peter Meehan camping at the site awakened one morning and found his dog "Boney" dead at the door of the hut. Peter accorded his dog a careful burial and for over 100 years the site was known in the locality as the Dog's Grave. However, researching this story amongst the Cobungra Station folk provided a second version of the story.

Mr Charles McNamara, alive and well today, grandson of the owner of Cobungra at the time of the incident, asserts that his story is the true one. His story is supported by many Omeo folk and generally has been accepted down the years by the Cobungra story tellers. He states, "There never was a hut at the time of the death of the animal. The dog was not "Boney" but "Angus", not an Australian Kelpie but a stumpy tailed Smithfield. The drover who owned the dog was Johnny Crisp, well known in Omeo where he kept a hotel and later on was a cordial manufacturer in Omeo. Peter Meehan, John Crisp, Ned Gray, Ned Gunn, Tom Worchester and Jack Tolland, all Cobungra station men were mustering in the area when "Angus" picked up a bait that had been carried by a dingo. The dog died. Crisp buried his dog with much care, placed two layers of stones over the plot and erected a fence with bush timber. On a piece of bark he wrote the following verse:

> Once he came across the plain
> Wild cattle to surprise
> Now he's slain
> By Strychnine laid
> And never more to rise.

Whether the facts have been confused with the passage of time or which of the stories is the true one matters little. What does matter is that the memory of the pioneers and their dogs has been perpetuated in a fitting manner at a fitting site. The Giannarelli monument is a tribute not only to drovers and their dogs but also honours the early pioneers.

(Acknowledgement is made to Miss Flora Johns and Mr O.S.Green for material used in this article. Ed.)

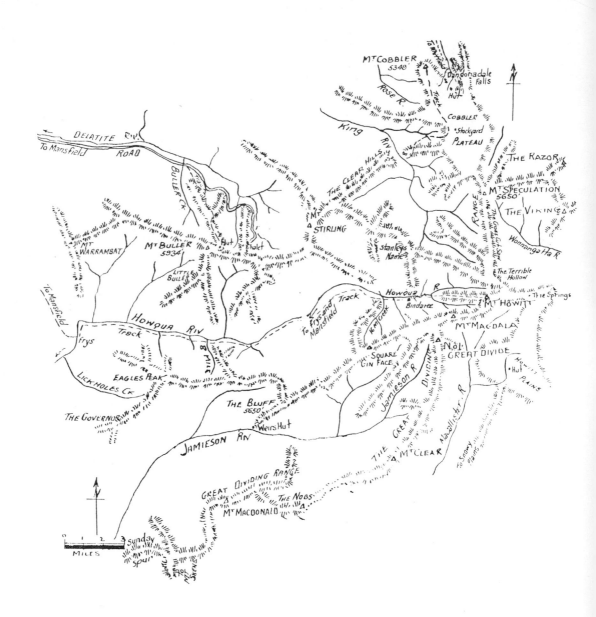

Bushwalkers' Map of the area between Mts Buller and Howitt, and Mts Macdonald and Cobbler. Prepared probably in the early 1930s, this and similar maps of other areas circulated amongst walkers of that period, and provided ample information for extensive trips to be undertaken. The originator of this map is unknown, but it was likely the joint efforts of members of the Melbourne Walking Club.

The Buller–Howitt Country

MT HOWITT, named after one of Victoria's greatest bushman-explorers, Dr A.W.Howitt, occupies a unique position at the hub of a series of rugged ridges which radiate from its summit — and the streams which have their birth in the precipitious valleys between are amongst the finest in the state.

The view from Mt Howitt's summit begins with the Crosscut Saw leading to nearby Mt Speculation, the commencement of the Barry Mountains which wind past The Viking and The Razor, on to Mt Selwyn, and thence to Mt St.Bernard visible on the horizon. Terrible Hollow, birthplace of the Wonnangatta River, is formed by the sheer drop from the Crosscut Saw, with Speculation and Howitt at either end.

Turning clockwise the viewer looks across a narrow ridge to Macalister Springs, headwaters of the Macalister River, with the Howitt Plains stretching away to form the ample watershed between the Wonnangatta and Macalister Rivers. Further around, the Great Divide which has reached Howitt via the Barrys and the Crosscut Saw continues towards Mt Clear and Macdonald with the valleys of the Macalister and Barclay to the left and Jamieson Rivers on the right. The viewer turns next to the Magdala, Square Gin Face, Bluff divide, gently sloping to the Jamieson fall but presenting rugged cliff faces which form the bastion of the Howqua River valley.

Facing the Bluff, across the Howqua is the Stirling-Buller ridge, connected to Howitt by Stanley's Name Spur. From Stirling, the Clear Hills lead down to the King River, with the head of the Delatite valley behind. The King River rises at the junction between the Stanley's Name Spur and the Crosscut Saw, and drains, beyond Speculation, a portion of the Cobbler Plateau, with the dramatic peak of Mt Cobbler piercing the skyline. And so, the viewer returns, full circle to Mt Speculation.

If this is not the most spectacular panorama in Victoria, it could, arguably, be surpassed only from the vantage point of nearby Mt Stirling's summit.

Before the coming of the timber millers, spearheaded by old Christensen who, having failed as a farmer, wandered into the Delatite valley under the shadow of Mt Buller, in early 1933, and whose logging roads have brought in the 'easy riders' with their trail-bikes, four-wheel drives, and fun machines, the entire area was the province of a few long established cattlemen and the inevitable sturdy-legged bush walkers.

The area is well served with a number of delightful snow plains, fringed in most places by snow gums to provide a park like environment well suited to cattle grazing. These plains extend from Howitt along the ridge to the approaches to the rocky summit of MacDonald, along the Jamieson fall of the ridge to the Bluff, from Buller to Stirling and across the Clear Hills towards the King River, and, of course, across the broad expanse of the Cobbler Plateau. Extending, too, from Mt Howitt, are the Howitt Plains, but traditionally these have been linked with the Wonnangatta Station, whose cattle have grazed the plains since the days of Oliver Smith and the Bryce family, a hundred and ten years ago.

SNOWPLAINS and MOUNTAINS

In an area of indescribable beauty, the riders climb Mt Magdala from the Howqua Valley, with Mt Buller in the background, and The Bluff away to the left.

HEARNS

John Hearn, his wife Catherine and their two children Jeremiah and Norah arrived by bullock dray in 1862 to take up their selection "Booralite" on the Delatite River near the present day Merrijig. They developed a property and in the years to follow ran a dairy herd, sending their cream all the way to a butter factory in Flinders Street, Melbourne (long since demolished) and also breeding Herefords for the fat cattle market.

Bill Hearn rode the mountains with his long-time companion Jim Fry of Howqua Hills, and together they participated in the search for Bamford, after the Wonnangatta murder in 1918, and were also in the small party that eventually discovered the hapless Bamford, earlier prime suspect in Barclay's murder, but himself victim of a killer's bullet.

Bill's mount must many times have looked enviously at Jim Fry's pony, because while Jim was a lightweight, Bill tipped the scales at around 20 stone. He always wore his boots unlaced, not because of forgetfulness, but because his ample avoirdupois made the bending to lace or unlace them a difficult, if not impossible task! Bill worked for a time, after Phillips and Ritchie sold out to the Alexandra Syndicate, on the Wonnangatta Cattle Station.

Jim Hearn with his nephew Jack Hearn and Jack Seymour had a grazing lease on the Clear Hills and Hearn's Hut, built by them, was a landmark midway down the hills, between Stirling and the King River Hut.

COW CAMP HUT

Situated on the ridge between the summit of Mt Buller and the old Buller Chalet.

LOVICK'S HUT
The Mt Buller log hut built by Jack Lovick snr., snowcovered in a winter of the late 1920s.

LOVICKS

William Mitchell Lovick arrived at the Delatite valley and paid £10 for a publican's licence for the Hunt Club Hotel on 2nd September 1873. He also operated a hotel-store for a short period at Howqua Hills -- until the optimism generated by the 'rush' to that field waned and the 'pot of gold' proved to be no closer than the one at the end of the rainbow.

W.M.Lovick earned a reputation for his magnificent garden, his small apple orchard (with a prize-winning apple of 1 lb 5 oz) and his fishing expertise. He introduced trout to the Delatite River, driving a horse and vehicle to Euroa or Benalla to take delivery of spotted and rainbow trout fingerlings to be released into the Delatite.

William had nine children, and of the four boys, Jack, Frank and George all ran cattle in the mountains. Jack had the Mt Buller run from 1919 until his death in 1939, the cattle being driven up from the Delatite side via the old track from Buller Creek (later the site of Christensen's timber mill) which in turn grew into the township of Mirimbah.

Lovick's original log hut, a small one, was located about a mile from the summit. This hut was built by Jack Lovick in 1925 and was used until it succumbed to a bushfire. Nameless during its useful life, it became known after its demise as the 'Burnt Hut'.

A second hut on Mt Buller, originally intended to be erected at Buller Creek, was erected by the Mansfield Tourist Association but this, unfortunately, was destroyed by fire before the winter of 1933. The Ski Club of Victoria raised the necessary funds to build a replacement hut and this was repositioned on Boggy Creek only a quarter of a mile from the summit. This hut was built by Mr Robert Klingsporn at a cost of £57, after he had packed in all necessary materials along the testing Buller Creek — Summit track.

Bert Walker and Jack Lovick Snr. packing iron sheets in for the hut on Burnt Hut Spur, in 1926 or 1927

The approach to these huts was by a bridle track, part of which was cut by the Klingsporn brothers; the main portion was formed by working bees from the Mansfield Progress Association. It was steep and it traversed and climbed steadily until on rounding a sharp corner on a narrow spur, the first glimpse of the crest of Buller was obtained. Here everybody rested to have a breather and enjoy the summit view. It was appropriately, if irreverently, named "Thank Christ Corner" by walkers and appeared as such on old maps.

BOGGY CREEK HUT
Built by Robert Klingsporn a quarter mile from the summit of Mt Buller, this hut replaced a hut situated a short distance away, until burnt in 1933. It was reached via the foot track from Buller Creek and was used regularly by bush-walkers and skiers.

Frank Lovick (Jack's brother) took up the Bluff grazing licence in 1919 and ran cattle there until 1934. The cattle were taken in via Fry's at Howqua Hills and up the Howqua River to the track which led around the end of the Bluff to the snow plains on the Jamieson fall of the top. It was in this period that the well known 8 mile hut on the Howqua was built. From it a track provided a direct route, up the spur adjacent to 8 mile creek, to the Bluff. From here snowplains (and snowgrass grazing) extend along the ridge, mainly on the Jamieson fall, as far as Mt Howitt. A second hut, at the 16 mile mark on the Howqua River, provided a base for access to the top, the track coming out between Magdala and the Square Gin Face.

The Old Eight - Mile Hut on the Howqua

BINDAREE HUT
A solidly constructed log structure near the 16 mile flats on Howqua
River, built by Fred Fry, Harry Norris, Joe McIlroy and Harry O'Brien.

137

Jack Lovick (left) and Frank Hearn near Mt Howitt, looking across the Howqua Valley towards Mt Buller (centre skyline).

Jack Lovick (r.) outside the Bindaree Hut (c 1947)

139

KING RIVER HUT

Arriving at a wollybutt saddle, such as is often seen on our high mountain ridges, we followed a poorly blazed track descending into the King River valley. It faded away in the scrub and through this we pushed to the King River, which here was a typical mountain stream, fast flowing, its banks lined with vegetation and wildly beautiful. About a mile of walking downstream brought us to the King River Hut.

A.D.BUDGE 1938

George Lovick (brother of Jack and Frank) was grazing cattle around Buller in the early 1900s, his run being adjacent to Klingsporn's, and on Cobbler between 1910–1928. He was assisted by his son Jack (grandson of pioneer William Mitchell Lovick) in the latter period of his life. George died in 1940 and Jack jnr. took over the Buller run from his uncle Jack who passed away in 1939.

Access to the Cobbler plateau, for the Merrijig based Lovicks was along the Delatite River, via the Razorback, where Klingsporns had erected a fine log hut, across the Clear Hills to the King River at King River Hut and up on to Cobbler at a point near their stockyard. Bullock was associated with Lovick in operating the Cobbler lease from 1910–1924, when Sam Christopher and Gorman took over and continued until the late 1940s.

The original Cobbler hut was built, adjacent to the lake that fed the stream which plunged dramatically over one of the three Dandongadale falls, by Sam Christopherson, for the Gormans, who used to run stock on Cobbler in drought years.

COBBLER HUTS
The new Cobbler Hut with a corner of the old Cobbler Hut in the background.   A mantle of snow blankets the Cobbler Plateau in the winter of 1938.

COBBLER STOCKYARD
A winter 1938 photograph from Alan Bennie's (of Rose River) album.

COBBLER HUTS
*About two miles from the summit we turned north on a faint pad
which brought us to the Cobbler Huts. (A new one has been built
near the old one.)*
*The Dandongadale Falls nearby are perhaps the most breathtaking sight
of their kind in this State. One of the heads of the Dandongadale
River flows past the huts, but the main stream is a short distance to
the west. This flows through a dark gorge filled with strange holes and
gutters and arrives at the cliff edge. As R.H.Croll wrote, it then seeks
"its better known bed many thousands of feet below by the heroic
method of leaping from the cliff top."*

A.D.BUDGE 1938

Victor Tiernan was grazing the northern end of the extensive Cobbler
Plateau from the early 1900s. His home property was the Mt Typo Station,
which was adjacent to the holding that Alan Bennie, his one-time stockman
purchased in about 1919.

The Lovick family retained the license of the Hunt Club Hotel for more
than 75 years, finally relinquishing it in 1948. The grazing areas have been
reduced by the influx of timber millers and the skiers and Snow bunnies at
Buller. Jack has retained the 1400 acre home property and runs about 800
beef cattle. He has put his unrivalled knowledge of the mountains to good
use, by developing a Mountain Safari business which caters for bush lovers
who wish to spend 4, 6 or 8 days riding in an area that includes the finest
mountain scenery in this state, under the guidance of a third generation
bushman.

Cattleman Jack Lovick leads an injured skier down the Howqua River.

It is of interest to note that two of William Mitchell Lovick's daughters, Nellie and Tilly, in company with a friend Maria Drain were the first white women to climb Mt Buller. The ascent was made in March 1892. Baron von Mueller made the first ascent by a white man, climbing alone in 1853.

The pause that refreshes. Dargo Hotel.

RAZORBACK HUT
Robert Kilngsporn's Razorback Hut between the Delatite and Mt Stirling. Photographed in thick fog at Easter 1933.

The Delatite is a fine stream . . . after several crossings the track rises on the northern side and finally ascends a spur between two gullies. On topping the ridge, there is a junction – one branch leads to the west along a razorback to the Bullock Ranges; we followed the other and in about half a mile it brought us to Klingsporn's Hut.   We had been in dense mist for some time . . .
A.D.BUDGE 1938

KLINGSPORNS

Frank and Robert Klingsporn settled on a river property on the upper Delatite (for many years their property marked 'the end of the road') and like the Hearns ran a dairy herd, and as early as 1873 leased a cattle run on Mt Buller, taking the first cattle to Cow Camp in that year.   Their access route was up the Delatite to the Razorback, then up on to Stirling.   They held the lease until it was terminated with the development of the Buller ski fields.   Klingsporn's hut on the Razorback was a substantial log structure, which the writer had reason to appreciate at the onset of winter in 1933.   With Stirling blanketed in dense fog, a chance meeting with the Klingsporns, father and son, led me down to the Razorback Hut to enjoy their company for two days during which time the fog remained, and then with mustering (and bushwalking) impossible, we all returned to their home where their hospitality continued for another day.

The "Melbourne Walker" paid this tribute in 1960:

"With the passing of Robert Edward Klingsporn, at the age of 83 years, Mansfield lost an old and highly respected citizen who played an important part in the early settlement of the district and the opening up of Mt Buller.

144

About 75 years ago (it was 87 years, H.H.S.) R.E.Klingsporn, accompanied by his brothers and sisters, came from the Woods Point goldfields and took up a selection in the Delatite valley. They were the first people to take cattle on to the mountains and they blazed a track for that purpose. By 1915 about two miles of good track had been cut to Mt Buller, and, in order that tourists might reach this track, it was necessary to construct a road from Klingsporn's homestead to Buller Creek (now Mirimbah), where the track commenced. Mr Klingsporn was largely instrumental in obtaining financial assistance for the work and for the completion of the track to the summit, thus making Mt Buller accessible from Mansfield. Walkers and skiers visiting Buller in the early days will recall the long, arduous walk from the end of the road at the Klingsporn homestead. Since the completion of the road to the ski village on the upper slopes of the mount, the old tracks have fallen into disuse.

Mr Klingsporn rebuilt the cattlemen's hut that was burnt down in 1933, near the summit and which was later used as a club-house by the Ski Club of Victoria. He had also packed in all materials for the building of the first Buller Chalet in 1929. It was in the capacity of guide and supplier of pack horses that walkers first became acquainted with Robert Klingsporn.

With the passage of time, walkers are losing many old friends in the outback, but their hospitality and many kindly acts, and their names will be remembered.

The Klingsporns pioneered the cattle industry in the area but have left their Delatite property. They opened up the Buller ski fields with their access tracks and huts, but the development they initiated grew to the point where cattle grazing was discontinued and their licence cancelled.

WARES

John Ware came from Jamieson to Merrijig and married Robert Klingsporn's sister Hanna in 1894. They had three sons, Jim, George and Jack.

Jim took up a selection on the Howqua River "eleven crossings down from Fry's". At each crossing of the winding stream, there was a grassy flat on one side and a steep bank on the other. Jim ran cattle on leases around the head of the Jamieson, his main access being up the Howqua to Bindaree and then over the Howqua—Bluff ridge to the upper Jamieson. He wintered cattle below the snow-line and along the flats between Frys and his home property. The winter flow of the Howqua flooded the crossings and marooned Jim on his property for long periods. He moved out to Merrijig, close to the Delatite, about 1929 and married Catherine Hearn. Jim retired in 1936 and is now living in Melbourne.

Jack Ware, who had shared the leases with Jim, stayed on at the Howqua until 1965, sharing the run with Hedley Stoney. He died in 1979 at the age of 86.

George, the third brother, did not join Jim and Jack with cattle, but moved out of the district to take up shearing.

The old Ware leases are today being operated by Graham Stoney.

John Ware Snr.

Jim Ware at the Jamieson Hut.

Jim Ware.

Mt Clear Hut
Jack Doherty in the shadows at left.

STONEYS

Edley Stoney of 'Minto Park', commenced grazing by sharing the Ware leases and they built the new Bluff Hut on the divide between the Bluff and the Square Gin Face. Edley took over the leases when Jack Ware retired in 1965. His cattle ran from the Bluff end to King Billy, their run neighbour being Jack Lovick. Graham Stoney, who had assisted his father from the beginning, took over when Edley died in 1972. As a tribute to his memory, the high peak directly behind the Bluff Hut was named Mt Edley Stoney.

The Baw Baw Plateau

The 19-mile tree on the Old Baw Baw track.

THE BAW BAW PLATEAU has a major axis of almost ten miles, extending in a south easterly direction from Mt Whitelaw (4875 feet) to Mt Erica (5000 feet), with a minor axis of about four miles running from Mt St Phillack (5140 feet) the highest point and midway along the plateau, southwards to Mt Baw Baw (5130 feet).

An extensive snow plain area, totalling 20,000 acres, surrounds the main peaks, extends the length of the plateau and includes well watered sections at Mustering Flat and Tillicouty Glen.

On the earliest maps, the name appears as Bo Bo (native for Big) and later Baw Baw (native for Echo).

A cattle grazing lease was first issued for the Plateau in 1860, Thomas Hamilton being the first holder. Little is known, however, of early grazing activities. George Rawson began farming at Parker's Corner in 1874 and of his family of six sons and two daughters, Charlie and Harry took over the Baw Baw lease and built a chock and log hut near Mustering Flat before 1907. They had no knowledge of earlier run-holders, but they managed to muster a few white bullocks judged to be about seventeen years old.

1907 was a year of activity on the Plateau. Inspired by the thoughts of the area's potential for tourism, the Tourist Authority authorised the cutting of a track which commenced at McVeigh's old hotel on the Upper Yarra, followed the Yarra valley to its head, crossed the divide to the Upper Thompson River and climbed to reach the Baw Baw Plateau near Mt Whitelaw. It continued across the length of the plateau to Mt Erica and then dropped down to eventually reach Walhalla. Three huts were constructed, the Yarra Falls Hut of split palings, iron roof and earth floor, in April 1907, an iron hut with concrete floor at Mt Erica and before the end of the same year, a split paling, earth floored shelter near Mt Whitelaw.

147

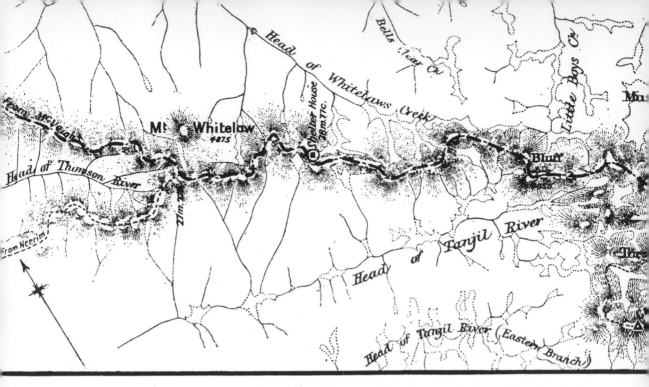

Reproduced from portion of the original Baw Baw Tourist Map.

Anticipating an influx of tourists on horseback, each hut had a nearby stable and wire fenced paddock for horses. However, it was left to two parties of bushwalkers to make the first crossing at Easter 1907 and in the same year, with a thick mantle of snow covering the snow plains, a party of three attempted the first winter crossing. Bad weather thwarted their attempt but they returned and made a successful crossing in the winter of 1908.

Coinciding with the cutting of the track and erection of shelter huts the Tourist Authority published a Tourist Map, a section of which is reproduced here. Rawson's Hut appears on this map.

Harry Rawson Jnr., grandson of George and son of Charlie, first rode up to the high country with his father, as a boy, and he recalls that Rawson's Hut had already been burnt down when he first visited the hut site. The Rawsons last license is believed to have been issued for 1913 and the lease was then taken up by Fred "Curly" Jans. His nephew, Norman "Bluey" Jans. commenced riding the mountains with him from the age of nine years and later shared and then took over the run. The Jans built a hut on the plateau, but its location is not known.

The Jans had 611 cattle on their lease when the 1939 fires swept over the Baw Baws. Eight survived. The remainder suffocated in the smoke laden atmosphere. The same fire destroyed the Jans' Hut, the Falls Creek and Whitelaw shelters and a new hut, erected in 1938 at the Thompson River crossing. The Erica Hut had been demolished during a severe storm in 1938.

Hec Stagg of Maffra took up the 60,000 acre snow plain and forest lease in 1958 and grazed cattle there for the next twenty years.

148

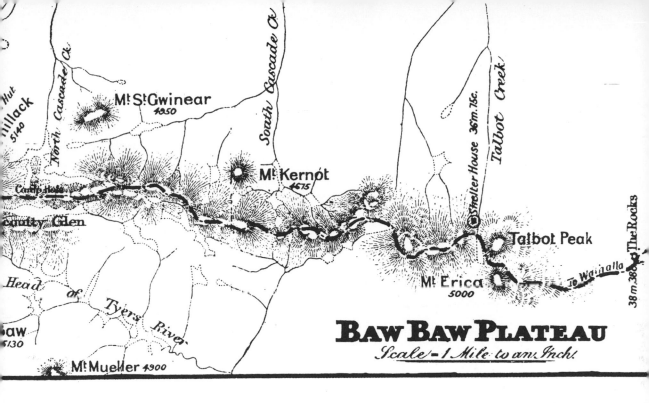

Map labels:
Mt St Phillack 5140
North Cascade Ck
South Cascade Ck
Mt St Gwinear 4950
Mt Kernot 4675
Shelter House 36m.75c.
Talbot Creek
Camp Hole
Equity Glen
The Rocks
Talbot Peak
Mt Erica 5000
To Walhalla
38 m 38c
Head of Tyers River
Baw 5130
Mt Mueller 4900

BAW BAW PLATEAU
Scale = 1 Mile to an Inch.

In 1962 an area of 7,000 acres above the 4,000 feet contour, including Mt St Phillack, Mustering Flat and Mt Whitelaw, was reserved and gazetted as an Alpine Resort, and in 1964 a further area, including Mt Erica was gazetted for the same purpose. The National Parks Association 1969 proposal for an Alpine National Park included the Baw Baws as a wilderness area and this proposal was implemented, all lands above the snowline (4000 feet contour) being declared a reserve.

The last grazing lease was withdrawn in 1978 and today only about ten of Hec Stagg's cattle remain. They are playing 'hide and seek' in the snow-gum forested slopes that surround the high plains, and National Park authorities, anxious for their removal have proposed to shoot them from a helicopter, lift out the carcases and send the bill to Hec Stagg! A more reasonable proposal would appear to be to allow them to remain and end their days in the mountains that have provided a pasture for their forebears since 1860.

The old foot track and stock route from the foot of Mt Erica is now overrun with blackberries and is impassable. New roads provide access to the developing snowfields and heated ski-lodges have replaced the old huts, but one record of the cattlemen's occupancy will remain. Board of Works development that came with the construction of the Thompson River Dam located a settlement near Parker's Corner. The proposal was that it should be named Robinson, after the Board's Chief Engineer. The locals received the suggestion with something less than enthusiasm and the name Rawson was finally adopted, thus perpetuating the memory of an early cattle family of the area.

BAW BAW PLATEAU

The 4000 ft contour outlines the shaded area and the 4500 ft contour, within which are enclosed the snowplain areas is indicated inside the shaded area.

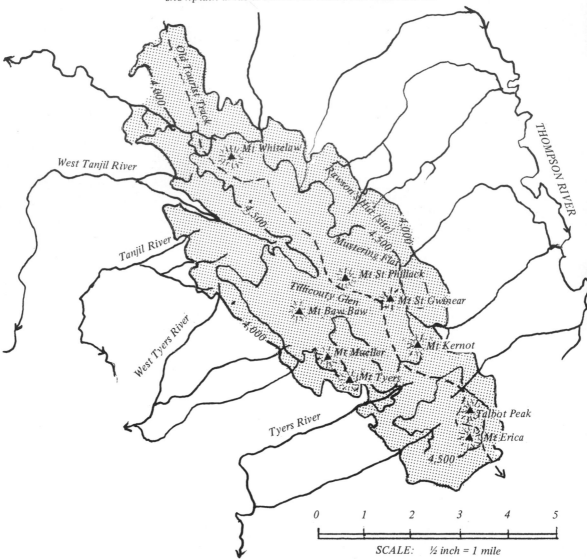

SCALE: ½ inch = 1 mile

As with other high plain areas, the official documentation does not relate very closely to the actual occupancy. There is no doubt about the Rawson, Jans and Stagg family grazing, although memories may be inaccurate to within a year or so.

Lands Department records suggest that Thomas Allen, a hotelier, grazier and cartage contractor, held a grazing licence on the Baw Baws between the years 1908–10, and 1915–20.

RAWSONS' HUT
Harry Rawson (in suit) and Charlie Rawson (wearing leggings) seated on either side of a couple outside Rawsons' Hut (pre World War I).

On Baw Baw Plateau.

Keppels of Lake Mountain

*T*HE CLOSEST ALPINE AREA to Melbourne that has been grazed continuously was the Lake Mountain - Federation - Torbreck heights and the slopes at the headwaters of the streams that drain them, the Rubicon, Royston, Big Rivers and Snobs Creek. Access to the Lake Mountain end was gained from Buxton and Marysville (the Cumberland) and the Keppels ran their cattle and sheep there from the mid 1870s until 1963.

From the northern approaches the Nicholas, Newman, Robb and Findlay families took in sheep and cattle to graze the Blue Range, Torbreck and Federation - as far as Stockman's Reward.

Maurice John Keppel came to Australia in the good ship "Joshua" in 1851-52 and first settled in Melbourne. He married Mary Grainger and moved to Marysville, where he took over the Marysville Hotel. In 1864 a sub-division of township allotments of land on Paradise Plains was offered for sale and Maurice John Keppel was one of the first purchasers. The original title is still in the possession of his grand-daughter, Miss Keppel.

Paradise Plains, a delightful pocket of snow-plains on the Great Divide, south of Marysville, was on the Edgar Track, a pack-horse route from Warburton to the Woods Point mines. It left the present Acheron Way at Acheron Gap, a low saddle on the Divide, climbed on to Smith's Hill, and turned north to follow the top of the Poley Range towards Mt Strickland and Mt Bismark (later re-named, with some degree of patriotic fervour, Mt Kitchener). Hereabouts, was a staging point on the Paradise Plains and the locals had high hopes for its future as a township. A packer, Robley, however shattered the real estate dreams when he discovered a better route down the spur which now bears his name.

Paradise Plains, aptly named, returned to its solitude and John Maurice Keppel (and a few others) were left with Titles to acre lots that had cost them £2 each.

Original Title to a subdivision block on Paradise Plains near Marysville, purchased in 1864 by Maurice John Keppel.

Marysville, however, being on the coach road and a depot for produce coming from Alexandra and Thornton to the Woods Point goldfields, was a thriving township.

Maurice and Mary Keppel had four children, John Maurice, Jeremiah Francis, Catherine Mary and Michael David. The two elder boys, Maurice and Jerry (then aged 17 years) became partners in the grazing of cattle around Mt Margaret and Lake Mountain. Access was via Keppel's track along Keppel's Creek from the home property at Buxton to Mt Margaret.

Six members of the Keppel family acquired 1150 acre selections of well watered grazing flats, all adjoining, at Buxton, and in due course took up the options to each purchase 640 acre freeholds. Their name also became synonymous with the Australian Hotel, Buxton, which they conducted.

The brothers grazed Hereford cattle and sheep. They rode up weekly to shift the cattle from one pocket of snow-grass to another, as fallen trees and other obstacles made the cattle reluctant to move to fresh pastures without persuasion. The Keppels built two huts - one, "The White House", on Mt Margaret and the second, "Wild Oat Hut", on Lake Mountain.

The cattle were not mustered before the snows, but wintered in the timbered heads of the valleys below the snowline. This practice was eventually discontinued as cattle duffing became prevelent. Winter snow on the tops prevented regular visits to check the cattle but the duffers managed to drive out stock from selected valley heads.

The original Australia Hotel at Buxton.

On one occasion, veteran auctioneer, Norman Chester, when conducting a sale at Maffra, recognised cattle he rightly suspected as belonging to the Keppels and he stopped the sale.* The cattle had 'found their way' via Woods Point to the Gippsland market!

Maurice and Francis Keppel

* The Keppels marked their cattle with a recognisable cut on the dewlap (the fold of skin that hangs from the throat of cattle, and laps the dew in grazing) and it was this identification that alerted Norman Chester of their rightful ownership.

KEPPEL'S HUT
The second Keppel's Hut at the head of Keppel's Creek, Lake Mountain. Burnt in the 1939 fires, it was replaced by the third Keppel's Hut, which still stands.

The practice of mustering in late Autumn was adopted and the cattle were sold as "stores" for winter agistment elsewhere. Regular buyers about 1900 - 1910 were the well known Daws of Broken River. The best Keppel cattle, however, were left to winter in the Mt Margaret area, as it was below the snow-line, close to their home property and carried an abundant crop of wild oats. Close by, at the head of the Royston and Torbreck Rivers, an eminence still bears the name, Wild Oat Hill.

The Keppels (and the Forestry officers of their time) believed that the country was best nurtured by a series of slow, 'cold', burnings of the dry growth up to the snow-line, in early spring, thus cleaning the forest floor of 'rubbish', promoting a fresh growth of grass and wild oats and minimising the danger of a big summer fire. In December 1938, the Keppels were puzzled that a fire in the Taggerty forest area burnt for more than a month without any serious attempts being made to extinguish it. Then, in January 1939 it blew up and spread to cause the devastating fires that enveloped the Marysville area. The huts on Mt Margaret and Lake Mountain burned in this holocaust. The Mt Margaret hut was not replaced, but Jerry's two sons, Maurice and Francis, who had joined their father and uncle around 1910, while still schoolboys of ten or eleven, built a new hut on Lake Mountain. The Forestry Commission subsequently replaced the shingle roof with iron, and this structure is still standing today, forty years later.

Cattle duffing, however, was still a problem and in 1962 a scaffold was discovered on the snowplains with five butchered carcasses nearby.

The Keppel brothers

The sheep which the Keppels had grazed from the beginning, were permanently tended by shepherds who lived in the huts. In the 1890s, the Keppels regularly drove their sheep the 65 miles to Newmarket, for shearing at Dalgety's shed and then for sale. They used to recall the consternation of the council parks and gardens men when the sheep reached the best grass they had encountered in a week - between the rockeries in Royal Parade, Parkville!

The Keppels eventually became disenchanted with alpine grazing of sheep. Eagles, as many as 50 were counted in a single flight, and the increasing activity of dingos and more particularly dogs, which were using the newly cut timber tracks to gain access to the sheep grazing areas, finally persuaded the brothers to "go out of sheep".

They continued with cattle, driving some to the railheads at Warburton or Healesville, supplying the local market and trucking numbers to Melbourne, but relying mainly on the saleyards at Alexandra for their outlet.

Jerry died in 1955 and when his eldest son Maurice passed away in 1963, an almost 90 year affair with grazing the Lake Mountain area came to a close. Miss Keppel (sister of Maurice and Francis) on relinquishing the lease to the Lands Department was told that the Keppel family's grazing license had been one of the longest held in the history of Victorian alpine grazing.

The cattle are gone, but the Keppel name will live on in the Marysville district with Keppel's track, Keppel's Ridge, Keppel's Creek, Keppel Falls and Keppel's Lookout to survive even when the present Keppel's hut is gone.

An old "hatter" who lived on the slopes of Mt Kitchener

* Norman Chester recalls:

Norman Chester, recalling the incident in 1980, elaborated: He had noticed the cattle when they were being driven in to Heyfield a day or two before the sale. They were placed in a holding paddock until Sale day and Norman contacted one of the Ross brothers of Mansfield. On arrival Ross confirmed that the cattle had been purchased by the Keppels and himself at Wodonga and branded with the Keppel's distinctive cut on the dewlap. The Keppels were then summoned from Marysville and confirmed Ross's identification of the cattle.

NICHOLAS

When, in 1919, the Eildon Dam, in its first stage, flooded the valley of the Goulburn River above Upper Thornton, the waters of Jerusalem Creek inlet submerged the home of Henry Thomas Nicholas, and he re-settled at Thornton.

Born in 1857, he had tried his hand with cattle and sheep at Eggleton, had been a butcher at Mansfield and then went back to the land at Darlingford, before settling on the property at Jerusalem Creek. Around 1890, or possibly a little earlier, Nicholas took out grazing leases for the timbered valleys at the heads of the Royston, Rubicon and Big Rivers and of Snobs Creek, and also ran on the fine snowplain areas that extend from around Mt Torbreck (4,968 ft.) to Mt Federation.

He was thus a run neighbour of the Keppels of Lake Mountain and his sheep and cattle roamed over an area of some 80,000 acres that extended as far as Matlock, and sometimes wandered as far as the Jordan. Nicholas ran from 8,000 to 10,000 sheep and 400 head of cattle, and after mustering, drove his mob through Whittlesea to Newmarket saleyards.

In the early years of his occupancy, Torbreck Station, with its two home-steads and woolshed was located on Running Creek, near its confluence with the Big River, and was stocked as a sheep station. Later, after it was abandoned, the old homestead and yards were used by Nicholas's stockmen and drovers. Another property, Clifton Station, was also, at one time, located on the Big River.

Les Nicholas on the grey, and Alec. Reddich.

STOCKMAN'S HUT
Located below Mt Federation on river flat at Stockman's Reward.
Built by the Nicholas run-holders prior to 1913, it was burnt in the
1939 bushfires.

Jim Fry, Arch Nicholas and Les Nicholas of Thornton, in 1945. The
pack-horse "Ruby Light" was a thoroughbred who had raced in
Melbourne. (Note: Jim Fry was from Thornton. He was not the Jim
Fry from Howqua Hills. Ed.)

Further upstream, Nicholas built a hut (and later a second one) at Stockman's Reward, about seven miles south east of Mt Federation, at the junction of the Torbreck and Big Rivers. Off Federation, between the heads of Snobs Creek and the Royston, another hut (Hoban's) was situated. At the foot of Mt Torbreck, on the western fall, Sir John Barnswall ran sheep on an area known as Barnswall Plains, and he had a hut there, on the west bank of Snobs Creek.

The holocaust of 1939 burnt all the huts in the area, including the Keppel's, on the adjoining Lake Mountain leases, and stock losses were heavy. Henry Thomas Nicholas died in 1940 and his son Les, who had worked with his father on the runs since boyhood, took over.

The leases were gradually relinquished about 1947-48 but Les ran cattle on agistment on Federation until about 1952. He is now living in retirement in Thornton.

Abandoned settlement at Jerusalem Creek

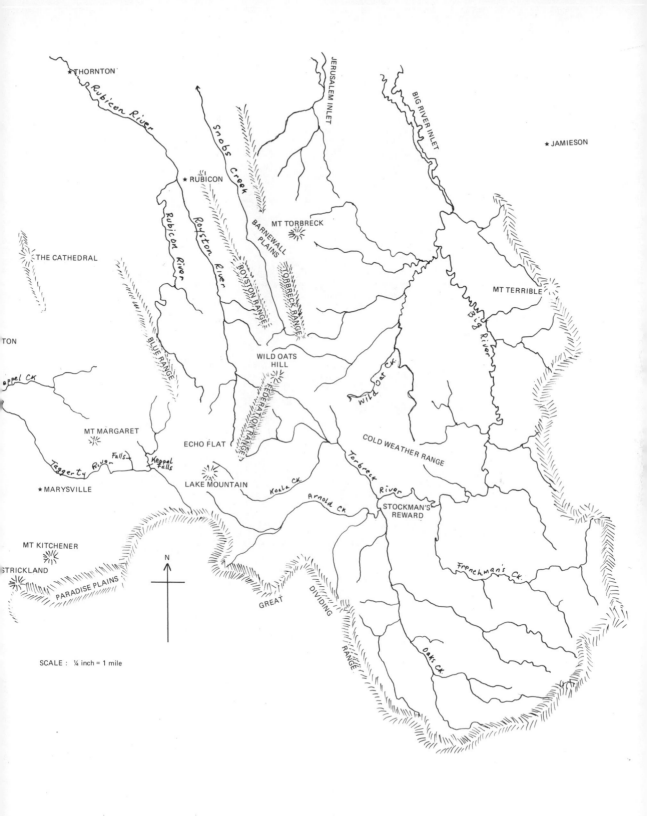

★ THORNTON

Rubicon River

★ RUBICON

Snobs Creek

JERUSALEM INLET

BIG RIVER INLET

★ JAMIESON

THE CATHEDRAL

Rubicon River

Royston River

ROYSTON RANGE

BARNEWALL PLAINS

MT TORBRECK

TORBRECK RANGE

MT TERRIBLE

...TON

BLUE RANGE

appel Ck

Big River

MT MARGARET

WILD OATS HILL

FEDERATION RANGE

Wild Oat Ck

Taggerty River

Falls

Keppal Falls

ECHO FLAT

COLD WEATHER RANGE

Torbreck River

★ MARYSVILLE

LAKE MOUNTAIN

Koala Ck

Arnold Ck

STOCKMAN'S REWARD

MT KITCHENER

N

Frenchman's Ck.

STRICKLAND

PARADISE PLAINS

GREAT

DIVIDING

RANGE

Oaks Ck.

SCALE : ¼ inch = 1 mile

The site of the old Torbreck Station

The Buffalo Plateau

*T*HE *BUFFALO PLATEAU* is a granitic mass located between the Buckland and Buffalo Rivers and bordered on the north by the Ovens valley. A connecting ridge from the south links the plateau with the Great Divide, in the area of Mt Selwyn. The plateau has an average altitude of some 4,500 feet, with a number of peaks rising to heights between 5,000 feet and 5,645 feet. Buffalo has a length of about 7 miles and is about 4 miles across at its widest part, with a total area of approximately 8,500 acres.

Baron von Mueller and a companion John Dallachy were the first white men to climb Buffalo, when in 1853 they climbed the Horn and remained on the plateau for a week.

The sheer cliffs and forbidding rock walls had deterred many settlers and it was left to the miners of the Buckland valley to ascend the plateau by way of Goldie's Spur, in search of the elusive metal. James Samuel Manfield and his brother, John, are credited with having climbed from the Buckland valley in 1854 and they spent some days exploring the plateau.

On their return they spoke in glowing terms of the lush pastures, and it was not long before cattlemen, facing an insatiable demand for meat from the thousands of miners who had flocked to the Buckland, Buffalo and Ovens valleys, commenced to graze their herds there. Amongst the earliest to take cattle to the Buffalo pastures were Thomas Buckland, John Brady of Eurobin, Billy Weston of Porepunkah, the Manfield brothers (James and John), and Edward Carlisle of Wandiligong. The Lands Department believes that Thomas Goldie grazed up till about 1890 and in the period 1891 - 1922 leaseholders were A.H. and B.Weston, Richard Hughes and Brady.

The access route was from the lower Buckland valley and along Goldie's Spur, a distance of about 5 miles to reach the top, near The Horn, from whence the logical grazing areas would extend towards the north Buffalo.

The vegetation was a mixture of delightful snow-gum woodland, open snow plains and heathland, and alpine bogs where streams cross the plateau.

The early cattlemen were soon guiding parties of visitors to the plateau and it was this interest in tourism that eventually led to the rapid development of the area. Edward Carlisle was originally paid £5 per year to keep the bridle track open. Then members of the Alpine Club and the Shire Council collected £80 and employed a local man, Denison to cut a road from Porepunkah. Without a professional survey, the road was cut and formed and it is a tribute to the road maker that it approximated the route of today's highway.

A section of 2,880 acres was reserved as a National Park in 1898 and in 1908 a further 23,000 acres was added. In 1980 the Buffalo National Park was increased to a total

"Buffalo"Bill Weston and Mrs Weston

area of 75,000 acres, which in addition to the plateau area includes much of the surrounding forested slopes.

It is interesting to note that Grazing Licences were cancelled in 1908 when the additional area was added to the National Park, but the subsequent renewal of licences supports the Lands Department's opinion that no incompatability between grazing and the National Park's recreational usage was perceived at that time.

Grazing, however, was phased out after 1922.

A winter scene on Buffalo in 1890s

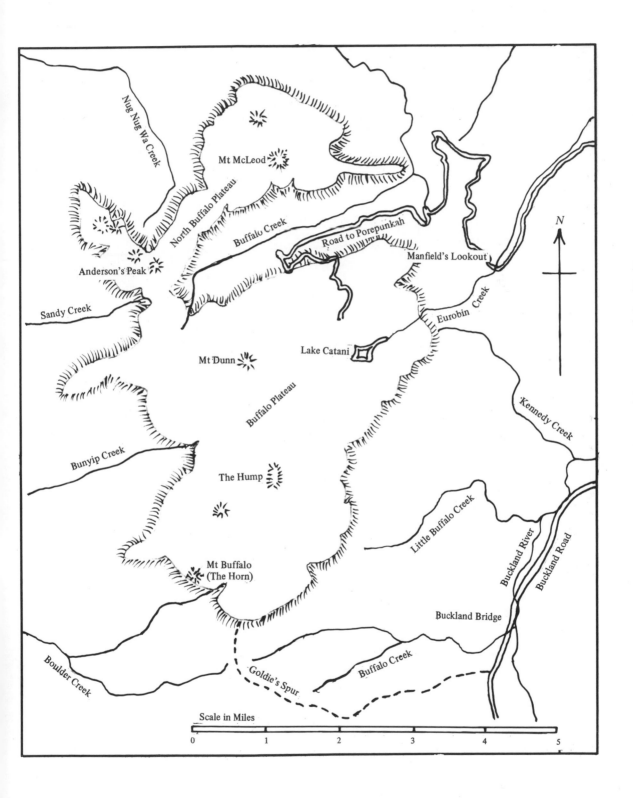

Nug Nug Wa Creek

Mt McLeod

North Buffalo Plateau

Buffalo Creek

Road to Porepunkah

Manfield's Lookout

Anderson's Peak

Sandy Creek

Eurobin Creek

N

Mt Dunn

Lake Catani

Buffalo Plateau

Kennedy Creek

Bunyip Creek

The Hump

Little Buffalo Creek

Buckland River

Buckland Road

Mt Buffalo
(The Horn)

Buckland Bridge

Boulder Creek

Goldie's Spur

Buffalo Creek

Scale in Miles

0   1   2   3   4   5

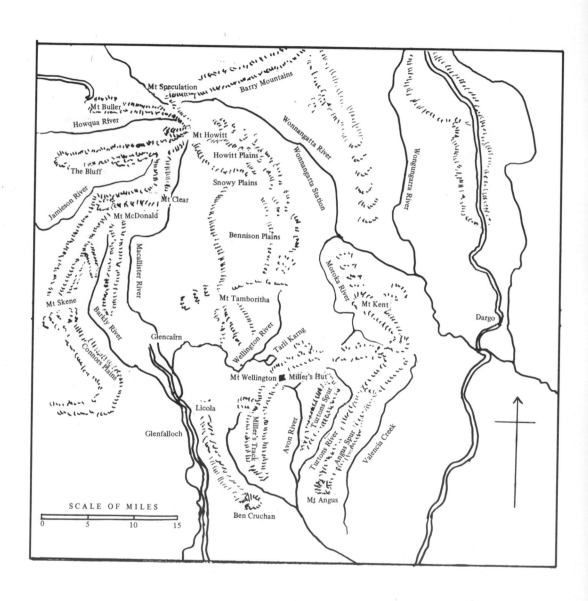

SCALE OF MILES

0   5   10   15

166

Glenfalloch & Mt Wellington

*T*HE *GLENFALLOCH B STATION* of 20,000 acres, situated on the Macalister River, some 12 miles north-west of Stratford, was taken up by Maurice Mayrick in 1846 and then by Malcolm Macfarlane in 1847. Macfarlane was probably the first man to move up into the mountains north of his station and run cattle in the Mt Wellington area. He was a nephew of overlander James Macfarlane who had brought cattle from the Monaro to Macfarlane's Flat across the Murray in about 1834—5 and held Omeo B, Tongiomungie, Bindi and Tom Groggin for periods between 1835 and 1860. He moved to Heyfield where he owned property from 1841 till a few months before his death in 1870.

Malcolm Macfarlane built a hut on the North Wellington plain and bush-walkers of the 1930s were familiar with the site although all trace of the structure had long disappeared. Macfarlane sold the Glenfalloch B property and also relinquished his holdings on Wellington in 1868 and died in 1870.

His name survives with Macfarlane's Creek which rises near Macfarlane's Saddle and flows into the Carey (or North Wellington) River.

George Gibson Harper (two years) and Thomas McGrath (four years) were brief occupiers before Edward Riggall acquired Glenfalloch B and the Wellington run in 1874 and with his son Sam held the properties until the Wellington run was later taken over by Henry Miller in 1900, and Glenfalloch B was sold to Bob Gilder III in 1914.

Early in his occupancy Edward Riggall built Riggall's Hut, a sturdy log cabin which was to survive as a serviceable shelter until the late 1920s and its ruins remained until the 1939 bushfires swept through the area. Riggall's Spur which leads up from the Carey River past Tarli Karng is a reminder of the old family, and it is noteworthy that Tarli Karng was discovered during his occupancy.*

* Refer to Dr A.W.Howitt's account of his visits to Lake Tarli Karng on page

MALCOLM MACFARLANE

Malcolm Macfarlane was born at Cowal, Argyllshire in 1810, he married Flora MacIntosh and left Greenoch, Scotland for Australia in the vessel "Minerva" in 1837 arriving in Sydney in 1838, having as one of his shipmates Angus McMillan the discoverer of Gippsland.

On his arrival he went to the property of his uncle James Macfarlane at Goulburn N.S.W. After a short time there he went down the Murray with the first mob of cattle to go from Goulburn to Mt Barker, S.A. The leader of this party was Charles Sturt and apart from overlanding 300 head of cattle to the Adelaide market, Sturt wished to fill in the relatively unknown course of the Murray above the Murrumbidgee Junction and prove that the Hume and the Murray were one and the same. They arrived at Mt Barker safely and without the loss of any cattle and had no trouble with the blacks. This trip took them about six months.

After staying for about two years at Mt Barker (Duncan Macfarlane's property) Malcolm Macfarlane was asked to go back to Melbourne to form one of Brodribb's party to take ship to go to Gippsland. They were the first party to arrive at Port Albert (Jan 1841). A few days later Angus MacMillan and his party arrived at the Port. Brodribb and Malcolm Macfarlane were the first to go up the Thompson River. They then went overland and justly claimed they were the first to go overland to Melbourne having no trouble in keeping well to the foot of the hills and round the Moe Swamp arriving at "Wedges" Dandenong and then on to Melbourne where they arrived in March, arriving before Strezleckie's party, which had trouble by keeping too close to the Moe Swamp. The track Brodribb and Malcolm Macfarlane made was for years known as Macfarlane's Track. On their arrival in Melbourne they met James Macfarlane who introduced them to Mr Wm. Pearson who went with Malcolm Macfarlane to Omeo to get stock to put on what today is known as Mewburn Park. When they returned they found it claimed by some one else who had put eight working bullocks on it* Malcolm Macfarlane then went up the Macalister River and took up Glenmaggie and Glenfalloch, He also took up Heyfield Station for James Macfarlane and managed this property for him for 14 years. It was then sold to Mr Firebrace and later to James Tyson, the celebrated "Cattle King" who developed it to a renowned cattle fattening property. Glenmaggie was named after Maggie Glen a friend of Mr MacMillan's in Scotland. Malcolm Macfarlane named Glenfalloch, Heyfield and Ben Crauchan.

While holding Glenfalloch, Malcolm Macfarlane held the Mt Wellington lease and ran cattle there until Edward Riggall took over Glenfalloch and the Wellington run.

---

* Mewburn Park was first selected on McMillan's first journey through Gippsland, by Dr Arbuckle for Captain Macalister. Shortly after selection, it passed into the hands of E.A.Johnson Boe, who named it "Mewburn Park".

THE RIGGALLS

Edward Sheens Riggall was the first of the family to migrate from England to Australia. Born in Lincolnshire in 1828, he arrived in Adelaide in 1851 as Mate on a sailing ship. The story has been handed down that the ship's Captain and Edward 'jumped ship' and set off for the goldfields. The ship was eventually re-crewed, sailed and was never seen again!

Edward was at the Castlemaine and Bendigo goldfields and was a storekeeper at Bendigo. He sold out in 1854. After farming the Loddon district of Victoria for some years, Edward came to Gippsland in 1874 when he purchased "Glenfalloch" Station, a property of 80,000 acres. He also had a farm at Glenmaggie and in 1885 purchased "Byron Lodge" at Tinamba. "Glenfalloch" was stocked with sheep but trouble with dingoes necessitated a change to cattle and horses, Edward having a preference for Shorthorn cattle, and some horses were bred for the Indian Remounts.

Some of the original buildings at "Byron Lodge" constructed entirely of red gum timber about 1868, are still in excellent condition.

Edward was a Maffra Councillor from 1886 - 1893 and from 1907 - 1912, being Shire President 1910 - 1912. He died in 1913.

"Glenfalloch" was sold in 1914, following Edward's death, but "Byron Lodge" remains in the possession of youngest son Samuel's immediate descendants, his son Haughton currently occupying the property.

William Riggall (1860–1932) one of Edward's sons married Violet Macfarlane, a daughter of Malcolm Macfarlane. Their only child died at birth.

William lived at Dargo, Victoria, which is in the mountains, and bred fine wool sheep with much success. He was a lay reader in the Church of England and because of the rugged nature of the country and the lack of roads in the early days when he first selected land, he held a "dispensation" to christen, marry and bury in the Dargo area. William related "that on one occasion I was called on to legalise the union of a couple who had been living in the hills for many years. On arriving at their log hut I found their eldest son, bigger than his father, ready to stand as 'best man'. In order to save another trip I did some christening as well!"

This story was told to Banjo Patterson and is believed to have inspired the Banjo's poem "A Bush Christening".

Samuel (1875–1951) was the last of the eleven children born to Edward and Martha a year after they had moved to Glenfalloch. His mother died of peritonitis in January, 1877, aged 38 years. An elder sister Mary played a large part in Samuel's upbringing. Sam eventually managed Glenfalloch for his father until its sale to Bob Gilder III in 1913. Samuel took over "Byron Lodge" in 1913, following his father's death and built the present homestead in 1930. In his book 'Memoirs of a Stockman', Harry Peck states that 'Samuel had greatly improved "Byron Lodge" and that its reputation was second to none as a cattle fattening property.' Samuel was a Maffra Shire

Councillor from 1921 to 1951, being Shire President 1925–1926 and 1949–1950. He married Annie O'Brien with three children resulting. Following his death in 1951, his eldest son Horton took over "Byron Lodge".

Richard Riggall (1861 - 1919) was thirteen years old when his father purchased Glenfalloch Station. He worked there with his brother Sam and his father for about twenty-four years, during which time he acquired a sound knowledge of the Mt Wellington country. He was the first white man to visit Lake Tarli Karng and he met and directed Dr Howitt to the lake on the occasion of the latter's fourth attempt to reach the hidden lake.

Richard married Ellen Macfarlane, daughter of Malcolm and sister of his brother William's wife, Violet. After a short visit to New Zealand, during which time a new home was being built, Richard moved to Cobungra station, a property he had purchased. Richard and Ellen had seven children, who were known in family circles as "Seven Little Australians".

Richard's tragic death at Cobungra in 1919, is recounted in the Cobungra chapter in this volume.

THE RIGGALLS

> *Thomas, Richard and Samuel (standing)*
> *and Edward Sheens and William (seated)*

Two 1914 photos of Riggall's Hut.   The riders have not been identified.

All that remained of Riggall's Hut in the winter of 1936.

For many years the route with cattle was up the Avon River, with its 32 crossings, then along a spur which took them over the very summit of Mt Wellington. This was tough country, but at this stage no alternative access to Wellington was available, as the "Gable End", or as the cattlemen referred to it, "The Big Hill", is ringed with precipitous cliffs and steep sides, and the only entry to the North Wellington plateau was along the top, off Mt Wellington.

It is possible that Riggall pioneered an alternative route to Wellington, following the Macalister River to its junction with the Wellington River and thence along this valley to the foot of Riggall's Spur, which led him up to the ridge between the Gable End and Mt Wellington just south of Spion Kopje — very close to the spot where Miller's Hut was later built.

Dr. A.W.Howitt in his endeavours to reach Mt Wellington and discover Tarli Karng, having heard of the lakes existence from aborigines, took a native guide "Billy" and in 1886 tried to follow the ridge between Ben Cruachan Creek and the Avon River, but was forced back by bad weather. Two later attempts were made to follow the Mount Angus Range, or the east side of the Avon (now Miller's Spur), but the way proved too rugged. Then learning that Johnny Snowden, one of Riggall's native stockmen had discovered the lake and that Dick Riggall was the first white man to stand on its shores, Howitt adopted the Macalister River — Wellington River — Riggall's Spur route, and at his fourth attempt, reached the lake with his native guide, at Easter 1887.

THE MILLERS

During the 1890s Henry Miller selected land at the top end of Upper Maffra West, where the Macalister River leaves the foothills and turns south-east across the rich Newry flats. Much of this land was rich river flat except for a rise where the toe of a spur jutted out from the hills. On this rise he built his homestead, "Bunyule", after his marriage to the sister of Frank Scott, who had settled on a farm block at Mewburn Park.

Land was cheap in those days, and Miller's rich river flat was selected for £1 per acre; but it had to be cleared of the huge red gums, swamp gums and silver tussocks before it could be sown with grass. When this was done Shorthorn and Hereford cattle thrived on it and grew fat.

Along the foothills of the Dividing Range there was much activity as land-hungry men selected blocks of poor, rocky bushland. One or two, becoming curious about the higher mountains, had travelled on foot or on horseback up to Mt Wellington and had returned with tales of rich, rolling plateau covered with grass in summer and snow in winter.

Henry Miller, who believed in action rather than words, in 1900 took over the Mt Wellington lease previously held by Edward Riggall.

With the help of two neighbours, "Yankee Dave" Geoghegan of "Beaver Meadows" and Andy Grogan, he succeeded in driving a mob of cattle through the Avon Gorge, up the Left Hand Branch, across the Little River, up Purgatory Spur on to the Razorback and so on to Mt Wellington. That autumn they rode up again, mustered the cattle and brought them down in fat condition for the market.

Henry Miller on right.

Bloor's Hut, in the winter of 1936.

However, there is a different version of the discovery of the Purgatory Spur route. It states that when Miller was mustering on the "Gable End", a mob of cattle were located. They took off down into timbered steep country, followed by horsemen. They disappeared through a gap in the rocks, and made off downward to the head of the Avon River. This is how access from Little River was located and eventually the stock route up "Purgatory Spur" was opened up, to provide a shorter and more convenient track.

The route was so successful that Henry Miller, Yankee Dave and Andy Grogan set to work and cleared a pack-trail all the way up — a great feat of pioneering. Grazing leases could be had very cheaply on the Wellington High Plains and the Horstman brothers, who were neighbours, put cattle in with Miller's and so helped with the droving and mustering. De Moulin who was from Boisdale, also helped. He is remembered at "De Moulin's Knob", the place where he suggested going over a steep hill on the south side of the river where the Left Hand Branch narrows between cliffs.

The grazing of cattle on Mt Wellington was not always easy; if the cattle were poor on the drive up, some would fall down and die, especially on the terrible steepness of Purgatory Spur; if the snow came earlier than usual, the cattle would descend into the maze of gullies in the heart of the mountains and go wild — some never to be found again.

Lower Block, half way between Golden Point and Huggetts.

In 1911 a catastrophe struck the hill settlers with the appearance of rabbits. A few of the lower settlers held on grimly until wire netting became available, but as the grass disappeared many others were forced to sell or simply abandon their blocks. Henry Miller bought Blore's Clearing near Ben Cruachan and used it as a resting place for his cattle. From this clearing he cut a pack track over the shoulder of Ben Cruachan to Golden Point where the Little River joins the Left Hand Branch. He employed men to clear a block at Golden Point.

The Hut known as Golden Point No 1 was a small structure on the opposite side of the creek from the present site, and Millers built a larger Golden Point No 2. This was eventually replaced by Golden Point No 3 (the present hut) using iron and whatever suitable materials survived from the earlier two.

Thus he established a safer and easier route to Mt Wellington; a route that was to become known as Miller's Track. However, as he still needed more lowland for winter grazing, in 1911 he selected the first part of the Thousand-acre Paddock at the foot of the hills.

Then Mrs Huggett sold him her block of 350 acres of land over the first range, on Navigation Creek, and her bark homestead known for many years as "Joanba".

The name "Joanba" was bestowed on the Huggett home after a visit by two of Mrs Huggett's nieces. They spent their holiday painting the home

175

*Henry Miller (left) and A. Waugh with pack and
riding horses, on way to Mt Wellington.*

and, pleased with their work, decided the dwelling should have a name. "Joanba" was selected as a combination of their three names — niece Joan, Mrs Anne Huggett and niece Barbara.

This was a resting place on the earlier track up the Avon Gorge. In order to make this track easier, Henry selected a block of land halfway between Huggett's and Golden Point. This was cleared and fenced, a bark hut built on it and became known as Lower Block.

Miller used Riggall's Hut on Wellington for about 16 years and then in 1916 Henry, his brother-in-law Frank Scott, and cattlemen friends built on the ridge midway between the Gable End and Mt Wellington, a sturdy slab hut with bark roof, which was later replaced with galvanised iron, packed in on the six-day trip by pack-horses. Today, sixty-four years later, the hut still provides shelter for cattlemen and bushwalkers.

Rex Miller joined his father in managing the Wellington lease and substantial log stockyards and horse paddocks were built, so that 700—800 head of cattle could be mustered and held on the Gable End until ready for the drive down to Heyfield.

Rex Miller

On occasions the Millers railed cattle from Queensland and New South Wales to Heyfield and then drove them up to Wellington for fattening. One year, the expected rains were late and sufficient grass was not available for a train load en route to Heyfield. The cattle were unloaded at Dandenong and while awaiting the rains and new growth of grass, the mob were driven slowly along the Princes Highway, grazing where roadside grass permitted. The cattle were left in the Haunted Hills, to be mustered later, with the loss of only a few head.

On another occasion Henry bought store cattle in New South Wales but on the way up to Mt Wellington they died — of pleuro-pneumonia.

In the 1930s Henry employed a well-known bushman and stockman, Denny Connolly, after whom Connolly's Soak on the Razorback was named. Another well-known drover and stockman, Bob Goldie, from Boisdale grazed a few cattle in with Miller's and helped with the droving and mustering.

Late in 1938, while branding cattle in the stockyard of his Thousand-Acre Paddock, Henry Miller was kicked in the stomach by a stockhorse and was taken to hospital with internal injuries. He lingered for a while and then died.

So passed away one of Gippsland's great pioneers; a thoroughly honest, clean living man who loved the mountains.

Rex carried on the Miller tradition until about 1960, when he retired to live at Mornington. Miller's Gap and Miller's Spur, two prominent landmarks, will be a reminder of the Millers, even if Miller's Hut someday succumbs to the ravages of time and the elements.

Golden Point Hut No. 1
Henry Miller and − Moreton
outside the entrance.

Golden Point No. 2 Hut

This was Golden Point Hut in 1936, when Alan, Frank and the writer passed this way en route for Wellington and a winter crossing to Mt Howitt and Merrijig.

The Golden Point Hut No. 3 in 1979. The hut
is now maintained by David Gunter, whose cattle
graze the Avon River area. Regrettably, as shown
below, the hut is accessible to motor-cyclists.·

A very early winter visitor to Miller's Hut. The roof, as indicated by the snow-line on the eaves, had not then been covered with iron, but retained the figuration of the bark, as shown in the photo below.

A large summer party at Miller's Hut.. Note the original bark roof with the substantial supporting log framework.

181

Denny Connolly and Rex Miller

A cattle holding yard on the Avon River approach to Wellington

MILLER'S HUT

From here to Miller's Hut is only three minutes, and between is a beautiful forest of snow gums, unlike, in colouring, any we have seen. The trunks are patterned like those of blue gums, but the contrasting colours are red and green on a cream ground. The predominant tone of red is that of the flame tree blossom, richer than terra cotta on brick, and softening into coral. The contrasting colour is apple green, deepening here and there to olive. A lovely wood.

Miller's Hut is in a small clearing, with a cattle stockyard hard by.

W.J.CLEARY 1936

A group outside Miller's Hut.   *Cleve Cole (centre) and Mick Higgins (right)*
They had accompanied Alan Bennie from Rose River.   *outside Miller's Hut*

Denny Connolly and Henry Miller
at Trapyard Hill

THE GILDERS

Following the death of Edward Riggall in 1913, Glenfalloch B was purchased by Robert Gilder III in 1914, for his son Robert Gilder IV who was away at the war. Robert III only lived at Glenfalloch for one year.

Robert IV resided at Glenfalloch 1922–1929 with his young family and then moved down to Maffra for the children to attend school. He had no mountain grazing leases at this time. He took out Doolan's Plain lease and the Butcher County lease in 1943 or 1944, when son Robert V was away at World War II.

Jack Kelly who had a run with his brother Jim Kelly on Holmes Plain took up the Glenfalloch cattle. On Robert Gilder V's return from war service he took over and gradually acquired additional leases at Gable End, Mt Wellington and the Mt Clear county (in Doladrook). In 1965 Wonnangatta freehold was purchased from Jack and Arthur Guy and the Wonnangatta leases were transferred.

Bob acknowledges the assistance given in his early years by the Kellys, Norman Chester and other cattlemen in the district, but after 36 years experience of running cattle on the High Plains, he is now one of the 'veterans'.

Glenfalloch is now about 12,250 acres freehold and 1,000 cattle graze on the High Plain runs (including Wonnangatta) in summer. The drive up from Heyfield to the top takes six days (three days from Glenfalloch).

The following excerpts are from a paper prepared by Dr A.W.Howitt, F.G.S., A.H.Lucas, M.A., B.Sc., and Arthur Dendy, D.Sc., F.L.S. and read before the Field Naturalists Club of Victoria, 9th February, 1891. In the paper are references to Dr. Howitt's several efforts to reach Lake Tarli Karng.

Tarli Karng

Dr A.W.Howitt, F.G.S.

A VISIT TO LAKE NIGOTHURUK AND THE MOUNT WELLINGTON DISTRICT, GIPPSLAND

This lake was unknown even to the blackfellows until somewhere about fifty years ago, when two natives of the Welwenduk tribe came upon it while in search of wombats. The Bundaurat tribe owned all rights of the Macallister basin, including the basin of the Wellington, which is a tributary. The Nigothoruk (Wellington Mountain) blacks claimed the neighbouring valley on the east, that of the Avon and its tributaries, which drain the plains over Mount Wellington. It was the Welwenduk division of this tribe which occupied the lower Avon, to which "Billy" and his father, the discoverers of the lake, belonged.

No white man had seen the lake until in 1886 a stockman named Snowden, working up the Wellington valley, saw the lake from the top of a spur, visited it, and made known its existence.

In the same year Mr. Howitt made a first attempt, with old Billy as a guide, to reach this "big fellow waterhole what creek go in and never come out again." They tried first to follow the ridge between Ben Cruachan Creek and the Avon River, but were forced back by bad weather. They twice afterwards endeavoured to force a way along the Mount Angus Range, on the east side of the Avon, but the country was so rugged that the explorers had to return.

Meanwhile news came of Snowden's success, and that Mr. Riggall, of Glen Falloch station, had also reached the lake. Accordingly Mr. Howitt saw that the Macallister and Wellington route was the most practicable, and in a fourth attempt succeeded in reaching the lake with his black friend, at Easter, 1887. Mr. Riggall later took up a party of thirty; they led down, however, only a single pack-horse to the lake. The Misses May and Annie Howitt, with their father, at Christmas time, 1887, made another vain attempt to reach the goal by way of the Mount Angus Range, but in the following February, 1888, they were successful, taking this time the Macallister route, and rode triumphantly down to the shores of the lake.

While a stream led into the lake from the Wellington Snow-plains, no communication had been found between the lake and the Wellington River in the valley below.   The lake was formed by a comparatively low and level barrier of rocky boulders but Howitt had been unable to examine fully the nature of the barrier or descend to the valley below.   He, therefore, led another party which included A.H.S.Lucas, M.A., B.Sc. and Arthur Dendy D.Sc., F.L.S. and set out on 23rd December, 1890 determined to more thoroughly examine the geological features of the lake.

It may be of interest to any member of the Club who propose to go on a similar expedition to know what we took with us.   The objects we had in view were three — (1) to make a more complete exploration of the lake and its surroundings than had hitherto been made;   (2) to take as complete a series of photographs as possible;   and (3) to collect natural history specimens.   Our baggage was accordingly somewhat elaborate.   For the first object we had to take — (1) horses and horse furniture, (2) tents and clothing, (3) provisions, and for the others appropriate photographic and collecting apparatus.

We took with us three riding horses and three packers, and also a youth, who provided his own mount.   Each of the packers was of course provided with a pack saddle, with surcingle, side straps, centre straps, and crupper, leading rope, bell, and hobbles.   Each riding horse had, in addition to the ordinary saddle and harness, a bell and hobbles.   We also took half a dozen horse-shoes (slippers) and shoeing tools, including "ready-pointed patent nails with countersunk heads."

When folded up, the tent and fly served as covers for two of the packs.   We provided ourselves with a large supply of American leather, for a first, second, and third necessity in the Gippsland bush is a waterproof, and manufacturered various strange and uncouth-looking garments to be worn on horseback in case of wet weather, and to lay on the ground at night to keep the damp from the blankets. We each had a "poncho", consisting of a large square of American leather with a slit cut in the middle to put the head through, and also an apron of the same material to protect the knees, and a valise of size convenient for strapping in front of the saddle in which to stow the private kit, consisting of changes of linen and sundries.   Of course, we all had large blankets.

As to provisions, we were well supplied with flour and baking powder, beet and bacon, tongues and sardines, cheese and butter, figs and prunes, jam and marmalade, tea, coffee and cocoa, with sugar but no milk.   The only culinary utensils we took were a spoon, a tin-opener, and three sizes of "billy", so that the small packed in the larger.   When our leader had occasion to bake he manufactured a beautifully clean white bread-board on the spot out of the bark of a white gum or other convenient tree by the deft use of a tomahawk.   Each carried a pocket knife of formidable appearance.

We took two cameras.   Mr. Howitt's was a half-plate with a lens of so extraordinarily wide an angle that we came to think it could take in objects behind the camera.   Dr. Dendy's was a very convenient travelling stereoscopic camera. The former used Ilford dry plates, Carbutt films, and stripping films, and the latter Fry's dry plates.   Mr. Howitt took what Dr. Dendy calls a diabolical invention known as a changing bag, and which he guarantees to produce more blasphemy in a given time than any other piece of scientific apparatus yet invented. The bag is made of two thicknesses of red cloth, and has three openings or sleeves, a single one at one end, and a pair at one side. In through the single opening are put the dark slides (containing the plates to be changed) and the box of fresh slides. Then the operator's hands are thrust into the two sleeves at the side, which clasp the wrists tightly by means of an elastic band, and there he sits on the ground, before beaming spectators, in the roasting sun maybe, or, worse, in the full smoke of the camp fire, both hands tied up in an irritating red bag, while he fumbles about for an indefinite period, trying in vain to make the plates go into their proper places without getting confused, while the perspiration streams from his face, and his utterances are frequent, brief, and emphatic.

24TH DECEMBER (CHRISTMAS EVE) — We got up about 4.30 a.m., packed the horses, had breakfast, and rode away from Heyfield at 8 a.m. Our cavalcade consisted of our three selves on our respective horses, the boy Alfred (who was engaged as a kind of handyman for the trip), the three pack-horses, and an escort comprising Mr. Du Ve, of Rosedale, who had kindly assisted us in making our arrangements, and Mr. Cox, the mounted constable in charge of the district, who rode with us to Glenmaggie, perhaps to see us safe off the premises. The various eccentricities of our horses soon began to show themselves.

The three pack-horses we shall not soon forget. Boco was blind of one eye. Brownie had a "jinked back", i.e. was gone in the loins. Biddy went everywhere but on the track, and on coming to a tree took her pleasure in veering to the right if she saw you working to the left — a proceeding which leads to entanglement and unphilosophical language. But we shall discover more of the ways of packers as we proceed, and must not allow them to make us linger in our narrative as they did on our journey.

We had first to leave the basin of the Thomson, and cross the low watershed which separates it from the basin of the Macallister, the Glenmaggie Creek being a tributary of the latter. Here we parted with our friends and crossed the Glenmaggie Creek, more attracted by the big hills we could see in the distance, than by the rather pretty little township. After crossing another creek, our road lay along a long ridge, which runs parallel to the Macalister River at a distance of one or two miles and which culminates about a dozen miles to the north in the steep Blanket Hill. We continued to skirt the left bank of the river, the track narrower but still good and well worn.

At 1.30 p.m. we made our first ford of the Macallister River, 21 miles from Heyfield. Here we camped for lunch. Here we met Mr. William Riggall riding down from Glen Falloch, and his was the last outsider's face we were to see for a week. After lunch we pushed on, keeping near the river, our leader jogging ahead, anxious to bring us to the lake in good time.

At Hickey's Creek we left the river, which here comes from a considerable westward bend, and shortly after entered upon a southward projecting tongue of the Upper Devonian. This formation constitutes the whole of the district of the Upper Macallister and the Wellington rivers, including Mounts Crinoline, Tamboritha, and Wellington. It bends southward, on the west, the tongue to Glen Falloch and Hickey's Creek, and on the east a much broader stretch of country, comprising the Avon valley with Mount Angus and Ben Croachan. These summits, with Mount Useful to the east, formed the most conspicuous land-marks on our journey. Mounts Wellington and Tamboritha are over 5,000 feet high, and the Crinoline Hill is not of much less elevation.

Next over the Big Hill to Glen Falloch, with magnificent views on either side, and the deep ravines into which we looked down were seen to be in many cases bounded by steep, nearly vertical walls, the harder beds of rock standing out in often overhanging terraces, while the flat outline of the mountains appeared to be fringed by a single row of trees, so clearly was the folliage of the gums which grew close to the edge of the precipice projected against the sky.

We did not stay at Glen Falloch, as we had a good hour of daylight available. We pushed on, keeping close to the river, and camped on Herald's Flat.

25TH DECEMBER (CHRISTMAS DAY) — We were all up at about 4.30 a.m. It took us 3½ hours to get breakfast, collect, saddle, and pack the horses, and take a photograph of the camp, and at 8 o'clock sharp we were on the track again.

The branch of the Wellington River whose source we investigated rises to the north of the mountain, runs west to unite with the other branch coming still further from the north, then the united stream flows westward, till beneath the Crinoline Hill it turns south to join the Macallister at an acute angle. Hence our course up the Wellington track took pretty much the shape of an L — a northward line to the Crinoline, and then a line nearly due east to Mount Wellington.

Two miles jogging along the flats brought us to the last ford of the Macallister, and two more to the first on the Wellington. We had fine views of Crinoline Hill, so called from its shape and well marked terraces. At first it lay in front of us up the valley, and then on our left hand as we turned eastward at its base. We crossed the Wellington by an old camp of Mr. Howitt's.

The Wellington River has less extensive flats than the Macallister, and our mode of progression up the valley consisted in crossing a spur, longer or shorter, lower or higher, on one side of the river, fording, crossing a spur on either side, fording, skirting the river, fording, and so on unto nearly forty fords.

After passing the Crinoline Hill, and making some 15 miles from Herald's Flat, we camped for lunch at 12.30 on the Wellington River below Breakfast Creek, and near the turn-off of Whitelaw's track. The river here is very beautiful, a wide and winding rock-bedded stream flowing between high hills thickly coated with gum trees. We boiled the billy on a pebbly shore to avoid all chance of kindling a bush fire, and after lunch had a most refreshing bath in the river, which was rather too shallow and broken here for a good swim. We camped early for the night at the foot of what is known as the Gap or Saddle.

26TH DECEMBER — We were up again at 4.30, for one needs must rise early to make good stages in the bush. We had, however, to-day but a short march before us. Our track lay up the hillside and over the "Gap", then down again to the river. From the top of the Gap we had our best complete view of Mount Wellington, straight in front of us, with its two characteristic humps on the long summitt. We descended to the river, close to a ruined hut in which Mr. Angus Shaw once lived. We came on to the river again close to a deep pool, flanked by an enormous vertical rock, which we stopped to photograph.

We found the photograph-taking rather a labour, as it involved unpacking one of the pack-horses to get out the apparatus, and thus caused half an hour's delay each time. We continued our journey up stream till we had made about 10 miles from our last camp and found ourselves on a grassy flat near the junction of two branches of the upper Wellington, and almost at the foot of the mountain. Here we pitched camp at about 12.30.

About this camp the river flows from side to side of a broad, flat-bottomed valley, bordered by moderately steep grassy slopes.

27TH DECEMBER — We were up about 4 o'clock — indeed, our leader was up a good deal earlier. Our horses were getting used to the hobbles, and the two big riding horses showed that they meant to lead the others into mischief. Mr. Howitt was up between 1 and 2 o'clock and brought them back to camp; and yet when he rose at 3 they were nowhere to be seen. He and Alfred accordingly set out in quest, while the others got breakfast ready, &c. The five were found at no very great distance, but the two ringleaders had left the home track, and made up a spur several miles. Fortunately Mr. Howitt had all knowledge of horses and their ways in the mountains at his fingers' ends, and presently we heard the faint, far-off tinkle of the bells, and the runaways were ridden back without much mercy. This was our last camp before reaching the lake, distant about eight miles, and the worst part of the journey lay before us. In view of this we packed up all the luggage and provisions which we were not likely to want, and made a *cache* of it on top of a tall stump, out of the way of the dingoes, so as to lighten the loads of the packers as much as we could. Our camp was on the left bank of the river, and, after crossing it once more, and for the last time on our upward march, we made for a great spur of Mount Wellington, up which we struck. The spur was very steep in places, terribly long, and tolerably thickly timbered, and we had to proceed gently and rest the horses frequently.

At last we reached the top, and were indeed rewarded for our climb. Immediately opposite to us on the east side rose the main mass of Mount Wellington, towering in lonely grandeur above the surrounding hills, while far below in the hollow of the basin lay the little lake, known to the aborigines as Tali Kango Nigothoruka (the little lake on Wellington or Nigothoruk). It looked very small from where we stood, surrounded on all sides but one by precipitous and thickly wooded slopes. It really occupies an area of about 22 acres, but one end of it lay to our right, and was hidden by the trees on the mountain side below us. At this end should be the outlet, but it is blocked by a great barrier of rocks, of which we now had a good view, though the actual rocks are concealed beneath an abundance of vegetation. At the other end we could see the gully of a small creek (Nigothoruk) which enters the lake, flowing down from the high river plains above.

It looked an awkward job which lay before us, for we had to take seven horses down to that lake, through rocks and scrub into which even the wild cattle never venture.

Arrived at length at the bottom, we had next to push our way through the scrub and boulders along the edge of the lake till we came to a patch of level ground where we could hobble the horses. The thick scrub comes down on the mountain sides nearly to the water's edge, leaving a narrow shelving, rocky beach, which is probably covered with water when the snows on the mountains melt.

After lunch Mr. Howitt and Mr. Dendy went to look for the outlet of the lake. They made their way along the shore of the lake, and so came to the great barrier which dams the head of the valley. From the general lie of the country it was obvious that the lake must be connected with the Wellington River — indeed, that one branch of the latter takes its origin in the lake — and our explorers were now going to examine the valley below the barrier. They forced a passage through the thick scrub, which covers it and shows that the lake never bodily overflows. They crossed the barrier on the right, and found themselves at the head of a great

Set between two northward reaching spurs of the Gable End this delightful tarn reflects the sky and clouds by day and the stars by night. So steep are the banks in places that a rolling boulder will continue under the water, and can be watched quite easily down through the clear depths. A small waterfall pours the waters of Nigothoruk Creek into the basin, and it has been said that the rise of the lake varies but a few feet. This I know to be incorrect. On my first visit the waters were low and a wide beach fronted the lake at the barrier, whilst on the occasion of my second visit there was no beach — a rise of at least fifteen feet being evident.

RAY WHITFORD 1963

Snowden Falls

Lake Tarli Karng

A lake, like a jewel, requires a setting. That is what makes the charm of Tarli Karngo Nigothuruk, the hidden tarn of Mt Wellington in Gippsland. Climb 5,000 ft and you stand on the edge of the Basin, slip down 2,000 feet on the inside and you reach the margin of the waters. Solitude abides there; it is the home of ancient Peace.

R.H. Croll 1928

190

gorge which they named the Valley of Destruction.   Presently they saw through the trees on the left hand a great vertical cliff, a wall of naked rock, 400 or 500 feet high, towering above them in the distance.   This cliff is part of Mount Wellington proper and forms the south-east side of the gorge.   They now found that it was getting late, and in returning they kept to the left or south-east side of the valley, and found the ascent here very much easier than on the other side or in the middle.   They came back to the lake over the barrier again, close to the Mount Wellington side of the latter, and past a great twin gum tree near the water's edge, which forms a convenient indication of the best place to cross the barrier.

We all started at about 6 o'clock to make a determined effort to find the place of issue of the water.   We went down easily enough as far as Dendy's Heights, and then we rapidly scrambled down what appeared to be the principal gully. Presently we distinctly heard the water, and suddenly we saw in front of us a small still pool among the rocks, as clear as crystal, and fringed with a thick growth of ferns.   Into this pool a tiny streamlet trickled from between the rocks.   The mystery was solved, for it was evident that the water from the lake filtered through the barrier at the head of the gorge, and worked in underground channels between the rocks which partly fill the gorge, to come out here at length 550 feet below the level of the lake, at a point perhaps a mile and a half distant.   There are probably at least half a dozen springs distinguishable.

Mr. Howitt still considers that the most probable explanation as to Lake Nigothoruk is the action of a glacier which extended from the Mt. Wellington Plains down the valley.   He has been unable to observe any signs of landslips in the igneous rocks there.   The form of the dam, its structure, as well as the general character of Lake Nigothoruk strongly suggest to him a moraine blocking up the valley.   To positively determine the real nature and origin of the lake will require a detailed geological examination of the locality, which at present it has not been possible to make.

The Hidden Lake

In the Wellington River Valley.

Leaving the lake the party experienced difficulties with some of the horses, were enveloped in a fog on Mt Wellington and were caught in a heavy thunderstorm, before returning by the same route.   They recorded 35 crossings of the Wellington River (in 20 miles), met Mr Walter Riggall*who had ridden up from Glen Falloch to meet them and eventually reached Heyfield on 31st December.

TARLI KARNG

Howitt's reference to Walter Riggall is a mistake.   There was no Walter in the Riggall family.   Howitt suggests that Snowden, in 1886, was the first white man to see and visit it.   Johnny Snowden, however, was a native stockman employed by Dick Riggall of Glenfalloch.   He discovered Tarli Karng, having seen it from a distance, he refused to visit it, due probably to native taboos.   Richard Riggall was the first white man to stand on the shore of the lake, and he was also at Mt Wellington on the occasion of Howitt's visit.   Riggall directed Howitt to Tarli Karng, but even so Howitt had difficulty in locating it.   Unimpressed with Howitt's bushmanship, Dick Riggall re-directed him and Howitt reached the lake.   Howitt's account of the journey makes no mention of meeting Dick Riggall on Wellington!

The Lands Department first suggested that the lake be named Lake Riggall, but Richard protested and asked that it be called Snowden, after its discoverer.   This was not acceptable to the Lands Department, probably because Snowden was an aboriginal. They then settled for Tarli Karng which they believed was native for "the little lake". However, Dick Riggall after asking Snowden what the words meant, received the answer, "White man gibberish".   Snowden's name, however, is remembered by the stream and falls which enter the lake.

Sam Riggall, Dick's brother, later discovered the outlet from the lake.

Bush Ballads

SOME GIPPSLAND RIDERS
by Annie Bryce

Out back in Northern Gippsland, where Mt Howitt rears its crest,
   Where snow lies thick and deep on Reynard's side,
Where the snowy plains of Bennison go stretching further west,
   There are men who could teach "Clancy" how to ride.

There's Harry Smith, of Eagle Vale, who counted pretty fair,
   The horse was never foaled he couldn't back;
But for chasing the big "Mickies" in the rugged ranges there,
   They reckoned "Dargo Norton" was the "crack".

Like the "Man from Snowy River," he would never pause to think,
   But down the slope would race at topmost speed.
When the game was chasing brumbies in the scrub of Carey's Creek,
   'Twas "Dargo Jim" who always kept the lead.

There was "Goldie", wild Bob Goldie. 'Twas said that he could sit
   A bucking horse, and calmly have a shave;
But I'm much inclined to doubt it, for never saw I yet,
   On cheek, or chin, or lip a hair to shave or save.

There was Will Lee from the "Crooked", Tom Phelan and Culhane,
   They'd ride a horse until he'd slung his brand.
And they'd fill a pipe and light it, strike the match upon his hoof,
   And keep him bucking till he couldn't stand.

Talk of "Clancy of the Overflow"; I'd like to see him stay
   Till a horse had bucked his brand to "Holy Smoke";
And his droving mate once told me it was always Clancy's way
   To leave the saddle when the girth-straps broke.

But the "Man from Snowy River" is the man I'd like to meet;
   I'd give a pound to put him to the test;
If he galloped down Magdala without shifting in his seat,
   There's not a man that wouldn't give him best.

What a day we had last summer in Mt Darling's gullies deep
  (Where by rocky cliffs the way was often barred);
When we hunted the wild bullock that was outlawed on the run,
  And for fifteen years had never seen a yard.

How we raced him down the hillside on those horses mountain-bred,
  With a pack of dogs all eager for the fray;
What a noise of cracking stockwhips as we followed where they led,
  Till in the creek they brought the stag to bay.

There he stood and pawed the gravel, and glared around with firey eyes,
  Or charged the dogs, and roared with rage and pain,
But no more he'll lead the cattle to the salt-lick on the Rise;
  We left him dead upon the Wild Horse Plain.

Then the day we ran the "Wellington" we had a bit of fun,
  Tho' all of us got worsted in the chase.
But Dave Bryce sat in the timber for hours with the gun,
  But she never once looked near his hiding place.

The stockmen from the Bennison were there, a lovely lot,
  And we ran her till the horses all were done;
But we never got her yarded, and we never got her shot,
  For she knew each creek and gully onn the run.

Dargo Jim was close behind her when his horse gave out and fell,
  In the gorge by Holmes' fence where two creeks meet;
And no more the brave old stock-horse will be raced to wheel the lead,
  On the plains that day he ran his final heat.

But winter's snows came early and winter's snows stayed late,
  They covered the hill and hollow like a wrap;
And the filly from the Wellington that winter met her fate;
  In the spring they found her dead in Darky's Gap.

The new chums on the station ride round the waterfall,
  Or view the torrent from the topmost height;
They talk of the good scenery, say the stringy-barks are tall,
  And remark that mountain snow's a pretty sight.

But put them on a stock-horse, and they're out upon his neck,
  As he wheels, and twists, and doubles in the chase;
And they cannot share the feelings of the men they little reek
  Of danger in the hurried, headlong race.

O, there's music in the stockwhip, to the stockmen born and bred,
  And bounding life in every pulse and vein,
When he feels the horse beneath him, pulling hard to get his head,
  And chafing madly at the tightened rein.

And there's music in the lowing of the cattle on the ridge,
  In the sound of thundering hoof-beats down the rise;
And there's beauty in the bushland to the far horizon's edge,
  Where towering snow peaks cling to meet the skies.

Mustering

THERE IS MAGIC IN THE WORD MUSTERING. It conjures up visions of thundering mobs of cattle, the shouting of sun-tanned bushmen, whinnying of nimble-footed stock ponies, cracking of stockwhips and the eager barking of cattle dogs. Every autumn in the Alpine foothills the stockmen and their thoroughbreds assemble for the annual cattle muster.

Thousands of head of magnificent beef cattle, mostly Herefords, that have roamed the High Plain pastures from the Border to Gippsland unmolested for five months, fattening on the lush snow-grass, must be mustered, drafted and driven down from the snow plains to the winter pastures in river valleys, home paddocks or to the saleyards before the winter snows arrive to cover the high places with a mantle of white that will hold the mountains in its grip till the Spring thaw.

The muster varies somewhat in duration and method, from place to place. In some areas, such as the Cobbler Plateau, Mt Skene, Lake Mountain and Howitt Plains, the grazing rights might be the property of one station owner whose stockmen will muster the cattle from a defined area, drive the daily round-up to a holding, or stock-yard and finally drive the entire mob down to their winter pastures by one established stock route. There are other, often larger areas, with access routes from two or more directions, where holdings for different leasees adjoin, and here it is not unusual for the several stock owners to work together, rounding up all cattle from the entire area, driving to a common stockyard and on completion of the muster drafting the herd, according to brands or calves running with their mothers, into mobs belonging to each owner. These are then driven by individual routes to their respective lowland pastures. Such areas are Mt Bogong, the Bennison and adjoining plains, The Bluff-Magdala-Mt Clear, and the Dargo High Plains. The Bogong High Plains, however, sees the most complex and concentrated mustering with fourteen leaseholders mustering 4,200 head of cattle and after drafting, driving them out by seven different routes.

Mustering in the High Plains.

All combine to muster across the whole of the fenceless High Plains, yard the daily round-up in several widely dispersed stock-yards, draft the entire mob into fourteen different herds on completion and drive their cattle out by seven routes.

But the mustering in all areas has much in common.

Cattlemen leave their home properties well mounted, pack-horses loaded with a week's or more food and all necessary equipment and cattle dogs eager for the fray. They ride to their own grazing grounds or to rendezvous with other cattlemen at the bush huts, strategically placed in the High Plains and used, generally twice yearly — at Autumn mustering and again in early Summer, when the cattle are returned to pasture.

From Spring to early Autumn, the snowplain regions, mostly between 4,500 and 5,500 feet, but occasionally as on Mt Bogong, Hotham, The Cobberas and the higher parts of the Bogong High Plains, reaching to 6,000 feet, are known best to a privileged few cattlemen and bushwalkers. They are dramatically different from the plains of the lowlands, with irregular areas of coarse snow-grass flecked with masses of wildflowers in a glorious profusion of yellows, white, pinks, blues and mauves, clumps of white and green snowgums, branches twisted to grotesque shapes from bearing the burden of heavy winter snows, winding crystal clear streams edged with great boulders and bordered on all sides with sloping wooded spurs that are the stock routes to the plains below.

197

Mustering on Lankey's Plain.

The stockmen proceed in the first instance to round up the large and obvious mobs. In most of the alpine snowplain areas a deficiency of salt in the water and herbage makes the cattle 'salt-hungry' and it is an established practice for stockmen to scatter salt and announce its presence with the well recognised cry of S - A - L - L - L - T, to which the cattle respond, emerging from the cover of snow-gum thickets and secluded feeding places.

Although mustering does not necessarily require fast riding, it demands skilled horsemanship from riders and powers of endurance from the horses. There are sometimes long descents into log strewn gullies, leaps to clear a fallen tree, sharp manoeuvres to avoid low hanging branches and then steep ascents to bring the cattle out on to the tops. In all the work the well trained cattle dogs are invaluable, consolidating the mob, urging along the stragglers and racing to head off the recalcitrant beast that decided to "take off" in the opposite direction.

At the end of the day the cattle are driven into large stock yards of "dog-leg" or similar construction, which have been constructed from snow gum logs and are a permanent feature of the landscape. Once the cattle have settled down in the holding yards, the stockmen return to the huts for the evening meal, generally prepared on the larger musters, by camp cooks, or by one of the party appointed to that task (and "it better be good").

An evening around a blazing log fire — and there is no better than one of snow gum branches — a final brew of billy tea and the stockmen roll up in

Jim Treasure and Carl Wraith mustering on the Dargos.

their blankets to sleep on a large bench-type bunk that extends across the width of the hut.

Each day, after the more obvious groups of cattle have been mustered, the work becomes more difficult. Areas are allotted to pairs of stockmen who comb the less accessible spurs and gullies for stragglers. Often the men must resort to the unpopular "footwork" which means dismounting and leading the horses as they force their way through patches of hop scrub and undergrowth. Again the dogs are invaluable in poking the stubborn cattle from their retreats. Most beasts respond to the shouts and urging of the cattlemen and those that don't are generally brought to heel by the nip of a cattle dog or the crack of a stockwhip. Surprisingly, the tally for most musters is remarkably high, often only a few odd beasts are unaccounted for, and these are generally located and rounded up in the following year's muster.

Spectacular riding is sometimes seen towards the end of a muster, when a rider attempts to round up cattle which escaped last season's muster and have roamed for a year in the well grassed gullies below the snow-line. The eventual catching of these 'wild' cattle requires the best of both man and steed. The stockman must be fearless and the horse strong and agile to pursue the truant steer across hillsides pitted with wombat burrows and strewn with fallen timber. Horse, rider and dog are usually victorious!

Driving cattle around a difficult traverse between The Bluff and Magdala.

Prime "beef on the hoof" moving across snow-plains bedecked with summer wildflowers.

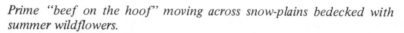

Mustering on Dargo High Plains.

Fortunately, falls are infrequent, and injuries to horse or rider, comparatively rare.

When the yarding has been completed, the task of branding and ear-marking the "clean-skins" is performed in a smaller, high-railed yard built for the purpose. The calves are herded into a small pen at the end of the yard, then leg-roped, ear-marked and hot-iron branded. And some of the brands of the pioneer cattlemen families have now been in use for more than a hundred years.

It requires speed, strength and agility on the part of the stockman to handle a bucking calf in a pen crowded with other cattle — and there is also the danger that an irate mother may charge to the assistance of her offspring. Then there is a scatter to reach the safety of the fence, climb the rails and avoid the horns of the pursuer.

A Long Wait

T*HE LAURIE SEAMAN MEMORIAL HUT* was erected by public subscription, in memory of W. Laurie Seaman, a skier who lost his life on Tuesday, 14th August, 1928. The hut is situated on the snow-pole line, on the north-east end of Etheridge Range, in a prominent position, about 1½ miles from the summit of Mt Kosciusko, Australia's highest peak.

The hut is a substantial stone building, of two rooms, and is stocked with rations, first-aid kit, blankets and firewood, for emergency use only. A telephone connects the hut with Charlotte's Pass Chalet and the Hotel Kosciusko.

Fifty years later, the hut perpetuates his memory, but how many of today's skiers recall the bizarre misadventure that took two lives with surprising suddenness in Australia's first skiing fatality.

On Tuesday, August 14th, 1928, a party of six skiers left Betts' Camp at about 10 a.m. with the immediate objective of skiing to Charlotte's Pass. Two members of the party, W. Evan Hayes and W. Laurie Seaman, intended to return to Betts' Camp for lunch and then go on to the Kosciusko Hotel for dinner and a committee meeting that evening. Accordingly they did not consider it necessary to carry any spare clothing or food. The weather was fine and sunny as had been the preceeding few days. The western slopes of the range were hard and icy and the eastern slopes were soft. Seaman and Hayes gradually drew ahead of the others and reached Charlotte's Pass about a quarter of a mile ahead. They waved to the others and skied on, and out of sight. They were never to be seen alive again.

The party of four reached Charlotte Pass, dismissed Seaman and Hayes from their thoughts and proceeded on towards the summit of Kosciusko. While climbing the Etheridge Range, a sudden blizzard overtook them, reduced visibility to a few yards and with wind and sleet at gale force, they turned to retrace their route to Betts' Camp. The time was 1 o'clock, and by 4.30 p.m. they were safely back. They were surprised to find that Seaman and Hayes had not yet returned and somewhat apprehensive, two of the party retraced their tracks. About half way to the Pass they found a scarf and glove belonging to Hayes, but failing light and worsening weather persuaded them to return to Betts' Camp.

By next morning the situation was considered grave and a search party was immediately assembled. An extensive search was mounted and a wide area covered in succeeding days, but by the evening of Monday August 20th, all hope of finding the skiers alive above the snow-line was abandoned. A slender hope was held that they might have reached the timber line where survival might still be possible. The only faint possibility of a clue was a single set of ski tracks and some boot marks on the summit and a single set of ski tracks running away towards the Ram's Head Range.

Although touring parties were frequently on the summit of Kosciusko, it was not until Sunday, 9th September, that Seaman's body was discovered, close to the summit and only 30 yards from the road. His skis were found a few yards away and an exposed film, taken from his camera was developed to show one print of Hayes standing beside the summit cairn, and another with Seaman in a similar position.

It was now certain that the two skiers had reached the summit of Kosciusko on the afternoon of August 14th. The evidence available indicated that the two had separated and Hayes, who was the more experienced skier, followed the road on skis right to the summit. Seaman, perhaps less sure of his ability on the final icy slopes, had removed his skis and walked directly up the final short slope, kicking steps (these were visible to the early searchers) and rejoined Hayes at the cairn, where the two photographs were taken. It is assumed that they again separated, Seaman to walk back to his skis and Hayes on skis to rejoin him at the foot of the slope. Seaman, following his footprints, made it to his skis and presumably sat down to await the return of Hayes to the rendezvous. He waited until death overtook him. Hayes, skiing in bad weather conditions, on an icy surface that did not assist him to retrace his upward route, missed the rendezvous, and skied on - into oblivion.

Hayes body was not discovered until two summers later, when it was found partly covered by snow at the edge of the Cootapatamba Drift, an unusually large drift at the edge of Lake Cootapatamba, a short distance from the summit of Mt Kosciusko. The snowfalls in the winter of 1928 had been unusually heavy and the spring and summer thaw had left a larger area of snow than usual at the Cootapatamba Drift. Lighter falls and a warmer spring in 1929 resulted in the body being partly uncovered for the first time in fifteen months. The set of ski tracks running towards the Rams Head Range, which the searchers in 1928 had observed, had been those of Hayes, for it was beyond their traceable end that the body was found. As the map indicates Hayes had obviously mistaken his direction after leaving the summit, missing the rendezvous point, and had simply become disoriented and lost.

On the night of August 9th, 1928, only a few days before the tragedy, a record low temperature of 6° Fahernheit had been registered in the area, and without food, warm additional clothing, or even the means to dig a shelter in the snow, Seaman and Hayes had paid the supreme price.

Seaman Hut and Etheridge Range.

The incident is recorded in order to emphasise a number of facts:

(i) The weather in Australia's high country can change from sunny and fine to blizzard conditions with alarming suddenness, as had happened to the combined party, setting out on a pleasant sunny day to enjoy a few hours skiing and being engulfed in a sudden blizzard.

(ii) For even a trip of only a few hours duration, some food and emergency warm clothing should be carried.

(iii) The first signs of approaching bad weather should be heeded and an immediate return to a sheltered position commenced. The main party of four wisely turned back to the safety of Betts Camp, whereas Seaman and Hayes were tempted to 'give it a go' for the summit, in spite of the weather change.

(iv) It is an inflexible rule of bushcraft that a small party should never separate, except in the direst emergency. Seaman and Hayes separated twice. Whether they would have made it back to Charlotte's Pass had they remained together is a matter of conjecture, but there is evidence to believe, however, that Seaman sacrificed his life by waiting in vain for a companion who, having lost his way, did not return.

The final observation, however, is that on the day in question, Seaman and Hayes were not equipped as ski-tourers, but were virtually day-trippers. Ski tourers would have been fully equipped with food, clothing, bedding and shelter - in fact all the necessary equipment to enable them to cope with such conditions that were encountered. As day trippers, Seaman and Hayes were simply not prepared for the extreme conditions that can be encountered at short notice in our high country.

Seaman Memorial Hut.

THE CLEVE COLE MEMORIAL HUT
CAMP VALLEY — MOUNT BOGONG

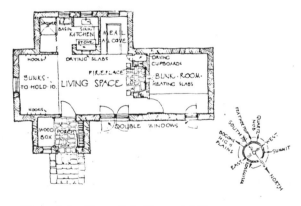

Plan of the Cleve Cole Memorial Hut
erected as a tribute to a pioneer skier

Cleve Cole

Cleve Cole's Last Trip

*I*N THE WINTER OF 1934, Cleve Cole, accompanied by Roy Weston, made a trip to Mt Bogong. They travelled with horses to near the head of Mountain Creek from where a direct ascent to Staircase Spur was planned. Leaving the horses at a height of 5,400 feet at 1.30 p.m. on July 29th they set out on a climb that would eventually take them to Maddison's "Aertex" Hut in Camp Valley. Cleve said, "It was with mixed feelings that we commenced the climb, partly owing to the weather conditions above, which, quite obviously were very bad."

Coming out of the timber at 5,800 feet, they encountered wind of hurricane force, and it was necessary to seek temporary rest behind the smallest shelter. The weather was so bad that a stay in the vicinity of the tree-line was considered. After a discussion, they decided to go on. Later, the question of turning back was discussed, but again they decided to continue. Their view was completely blotted out by fog, but once on the summit ridge they put on skis, which for greater safety, had been carried to this point. The wind was so cold that if a portion on the face was exposed, it became numb almost immediately.

Finally, at 5.30 p.m. the hut was reached. A week was spent skiing and exploring the area and a return to Tawonga was made in inclement weather, across the Mt Bogong plateau to the summit cairn and thence down the Staircase Spur to the snowline, which was reached 5½ hours after leaving "Aertex" Hut.

Cleve Cole, in the golden years of the early 'thirties, when much of Victoria's snow country was undeveloped and only partly explored, had justly earned the reputation of being one of our most competent and experienced ski-tourers and explorers. He had visited Europe on two occasions, skied in New Zealand and on all Victorian snowfields. He was a trail blazer and was the first to visit and ski in some remote areas. But of all the areas he visited, Mt Bogong was the Mecca that drew him back and received most of his attention. He explored the alternative approaches and was unceasing in his campaign for development of the mountain's snowfield. Cleve was a 'loner' and taking advantage of every opportunity that presented itself for an exploratory trip, his companions were whoever happened to be available at the time. On at least two occasions, to Mt Skene and across the Dargo High Plains, his sole companion was a mountain cattleman from the area. Cleve had grown up in the Boy Scout movement, and predictably he became Commissioner for Lone Scouts, a section which encouraged boys in isolated areas to participate in scouting activities.

But in spite of his adventurous spirit and distinguished record, Cleve preached the doctrine of 'Safety First'. He invariable carried compass, aneroid barometer, maps, alpine tent, storm-proof clothing, a margin of food for emergencies, and the standard camping equipment of the best quality obtainable. And his articles on 'Safety Precautions' appeared in Skiing and Walking Journals.

This, then, was the man, a master of his craft, who set out from Hotham on Wednesday, August 5th 1936, on what was fated to be his last trip.

Cleve Cole had reached Hotham Heights Chalet after a successful crossing of the Dargo High Plains accompanied by mountain cattleman Jack Treasure.

That trip, however, was not without incidents. During one night, spent in Gow's Hut, Jack left his boots close to the open fire, and during the night a log rolled out and burnt the side out of one of his boots. It was a mishap that prevented Jack Treasure from accompanying Cleve Cole across the Bogong High Plains and up on to Mt Bogong. Questioned about the trip recently, Jack said that had he accompanied the party, he would have got them down off the mountain to shelter below the snow-line. "There is no way", he said, "that I would have stayed for days in a hole in the snow".

Cleve Cole, unaccountably, was wearing new ski-boots when crossing the Dargos and he raised a severe blister on one heel. This considerably slowed the party and there were indications that Cleve was not in the best physical condition, causing the party to travel slowly. "At one point", recalls Jack, "Cleve paused and removed his skis. Laying them down on the snow, one slid away down hill, and I went after it and brought it back". Cleve was to repeat this elementary error on Bogong, and on this occasion, the ski was lost. Surely, not the practice of a master of his craft!

Cleve was joined at Hotham Heights by Mick Hull and Howard Michell. Mick, an experienced skier, was Treasurer of the Ski Club of Victoria, and

Cleve Cole photographed by P.E. "Mick" Hull, at 7 a m. outside Fitzgerald's Hut.

his name appeared regularly among the top runners in the club's racing championships. Howard Michell, a South Australian, was not so well known on the Victorian snowfields, but as events proved, he was the strongest and fittest of the party.

The three, who individually had earlier sent food supplies to Hotham, Fitzgerald's Hut and Maddison's 'Aertex' Hut conceived the idea of a trip across the Bogong High Plains, an ascent from the Big River to 'Aertex' Hut and thence over the summit of Mt Bogong to the Staircase Spur to Tawonga, a route which was known and had been travelled in its entirety on previous occasions by Cleve Cole.

All three seemed fit,and well-equipped with standard and emergency gear when they left Hotham at midday on August 5th, carrying 2½ days food. Fitzgerald's Hut and an additional food supply was reached in 1½ days, after they experienced relatively poor weather conditions.

On August 7th they left Fitzgerald's Hut in fine weather, carrying food for three days. Fog closed in on the party near Mt Nelse, lifted briefly, and descended again before they reached Big River at 3 p.m. They camped here for the night.

The party was fit, on schedule and with two day's food in hand had a short day's climb ahead to reach Maddison's "Aertex" Hut on Saturday August 8th.

They left Big River in good weather, faced with a climb of 3,500 feet. As they climbed the weather gradually deteriorated and they became enshrouded in dense fog at the western end of the plateau which leads to the Summit Cairn. Progress had been satisfactory and climbing was almost completed after five hours travel. However, poor visibility, a strong wind and driving snow made conditions and route finding difficult.

In icy conditions, Cleve removed his skis, dropped one and it slid away down a steep slope and was lost. Unable to find the Summit Cairn, they decided on the safest option open to them - they attempted to return to Big River, a sheltered, timbered location, below the snow-line. The dense fog defeated them. Every spur they attempted ended in an impossibly steep drop. At 5 p.m., they wisely halted and scooped out a dugout (an unenviable task, using enamel plates for a shovel) in which to shelter for the night. The dugout was 4 feet wide, long enough to lie down and had a roof constructed with a frame of skis and sticks, over which was spread a tent with snow over it. Mick's hands became numb and powerless during this operation and they remained in this condition for the remainder of the trip. Cleve was extremely tired, and Howard was the strongest of the three.

They prepared a hot drink of 'Oxo', heated over 'Meta' fuel (chalk like strips impregnated with methylated spirit), changed into dry clothing and settled down for a cold night.

On Sunday, August 9th Howard and Cleve searched for the Summit Cairn but appaling conditions defeated them. After a discussion they decided to 'stay put'. As the prevailing weather had defeated their attempts to return to Big River or reach the summit, they scarcely had any other option. They calculated that they had food and sufficient Meta fuel for 1½ days.

On Monday August 10th, Howard and Cleve again searched for the cairn, but driving snow, strong wind and heavy mist not only hindered their search but made them apprehensive of finding their way back to the dugout, and after 2½ hours, they abandoned their attempt. Mick, whose hands and feet were frostbitten, had again remained in their shelter, and by now their sleeping bags were saturated.

During Thursday, August 11th, they all remained in the shelter and with food almost exhausted, they wrote farewell letters to friends.

On Wednesday, August 12th a decision was reached to make a 'do or die' dash for the summit. Sleeping bags (saturated and useless), Skis (walking was preferred) and other equipment deemed unnecessary were all abandoned and carrying two compasses, maps, cameras and little else, they left the dugout and set out. They believed they were on the western side of the cairn and the southern side of the mountain. An easterly course should take them to the cairn and if this was missed, the course should take them in a further two miles to Camp Valley and the "Aertex" Hut.

When they reached the top of the ridge, they had to contend with strong wind, falling snow and dense fog allowing a visibility of only 20 yards. Linking arms and checking compass direction every 25 yards, they proceeded about a mile or 1½ miles and then walked right up to the Summit Cairn. They were jubilant, and halted for a brief rest.

The Staircase Spur led to Bivouac Hut, 1½ miles away, with its promise of food, warmth, rest and safety. Cleve had traversed the spur on numerous occasions and he led the party from the summit. Their route, to avoid dangerously steep slopes to the north of the cairn, was plotted as 100 yards east, 100 yards north-east and then 100 yards north, to bring them on to the head of Staircase Spur. In icy conditions, it was necessary to kick steps. The course was set by compass, but after several attempts ended in steep rocky drops, they decided to return to the summit and drop down a gully which they thought would lead them to Mountain Creek and in due course, into Tawonga.

At this point, let us look at a map of the summit area and trace the course they plotted.

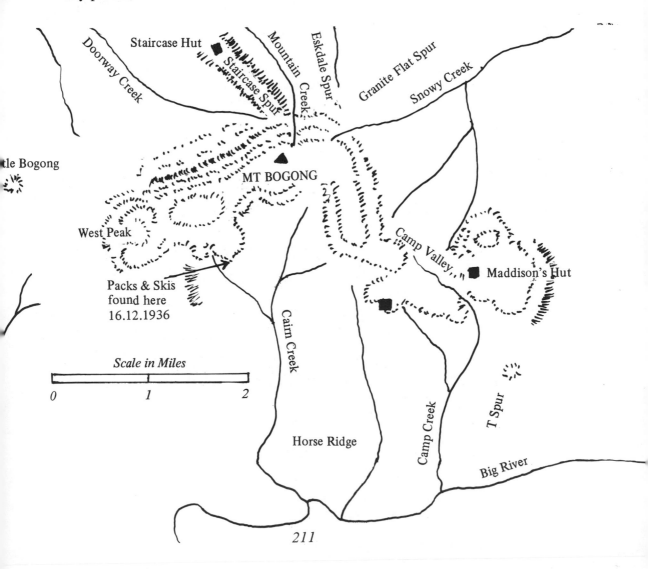

211

The ridge they followed back towards the summit swung into another spur and a descent was made into a gully where soft snow was encountered. This , said Mick, ended hours of step kicking. So, their unsuccessful effort to reach Staircase Spur from the summit, following a 300 yard plotted course, and then returning towards the summit, had cost them 'hours'. They linked arms, descended 500 feet rapidly and then traversed with the hill on their left, bringing them to what they believed should have been Staircase Spur. The wind was unbearable and as they continued, they realised they were not on Staircase Spur. They continued on through darkness, meeting small streams, walked out of the snow and reached a large stream. Finally a sizeable tributary stream barred their path in the darkness and they stopped at 2 a.m.

For a party, who must have been in poor shape at the beginning of the day, after having battled against tremendous odds since leaving the Big River on the morning of 8th August, four days and nights ago, this incredibly long day's journey, lasting through the night to 2 a.m., must have taxed their endurance to the very limit.

On Thursday, August 13th, after a few hours sleep, they continued down the valley, and by 5 p.m. had covered possibly ten miles. For some time the general direction had been easterly and they were now convinced that they

BIVOUAC HUT
The Staircase Spur hut which provided shelter for bushwalkers and ski-tourers en route to the summit of Mt Bogong. This was the hut which the ill-fated party of Cleve Cole, 'Mick' Hull and Howard Michell were seeking after leaving the summit of Mt Bogong in August 1936 and the hut from which Georgine Gadsen, John McRae and Ted Welch left in their unsuccessful attempt to reach the summit hut in 1943. It has since been burnt. (Photo 1937)

were in the Big River valley, and not Mountain Creek, as they had hoped. During the day Cleve had trouble with his eyes and Mick wrenched his left ankle. They sheltered for the night with what comfort a hollow log and an overhanging tree provided.

Next day they continued and made reasonable progress. Cleve had one bad fall which slowed the party. Then after he fell again the party camped, again finding such comfort as they could in a hollow log. They were, of course, completely without food, and with matches sodden, unable to light a fire.

Next day, Saturday 15th August, they made very slow progress for 1½ hours and then after a discussion between Mick and Howard, it was decided that Howard should go on alone to seek help. Mick and Cleve made camp soon after Howard left, Mick making Cleve as comfortable as possible. They remained at the camp that night and all through Sunday. Then at 7.30 on Monday morning they heard the welcome calls of a rescue party.

Top left: W.F. "Bill" Waters helps to carry "Mick" Hull on stretcher.
Top right: E.C. "Eddie" Robinson and miners with lamps for night searching. Lower left: Miners who played a major part in the search.
Lower right: Ski Club members and miners in search party.

Howard, after leaving them on Saturday morning, had travelled some 20 miles down the valley to reach the home of Mr Batty, a cattleman of Glen Valley on Monday morning, August 17th. A rescue party consisting of the Batty brothers, mine workers from the Maude and Yellow Girl and others quickly set out to bring Cleve and Mick in to safety. It was typical of the rescuers that the foremost waited only long enough to don overcoats and collect some food before setting off on a mission that they knew would keep them out for one or possibly two nights. After spending Monday night without blankets, around camp fires, they reached the two skiers early on Tuesday morning, constructed make-shift stretchers and commenced the journey back. They were soon joined by additional helpers, but it was still necessary to camp that night some 10 or 12 miles short of Glen Valley. Cleve's condition was causing alarm, but they made him as comfortable as possible with blankets, at a safe distance from the fire.

Cleve's condition had deteriorated further by the morning of Wednesday 19th August, and carrying in relays, the rescuers made the best time possible to the end of the road where transport was waiting to take Cleve to hospital. After a short stay at Mrs Bittner's guest house, where he received attention, Cleve was rushed to the Omeo hospital, where, despite receiving massage and every possible attention, he died at 9 p.m.

Mick's party brought him in later and he received attention for frost-bite and exposure. He lost several toes, but otherwise made a complete recovery. 'Iron man' Howard Michell quickly recovered from his ordeal.

Memorial tablet, hand chiselled, on wall of Cleve Cole Memorial Hut, Camp Valley, Mt Bogong. (Photo 1937)

Bogong Tragedy

*A*UTUMN OF 1943 ushered in what was to be one of the heaviest and stormiest snow seasons in memory. The first fall was recorded in February and heavy falls followed in April. Blizzard conditions occurred throughout the winter and August provided the coldest temperatures yet recorded. During the first half of this month heavy falls and severe conditions occurred and built up drifts of tremendous depths, while ice formations were accentuated by the abnormally low minimum temperatures.

On Monday, August 2nd, eight skiers were at the Bivouac Hut on the Staircase Spur, Mt Bogong, waiting for the weather to clear. Their objective was the 'Cleve Cole' Hut, to which six of the party had food packed in before the winter, for a fortnight's stay. Two other skiers had joined the six the previous day. They were carrying their own equipment and food. Five of the eight were experienced skiers and three were novices.

Outside Bivouac Hut, situated at a height of 4,900 feet, visibility was bad and it was snowing heavily. With no improvement in the weather after lunch time, three of the party considered the conditions difficult but not hazardous and they decided to move on up the mountain. They were John McRae and Miss Georgine Gadsden, the two who had joined the party the day previously and Ted Welch.

McRae had visited Mt Buller and had touring experience in New South Wales snowfields. Georgine Gadsden's experience included skiing in Switzerland, at Mt Kosciusko, Mt Hotham and Mt Buller. Her equipment was excellent and she was superbly fit. Ted Welch, with previous knowledge of Mt Bogong, was to lead the party.

Georgine Gadsden's pack weighed 33 lbs, John McRae's 40 lbs (both reasonable weights), and Ted Welch carried the steadier (considering the unfavourable conditions and soft snow) of 50 lbs. Their plan was to climb on skis the steep mile and a half (and 1500 feet vertical rise) to the Summit Hut at 6410 feet, and hopefully continue a further two miles to the Cleve Cole Hut, at 5,800 feet.

Ian Lenne, with two previous winter trips and one summer visit to Mt Bogong, with his experienced friend, Jack Kelaher, and the three novices, Mrs Peggy Lenne, Mary Brown and Bob Moss were to follow the first party if the weather did not deteriorate and if the leading three had not found it necessary to return.

At 2.30 p.m. Ian Lenne's party left Bivouac Hut, but after going only a short distance they decided to return. It was snowing heavily, visibility was poor and a strong wind was blowing. Under the conditions and with three novices in the party, they made a wise and responsible decision.

Next day, Tuesday August 3rd, at 10 a.m. Lenne's party of five left Bivouac Hut again, en route for Cleve Cole Hut. They walked, carrying skis and packs. The weather had not improved, it was snowing heavily and there was a strong wind. As they climbed the conditions worsened and by 4 p.m. - four hours after leaving Bivouac Hut, visibility was reduced to only ten yards they were still short of the summit of Bogong and with the likelihood that Summit Hut was completely snowed under, they wisely decided to return to Bivouac Hut. In six hours they had failed to cover a mile and a half!

After overcoming difficulties with route finding, they finally reached Bivouac Hut, in darkness, at 6.30 p.m. During the night an additional eighteen inches of snow fell around the hut.

On Wednesday, snow continued to fall all day and the party remained at Bivouac Hut. Next day, Thursday, snowing continued but the wind had dropped and visibility had improved. A decision was made to leave for the Cleve Cole Hut. They left at 9 a.m. and two hours later reached their skis, which had been left when on their return from their summit attempt on Tuesday. Visibility had worsened and three of the party waited while Lenne and Kelahar went ahead. At 1.30 p.m. they reached the first snow pole in Gorge Gap (four and a half hours after leaving Bivouac Hut) and found, standing upright in the snow, the skis of Welch, McRae and Gadsden, which had the appearance of having been there for some time..

Lenne and Kelahar returned to their party and brought them up to the first snow pole. From here, with visibility still bad, Lenne moved forward and told the others to follow carefully. Near the fourth snowpole, he discovered the bodies of McRae, Welch and Gadsden. They were 500 vertical feet above the point where they had left their skis and only 80 yards from the Summit Hut, which, however, may well have been completely snowed under and invisible.

The position of the bodies was puzzling. To quote the A.N.Z. Ski Year Book:

> Welch lay face downwards, head about 3 ft. west of the pole, feet down-hill His pack was still on; the sleeping bag, out of its waterproof cover, protruded from the top. The top flap of the pack was fastened across the bag. His right hand clasped a stock. The other stock was near his left hand. On his right was an empty rum bottle, without a cork, pointing down-hill. His face, buried in the ice, was not visible. Trousers, pack, and parts of his body were iced. A hood or cap covered his head.
>
> Eight feet further up, slightly to the right, lay McRae, huddled against his pack. One stock was between his legs, grasped in his left hand, his foot against the bottom of it. The other stock was missing. His right hand held a small flask, a small amount of brandy in it. His rucsac was still strapped to his back. His jacket hood was over his head, but his face was showing.

Four feet to the left, but further up the slope, Miss Gadsden lay on her back, leaning slightly towards McRae. The hood of her jacket was pulled up, leaving a small opening, showing her face, partly covered by a vizor. Her left arm reclined beside her, a ring on her finger showing clearly.

Lenne, after his grim discovery, could not find the hut so his party decided to leave the bodies untouched and return to Tawonga. They reached Bivouac Hut at 5 p.m., stayed the night and were in Tawonga the following afternoon.

The bodies of McRae and Welch were brought down on Saturday, but the party of 17 rescuers returned without Georgine Gadsden's body. It had mysteriously disappeared from its position when discovered by Lenne.

On Tuesday Lenne and others returned to the mountain and stayed the night at Bivouac Hut. Next day Miss Gadsden's body was found 450 vertical feet below its original position, it having apparently slid down the slope to the position where it was found. The search party also found McRae's torch, switched on, indicating that the party had been overtaken by darkness in their futile attempt to reach the Summit Hut.

Many questions remain unanswered. It may be reasonably assumed that the party, a strong one, found the conditions much more severe than expected. This is indicated by the fact that all three removed their skis, left them and continued on foot. The fact that both men's bodies were found with their packs on and rum bottle empty and brandy flask almost empty led to the belief that they were exhausted, stopped for a rest and sought the warming effect of alcohol. Miss Gadsden was a non-drinker and her body was found with her pack off. Had she, possible the strongest of the three at

BIVOUAC HUT
Situated on the Staircase Spur which leads up from Mountain Creek to the summit of Mt Bogong.

217

the time, removed her pack and searched ahead for the elusive hut while her companions rested? On her return, had exposure and exhaustion already weakened the two men to the point where they could not proceed? Neither had removed their packs to seek food or additional clothing, but Welch's sleeping bag was partly protruding from the top of his pack. He could not have reached for it with his pack on. Had Miss Gadsden, whose gloves were removed, attempted to get the sleeping bag for Welch?

No attempt was made by the party to seek a more sheltered position, nor was any attempt made to dig a hole in which to crawl into sleeping bags and spend the night. Nor had they made any attempt to return to their skis and possibly retrace their steps to Bivouac Hut, although in darkness, this would have been an almost impossible task.

The two men appear to have reached the end of their endurance at the point where they were found. Possibly Georgine Gadsden, unable or unwilling to go on alone, remained with them. But, why, if she had the strength to do so, had she not used her own sleeping bag?

The Professof of Physiology, Melbourne University (Dr. R. D. Wright) had this to say: "It is considered possible that a small quantity of alcohol, taken under the conditions described could cause complete collapse. Except under safe conditions, the use of alcohol should be regarded as dangerous, and in conditions of extreme cold and fatigue, the taking of a quantity as small as half an ounce might have fatal results."

Lenne's party of five, acted at all times in a responsible manner and it is unfair to criticise the three who lost their lives. They were experienced, well equipped and fit. They judged the conditions and believed themselves capable of reaching Summit Hut. It was a cruel stroke of misfortune that the conditions that overtook them within 80 yards of their goal were so exceptional, and even then it may have required only an ounce of luck for them to have covered the final short distance to Summit Hut and safety. A brief break in the heavy mist, a fleeting glimpse of an exposed corner of the hut and the tragedy that took their lives would not have occurred.

The fact that Welch and McRae were carrying a small quantity of rum and brandy respectively was not unusual. It was, in fact, a normal practice for at least one member of a touring party to include in his pack, a flask of brandy for use in an emergency. The dangers, as outlined by Dr. R.D.Wright were unknown to bushwalkers and ski-tourers until his warning was made known, after the tragedy. If, as he suggested, the consumprion of a small amount of alcohol did contribute to the deaths of Welch and McRae, it is quite certain that they acted in accordance with what was almost a standard practice at that time.

Bogong Tragedy

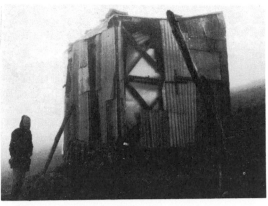

SUMMIT HUT

The Mt Bogong Summit Hut, situated well above the timber line, offers a chill welcome in severe winter conditions. Top: Snow has covered the roof and only a corner is showing. Left: Snow encrusted interior. Below: The ice-box on the roof of Victoria.

The report below, is an extract from a ski-touring party's story of their experiences some years before the Gadsden tragedy. It emphasises the extreme conditions which may be encountered in winter, on Mt Bogong.
In 1978, three huts on Mt Bogong were deliberately burnt (Maddison's, Summit and Bivouac), thus ensuring that ski-tourers visiting Bt Bogong in winters to come, will place their lives at risk.

> . . . we went back to the Summit Hut, intending to return from there to the Bivouac Hut, but cornices and ice on the narrow Staircase Spur made us abandon the attempt.
> As we could not light a fire at Summit Hut we spent a cheerless night there. Next morning we dug our way out and made another attempt to reach the Bivouac Hut . . . owing to fog and falling snow and a terrific wind we could not go on and had to get back again to the Summit Hut . . . we were prisoners there for four days.
>
> D.J.SMART 1939

The Bogong High Plains

DISCOVERY

EARLY GRAZING

CATTLEMEN AND FAMILIES

HUT PLANS

ACCESS ROUTES

FITZGERALD'S OF "SHANNONVALE"

COBUNGRA STATION

The Bogong High Plains

THE DISCOVERY OF THE BOGONG HIGH PLAINS

By Stella G. M. Carr

THE BOGONG HIGH PLAINS were discovered by two stockmen, James Brown and John Wells, who were employed to look after the run at Cobungra which was taken up by George Gray in 1851. Gray, accompanied by Brown, Wells and two others, brought his cattle to Cobungra from a property called 'The Pelican', near Wangaratta. The move was undertaken immediately after the bushfires of Black Thursday (13 February 1851), when it became necessary to find grass for the cattle which survived. (Mr. George Fitzgerald, of 'Shannonvale', Omeo, believed that there were 1100 cattle in the mob that left Wangaratta.)

They went first to Lockhart's Gap, but finding no grass there they went on to Mitta Mitta Station, then held by Bowler. (This would be Mitta Mitta No 1 Station, a property of 20,000 acres, 16 miles south of Tallangatta. It was held by Sam Bowler and later his son, Sam, from June 1839 to July 1877. Ed.). Again there was no grass available, but they fell in with an aboriginal called Larnie, who told them of Cobungra and offered to take them there. From Mitta Mitta they climbed the Gibbo Range, went down the other side to Hinnomunjie Station (a 36,000 acre property on the Mitta Mitta River, near Lake Omeo, and held since October, 1841 by Edward Crooke, Ed.), then on up Livingstone Creek to the Bingo Gap. From the valley of Bingomunjie Creek, they crossed into the valley of the Cobungra and established their first camp at Dick's Creek (now Crown Allotment 28, Parish of Bingomunjie). In the course of the next few years they moved further upstream and settled on the Victoria River (Crown Allotment 11, Parish of Bingomunjie). The licence for the run is dated 4th June, 1851. Its boundaries are not defined but it can be assumed that a boundary was agreed upon between it and the territory held by Hinnomunjie Station.

Although Gray is officially the first to have held Cobungra he believed that others had been there before him. Andrews (1920) records that Cobungra was held by the Wells brothers in 1842, but the source of this information has not yet been traced. There is no local tradition to support the statement. It appears clear, however, that Gray and his party were the first to open up the track between the Mitta Mitta and Hinnomunjie. In the next few years it was much used by miners, by the Grays themselves, and by others who took cattle to market at Beechworth. The track also provided a useful link between the North-east and the track between the Monaro and Gippsland which had been established some years earlier.

After their arrival in March 1851, Brown and Wells were left at Cobungra in charge of the cattle and lived there for some years. Brown realised that the track over the Gibbo was circuitous and argued that there must be a shorter way to Beechworth. Larnie had described to them as well as he could the Bogong High Plains and had told them also that the Omeo and associated tribes of aboriginals went to the High Plains from their camp at the Bundarrah River via Bucketty Plain, that is along the spur which joins the High Plains at Mt Cope. Brown and Wells followed this track and, once on the High Plains, set off in the direction of Mt Nelse. From the Nelse end of the Plains they had a view of the great spur of The Fainter and decided that it was the one to follow. By doing so they found their way into the North-east. It is not known whether it was on the return from their first trip or on their second journey that they found the alternative route over Mt Hotham, but they established both routes before they had been at Cobungra for three years, and had also been over Mt Feathertop. Very shortly after the discovery of gold in Omeo (April 1854) the track over Mt Hotham was much used by miners and until recently there were in Omeo people still living who had been brought to the district as children over this track early in 1855.

Some of the names given by Brown and Wells to parts of the country still remain in use. Rocky Valley, Pretty Valley, Rocky Nobs, Mt Jim, Jim Stream, Mt Feathertop, The Fainter, The Niggerheads, The Razorback, Blowhard and Bucketty Plain are well known. Skiers at Mt Hotham know J.B. (Plain), where Jim Brown carved his initials on a tree, the Old Wangaratta Bridge and Australia Drift. Other names were not officially recognised but are still in local use. Brown called Mt Hotham 'Baldy', and Mt Cope 'Mt Jack'. The older cattlemen still regret that Mt Jack is not the official name. Jim Brown and Johnny Wells are remembered as very great bushmen. Of the two, it is said that Jim Brown was the finer.

As it is generally believed that Baron von Mueller discovered the High Plains his claim to this distinction will now be considered. The relevant portion of his report is given in Appendix 1.

He visited the North-east of the State in 1854, crossing the Dividing Range from the valley of the Dargo River 'near the upper part of the Cobungra'. At the time he thought he had discovered the highest mountains in Australia and claimed to be the first civilised man to visit the area. Mueller climbed two peaks, one of which he wished to name Mt Latrobe, on 3 December, and the other which was to be called Mt Hotham on 6 December. The identity of these peaks remained a mystery for many years, because the compass bearings on other, already known mountains which he took from Mt Latrobe could not be reconciled with the more accurate work of later surveyors. However, Wakefield (1949) following a suggestion made by Barnard (1904) showed that if Mueller's compass readings are corrected to $33\frac{1}{2}^0$ Mt Latrobe can be identified as Mt Loch and Mt Hotham as Mt Feathertop. The compass error is attributed to magnetic interference from the Older Basalt capping of Mt Loch. This explanation is a very reasonable one, but Wakefield's interpretation of the route by which Mueller reached these peaks is open to some doubt.

Wakefield, relying on an old, very inaccurate sketch plan (not Mueller's) dated 1864, and perhaps misled by the mention of the Mitta Mitta (actually the West Kiewa River) assumed that Mueller crossed the Divide near the site of the present-day Cobungra settlement, travelled by way of the Bundarrah Top to the High Plains and thence to Mt Loch. It is difficult to justify this explanation either on the basis of the extent to which the geography of the area was known in 1854 or from Mueller's very brief report. After mining began, there was a great deal of traffic between Cobungra and the Dargo but there is no record or hint of any link between the two districts in 1854. Mueller does not mention his sources of local information but it can be argued that he had access to more than he acknowledged. For instance, he knew the name of the Cobungra and that the Cobungra and Dargo Rivers have a divide in common. He also knew that the Cobungra waters reached the Murray — a point which would not be obvious at the first sight of the headwaters and, further, he was able to make his way from Mt Feathertop to Omeo. In the absence of local knowledge this would have been a complex and difficult journey, chiefly because of the curious stream pattern of the intervening country.

Mueller's report states that, on leaving the Dargo valley (a) he traversed a grassy tableland in a NE direction 'along the Cobungra downwards', (b) until the country to the N appeared practicable and that (c) the ranges were timbered with *Eucalyptus pauciflora*. It is not clear whether Mueller distinguished between the Cobungra and its major tributory, the Victoria, into which Spring Creek flows. If he did not do so he could have crossed the Divide anywhere between Mt Hotham and Mt Phipps. As the Divide and the major valleys all run approximately NW-SE in this area, the further he was from Mt Hotham when he made the crossing the more impossible it is that a course to the NE would have allowed him a view of Mt Loch to the N. This strongly suggests that he crossed the Divide as he said, near the upper part of the Cobungra itself.

A closer examination of Mueller's statement in relation to the geography of the area confirms this. In the Divide between Mt Hotham and Mt Phipps three parts can be distinguished: the Spring Creek section, the Victoria River section and the Cobungra section. Table 1 sets out the extent to which each of these sections satisfies Mueller's description of the journey.

It will be seen that the upper part of the Cobungra fulfils all the conditions. It seems most likely, therefore, that Mueller crossed into this area because the top and spurs on the Cobungra side form, in places, a broad tableland and some of the spurs and tributaries (Brandy Creek and Swindler's Creek) run N.-E. It seems reasonable that Mueller rode across the top until he could get a clear outlook and then made for Mt Loch. Once there, Machinery Spur would present itself as an obvious route to the foot of Mt Feathertop.

TABLE 1.

Section of main Divide	Grassy tablelands	Stream course	View of mountains to the North	Forest type
Spring Creek	Not extensive	NE	No	Higher parts *E. pauciflora* mostly mixed species.
Victoria River	In higher parts only	SW	No	Higher parts *E. pauciflora* otherwise mixed species.
Cobungra River	Extensive	Large tributaries NE (Brandy Creek & Swindler's Creek) Mainstream E of S	Yes	*E. pauciflora*

This explanation is also atisfactory in that if, as has been supposed, there was no link between the settlements in the Dargo valley and Cobungra at the time, once in the Dargo valley, Mueller would have had no reason (except the roughness and difficulty of the country) to leave it until he reached the headwaters. In conclusion, it is necessary to say that although there is no tradition that Brown and Wells saw Mueller on his way through, it seems likely that he made his way to Omeo by following the Cobungra downstream until he found their track leading to Omea. On his journey from Omeo to Mt Kosciusko and his return to Gippsland via the Buchan River, Mueller undoubtedly followed the tracks established when settlement was extended from the Monaro to Benambra and the N part of East Gippsland. To record these things does not detract from Mueller's achievement. His was a great and difficult journey, but it is more correct to regard him as the first official visitor than to accord him the status of original explorer.

REFERENCES

ANDREWS, A., 1920. The first settlement of the Upper Murray. *Sydney.*
BARNARD, F.G.A., 1904 Some early botanical explorations in Victoria. *Vict. Nat. 21: 17-28.*
MUELLER F. von, 1855. Annual Report of the Government Botanist, Melbourne.
WAKEFIELD, N. A., 1949. Baron von Mueller's Australian Alps. *Vict. Nat. 66: 169-176.*

JOHN MITCHELL'S VISIT TO THE BOGONG HIGH PLAINS IN 1843?

In a booklet published by the State Electricity Commission of Victoria *"Early History and Discovery of the Bogong High Plains"* TR–K 596–4, two statements appear – p.3 "Evidence of earlier visits could have been left by men like John Mitchell who made an exploratory journey up the Kiewa Valley to the Bogong High Plains in 1843 . . . ", and p.5 "In 1843 John Mitchell crossed the Murray near Thurgoona . . . He was guided by aborigines . . . on to the Bogong High Plains . . . this was the first recorded instance of such a visit."

Dick Johnson in his excellent *"The Alps at the Crossroads"* – p.36 says "The first recorded journey to the Bogong High Plains by a white man was by John Mitchell in 1843 . . . " The Land Conservation Council in *"Report on the Alpine Study Area"* say, p.16 "The Bogong High Plains were first visited by John Mitchell, who climbed from the Kiewa Valley in 1843 . . . "

"Overlander", September 1980 p.26 reports "Bushwalkers have been traversing the Alps since the 1850s (? Ed.) . . . they were preceded on to the Bogong High Plains by John Mitchell, who climbed up the Kiewa Valley in 1843".

The last three publications are unable to verify the source of their information, but believe it may have originated in the S.E.C. booklet. A letter to the S.E.C.V. seeking the source for their statement, dated 22nd May, 1980, remains unanswered as at 30th October, 1980.

The matter was referred to the Mitchell Library, Sydney, where all of John Mitchell's writings are held. They discounted any suggestion that John Mitchell visited the Bogong High Plains in 1843.

My suspicions regarding the authenticity of the claim stemmed from the fact that I was aware that in 1843 John Mitchell was 12 years of age. Ed.

APPENDIX I

Extract from von Mueller's Report (1855).

Left Avon on the 22nd November, thence up the Mitchell, Wentworth and Dargo Rivers and crossed the Dividing Range between the waters of Gippsland and the Murray near the upper part of the Cobungra. Thence I traversed the grassy tableland in a north-easterly direction, along the Cobungra downwards, until the country appeared practicable towards the north, to reach the highest part of the Bogong Ranges. The ranges hereabouts have never been traversed by civilised man. They are timbered with Mountain Gum-tree, *Eucalyptus phlebophylla** On the 3rd December I ascended the south-east of the two highest mountains of the Bogong Range, and believed it to be nearly 7,000 feet high. The much more abrupt and yet higher summit of the north-west mount I ascended from the Upper Mitta, which skirts the base, on 6th December; unquestionably several hundred feet higher. On both mountains mighty masses of snow lay far below the summit. Considering that mountains of such altitude, probably the two highest on the Australian continent, deserve distinctive names, I solicit His Excellency's permission to name the grandest of both Mt Hotham, and the second in height Mt Latrobe, as I trust to be entitled to the great honour of being the first man who ever reached these commanding summits of the Australian Alps.

* Now *E. pauciflora* Sieb.

APPENDIX II

A full account of the Gray's journey to Cobungra is in the possession of the author. It was given by Mr Michael MacNamara and his brothers, the late Edward and the late Patrick MacNamara, grand-nephews of George Gray. It was confirmed by the late Mr George Fitzgerald and the late Mt John MacCrae, both of whom provided information about the discovery of gold in Omeo. All these people knew Brown and Wells. The dates in the original account and the information given concerning the names of the owners and managers and the boundaries of the various stations in the early part of 1851 have been checked by reference to other sources, some of which are official documents. These provide other corroboration of the verbal evidence. The original licence issued to George Gray was seen at the Department of Lands and Survey, Melbourne.

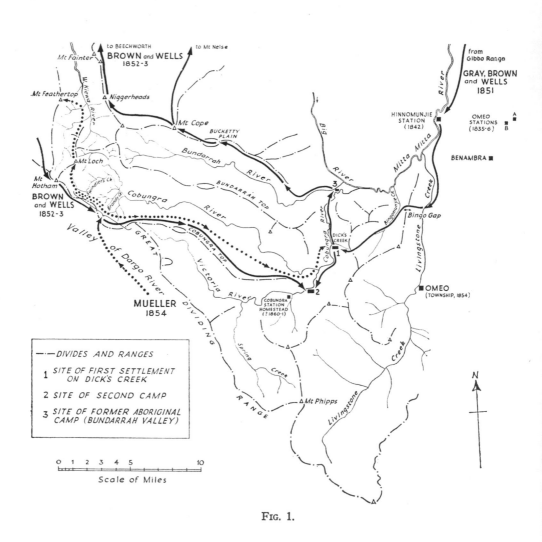

FIG. 1.

The Bogong High Plains

EARLY GRAZING

After Gray had depastured his cattle in the Cobungra area in 1851, and left his stockmen Brown and Wells in charge, some time may have elapsed before cattle were grazed on the Bogong High Plains.

It has been established that Brown and Wells climbed Mt Nelse and from this vantage point saw Mt Fainter and the spur that became the route down to Tawonga. They also explored the High Plains, named most of the prominent features and discovered the Mt Hotham — Ovens valley route to Morses Creek (Bright).

Baron von Meuller, however, believing himself to be the first white man to visit the area, saw no signs of cattle on the Bogong High Plains in 1854. It is possible, therefore, that Brown and Wells had not driven cattle up to the snow-plains by this time.

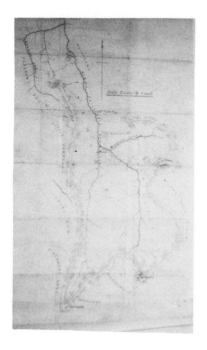

A photograph of the original lease document of the Tawonga area. Refer to copy overleaf.

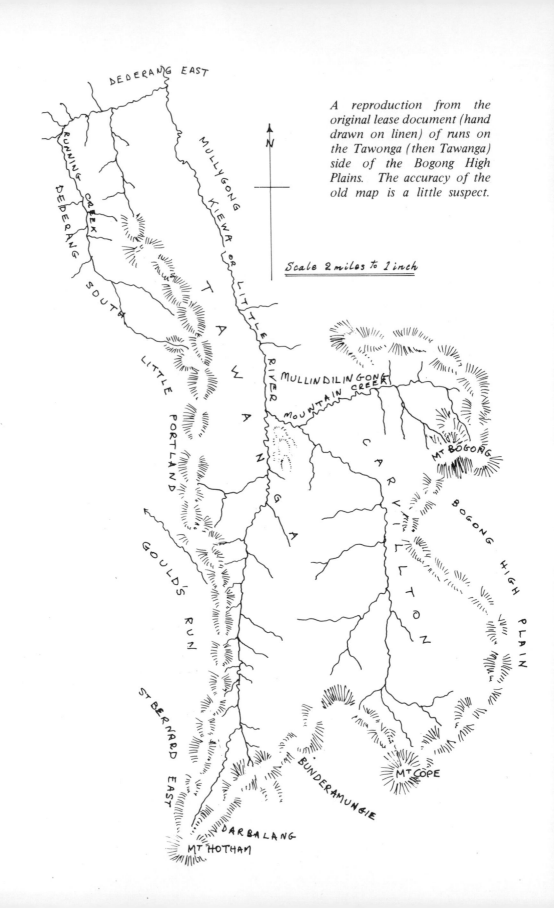

DEDERANG EAST

RUNNING CREEK

DEDERANG

MULLYGONG

KIEWA or LITTLE RIVER

T A W A N G A

N

A reproduction from the original lease document (hand drawn on linen) of runs on the Tawonga (then Tawanga) side of the Bogong High Plains. The accuracy of the old map is a little suspect.

Scale 2 miles to 1 inch

SOUTH

LITTLE PORTLAND

MULLINDILINGONG

MOUNTAIN CREEK

C A R V I L L T O N

MT BOGONG

BOGONG HIGH PLAIN

GOULD'S RUN

ST BERNARD EAST

BUNDERAMUNGIE

MT COPE

DARBALANG

MT HOTHAM

In the Upper Kiewa Valley, one of the first settlements was at Tawonga Station. It was taken up in December, 1841, by James Roberts, and transferred to John Rooth 1849, then to Thomas Ibbotson in 1854. Mr Ibbotson's manager was Mr.John Eyre, whose daughter, Mrs.Hobbs, lived in the homestead for 92 years. She died in 1949, so was the grand old lady of Tawonga for many years.

This property is the Tawonga pre-emptive right block, and the next pre-emptive block is 10 miles south, named Mullindolingong. From old records, this was occupied by Patrick Reynolds in 1846, transferred to W.Irwin in 1850, W.Muir in 1853, and then to Walter and Fred Roper in 1859. The property is still held by the Fred Roper family of Mount Yorke.

The first documented evidence of early grazing runs for the Bogong High Plains is:

Pierce, Jones & Williams	1866–1868	Henry Campbell	1878–1883
Malcolm K. McKenzie (Ensay)	1875–1878	Thomas McKnight Hamilton	1883–1887

at which later date the hitherto single Bogong lease of 90,000 acres was divided into nineteen separate grazing blocks.

It is, however, quite certain that the High Plains were grazed from the Tawonga side by about 1860. Local tradition is that from time to time every family in the Kiewa valley ran a small number of cattle in conjunction with their neighbours on the 'top country'.

Residents in the Kiewa valley by around 1857 included the Ropers, Ibbotsons, Briggs, Maddisons, Coopers, Ryders, Higginsons and Howmans and all were to become involved in mountain grazing. It is reasonable to assume therefore that most of them were using the High Plains by the 1860s. Charles Ibbotson is believed to have been there as early as 1854.

Prior to the 1887 split into Grazing Blocks, T.M.Hamilton held the Bogong run, Osborne Young held Bundaramunjie from 1879 and Peterson and Box had Darbalary from 1872. All were allocated grazing blocks in 1887.

Of those who became licensees in 1887 the following remained for some time:

Thomas McNamara	1887–1910	William Wallace	1887–1908
William Hollonds	1887–1926	Osborne Young	1887–1913
Marcus Hobbs	1887–1908	Andrew Sharpe	1887–1908
T.M.Hamilton	1887–1902	Patrick Duane	1887–1919

and P.J.Kelly, F.Roper, J.Higginson, George Maddison ran cattle without holding a license, but all except Higginson afterwards acquired one.

Among the better known cattlemen to later run cattle on the Bogongs were Frank and William Blair, from 1920, T.Briggs, 1919–1943, Ben Cooper 1921–1973, Arthur and Walter Dibbin 1908–1939, Lawlers 1897–1933, Dick Riggall 1901–1919 and Eric Weston 1929–1958.

The above dates are from Lands Department records which often vary considerably from actual date of occupation.

MADDISONS

The Maddison family were resident in the Kiewa valley at Tawonga, by the mid 1850s and would certainly have joined their neighbours in grazing on the High Plains.

Letters from Ensay Station archives reveal that George Maddison wrote in 1883 to Mr Campbell asking for a sub-lease of Mt Bogong. These letters, reproduced opposite, read as follows:

> Upper Kiewa
> April 1st, '83

Mr Campbell,
Dear Sir,
There being about two or three sections of grazing land on Mount Bogong and I have been informed that it belongs to you. And I can get a convenient road on to it from my place, I wish to know if you would rent it to me at how much per year.

> Yours truly,
> George Maddison

Mr Henry Campbell wrote to Mr Thomas McKnight Hamilton.

> Ensay
> 12th April '83

Dear Hamilton,
I herewith enclose Licence of Bogong High Plains, also a letter from a party wishing to rent portion of it.

> Yours faithfully,
> H. Campbell

A third letter supports George Maddison's request.

> Harrietville
> April 18th 1888 (sic.)

Mr H. & I. Campbell,
Gentlemen,
Mr George Maddison wrote a letter to you asking if you would rent him a small piece of the Bogong Plain at the east ind (sic.) of their he has got a track up a spur at the head of Mountain Creek this Part cannot be reached from any other Part of the Plains and if you will take Five Pounds £5.0.0 per year for it i will send you the Rent every year and it will do for me and Mr Maddison he asked me to write . . . lease. Answer this and . . .

> Yours respectfully
> Peter Ho

(The lower corners of the letter have been damaged and the remainder of the signature is missing. The name was Peter Howman, who later shared the Mt Bogong run with Maddison. Ed.)

And so, although there is no record of the answer, it would appear that the grazing on Mt Bogong, with access up Mountain Creek and the Staircase Spur, was commenced by George Maddison, probably in the early summer of 1883.

These letters are reproduced from the originals, by courtesy of Mr David Hamilton, custodian of the very extensive Ensay Station records.

George Maddison, when only a lad was employed as a station hand at Bowler's Mitta Mitta station. In 1864, bushranger "Mad Dog" Morgan paid the district a visit and took possession of one of Bowler's valuable horses. He then forced George to guide him through the bush until they came to country that Morgan knew. Here, he let the lad go.

The Maddison property was located in the shadow of the massive Mt Bogong and prior to 1883, when George wrote to Ensay, he was convinced that good grazing existed on Victoria's highest mountain. He voiced his intention of seeking a route up the Staircase Spur to the summit, but his good wife would not allow him to venture forth alone. So, George, accompanied by Mrs Maddison, who carried 5 years old son Tom on the pony in front of her, set out and reached the summit.

It was as a result of this trip that George chose Mt Bogong for his summer grazing — an area that was to be the Maddison domain for some eighty years. George built the original Maddison's Hut in Camp Valley, but the date is uncertain. Local tradition suggests that it would have been later than Tawonga and Wallaces' which originated in 1888 and 1889 respectively. Constructed of snow-gum logs, which fitted rather imperfectly, the hut was popurlarly known as "Aertex", after a 'ventilated' underwear material. The skillion roof, first clad with bark, was later renovated with a half dozen sheets of galvanised iron, but despite its austerity, the hut was a welcome refuge for bushwalkers and pioneer skiers.

The hut eventually succumbed to old age, and the Maddisons having relinquished the licence and transferred their interests to the Bogong High Plains, Wally Ryder, whose cattle were now grazing the area, and Bill Hodgekinson built a new hut. For this they packed in all the materials, including the roofing iron, which was folded double to facilitate cartage. This hut, still referred to as 'Maddison's' was financed in part, by the Tallangatta Ski Club. Its life, unfortunately, was relatively short, as it was deliberately burnt down, along with the Summit Hut and the Bivouac Hut on the Staircase spur, during a week-end of October 1978. The person or persons responsible have not come forward to claim the credit for their acts of wanton vandalism!

Tom Maddison, who had first ridden up to Mt Bogong in front of his mother in the 1880s, became the father of Tom jnr., Victor and Jack. Victor died on Mt Bogong. He rode out from the Cleve Cole Hut, suffered a heart attack, and his horse returned without him. Tom farmed the valley country but did not engage in mountain grazing. Jack, today, having anticipated the cancellation of Mt Bogong grazing leases, runs cattle on the Bogong High Plains.

Opposite: The tiny Maddison's Hut located at Camp Valley measuring only 12 ft x 8 ft 6 ins, was a welcome refuge in the event of bad weather. Named 'Hotel Aertex', the two illustrations opposite show the hut in mid-summer and mid-winter.

WALLACE FAMILY

David and Henrietta (nee Molyneaux) Wallace, of Doe, County Antrim, Northern Ireland, migrated to Australia in 1869 with their sons, Arthur, aged seven years; William, five years; and Stewart, three years of age. They left Liverpool in the famous sailing ship "Lightning" and having been obliged to provide their own food for the trip, they saw no land on the 72-day journey until Cape Otway was sighted. The Wallace family left Melbourne by coach at 4 p.m. one day and arrived at Beechworth the following day at noon, this fast trip being possible by frequent and rapid horse changes.

The family settled at Kergunyah and commenced grazing on 1000 acres of river frontage property. A slab hut with a bark roof and the interior lined with hessian and faced with newspapers was their first home. Mrs Wallace often sent the boys to catch fish for the next meal, and after baiting a line with small frogs they would return within a short time with either a Murray cod or bream sufficient for the whole family.

Arthur Wallace, who married Ann Magill, built himself a brick homestead which he called Kergunyah Park. The greater portion of this property was purchased from Richard Marum and contained 2000 acres of mainly river and creek flats. The Arthur Wallaces had six children — Mina, Martha, Bessie, David and twins Isobel and Ann.

Mrs Wallace died in 1900 and Arthur later married Gertrude Schroder and had a son, Marcus. The property was then sold to John Woodside and the Wallaces moved to Narrandera in New South Wales.

William Wallace married Ida McGeoch and they had three children, Norman, Geoff and Margaret. He purchased 700 acres of well cleared land from George W.Seymour and in 1909 built a brick home which he named Wallacedale, and later selected additional forest land.

Watchbed Creek on the Bogong High Plains received its name after William Wallace lost a watch and chain when his horse stumbled while running down an emu, and subsequent searching had failed to locate the watch.

After the death of his wife, William Wallace later married Lizzie Reid.

Stewart Wallace built the original "Warrawee" on a 640 acre river frontage property known as "The Selection".

Stewart married Alison Hamilton and bought a number of river frontage paddocks on the eastern side of the Kiewa River, opposite Warrawee. Of their two children Ian and Mary, the son, Mr.I.S.Wallace, still lives on the property.

WALLACE'S HUT

Wallace's Hut on the Bogong High Plains, was built in 1889 by the three Wallace brothers, Arthur, William and Stewart. There were few cattlemen up there that year, but the Wallaces had taken up a mob of cattle, and decided to fill their time usefully by building the hut. It measured 17 feet long by

WALLACE'S HUT
Built in 1889 Wallace's Hut is shown as originally constructed with split snow-gum sides and woolly-butt shingle roof. These photos were taken in the summer and winter of 1928.

9 feet wide. The uprights, rafters, wall plates and slabs were snow-gum, of which there was a plentiful supply in the immediate vicinity, and the roofing was of shingles, which were split from woollybutt which grew on the lower slopes. To obtain them, it was necessary to cut a track about 400 yards east, through scrub and down a gully to a branch of the Big River. The shingles were split there and brought up on pack horses to the hut. The snow-gums had to be split straight down the centre, and for this reason, it was necessary to select only those with a straight grain.

There are six upright posts. When five of these had been put in holes three feet deep, the builders sinking the sixth hole struck sandstone rock six inches below the surface. They had only a long handled spade with which to deal with this, but they persevered and succeeded in chipping away the rock to the required depth. This is the post in the south-east, opposite the door.

The roof was built up steeply in order that it would shoot off the snow and therefore it has not been called on to carry great weights, which has doubtless contributed to its longevity.

Wallace's Hut, under snow. Note iron roof covers old shingles.

One day, the brothers found a large, square flat stone about 4 x 2½ x 7 feet, out in Pretty Valley. They made a rough sleigh out of a forked sapling and brought it in to serve as the back of the fireplace. The inside of the fireplace was lined with stone and mud.

The hut took the spare time of five or six weeks to build.

William Wallace's Bogong High Plain leases extended from 1887 to 1914.

The State Electricity Commission assumed ownership in the early 1930s, when it was given a Crown grant over the land for the Kiewa hydro-electric scheme. The hut was re-roofed with corrugated iron and later the walls and chimney clad in the same material, and to complete the transformation a lean-to was added to one of the longer walls. Joe Holsten, an S.E.C. employee took up residence while a new S.E.C. architect designed hut was constructed nearby. The planners had underestimated the depth and weight of winter snow, however, and with the dwelling creaking and groaning, it was saved from complete collapse by the arrival of "Bill" Waters and a rescue party of Rover Scouts who shovelled sufficient snow away to save the hut.

After strengthening their hut, the S.E.C., having no further use for Wallaces, decided to retrieve their corrugated iron. Again "Bill" Waters came to the rescue. Not of the S.E.C. this time, but of Wallace's Hut. An appeal to a few Rover Scouts raised sufficient funds to enable us to purchase the second-hand iron from the S.E.C. and their financial watchdogs having been appeased, the iron was allowed to remain. In due course the Commission agreed to allow the Yarrawonga Scouters' Club Council to use and accept unofficial responsibility for the hut and its maintenance.

But Wallace's Hut, then 84 years old, with its original frame, sheathing and shingle roof hidden and enlarged, under an iron covering, was to be discovered in 1967 and classified as Category C, by the National Trust.

How much more appropriate, if, as a museum piece, it could have been restored to its original design and construction!

HOLLONDS

The Hollonds family of Tawonga and Omeo had a long association with High Plain grazing.

In 1883 William and Thomas Hollonds were running cattle and horses on part of the Ensay licence. Later their families' licences with the Lands Department covered the years from 1886 to 1949, embraced a total of eight separate grazing blocks and were held by seven members of the family. The family name has been given to Hollonds Nob, 5840 ft., a mile north west of Fitzgerald's Hut, and to Hollond's Hill about a mile and a half south of Mt Beauty.

ROPERS

John Roper, born at Gayton Thorpe, Norfolk on 29th February, 1820 was the first of the family to come to Australia. He left England in 1838 for New Zealand and from there came to Australia in 1843.

John is best remembered for his part in Leichardt's 1844 expedition to Port Essington in which he was speared by blacks and lost an eye. Roper River in the Northern Territory was named after him.

On his return he sent for his brothers and Walter and Frederick arrived in Australia in 1852. They settled in Yackandandah and ran store cattle at Alan's Flat and Kirby's Flat.

Frederick and Walter took over Mullindolingong, at the junction of Mountain Creek and the Kiewa River, from W.Muir in 1856 and in 1858 Frederick bought his brother's share and named the property Mt Yorke. 8½ acres of grapes were planted, but Fred's main interest was the breeding of Hereford cattle.

John Roper, 1820 – 1895, the first of the family to come to Australia.

Frederick Roper I, 1828 – 1904, who followed his brother John to Australia.

Frederick Roper II

Bert Roper (extreme left), Wal Ryder (third from left) and Fred Roper II (right).

Roper's Hut on Falls Creek in 1936.   Cleve Cole standing in doorway.

John, meanwhile, built the Globe Hotel in Albury (1860) and became Mayor of that city in 1861. He died at Merriwa (N.S.W.) in 1895.

Lands Department records suggest that Fred Roper grazed the Bogong High Plains from the late 1890s to 1908 without the formality of a licence. However, it is probable that Fred's involvement with the snow-plains commenced before this date.

Frederick Roper died in 1904 and his son Fred took over the property. He conformed to convention and took out a grazing licence for the High Plains in 1908 and held it until 1946. His son Bert also held a licence in 1912–13.

Fred Roper cut his own track up to the plains before World War I, after it had been surveyed by John Crossthwaite snr. a pioneer settler in the Kiewa valley.

A hut was built by Roper Hatch, on Mountain Creek, about 6 miles from Tawonga and close to the Mt Bogong track.

A second hut on Roper's Track was built in Rocky Valley on Falls Creek, about 19 miles from Tawonga, and in 1939 a third, on Reef Creek at the head of Duane Spur. This hut was built on the site of Duane's old hut, and replaced the Falls Creek Hut which was burnt in the 1939 fires.

Patrick Duane had been grazing cattle in the Rocky Valley area from 1887 and with Mathis Duane from 1901–1919.

HOWMAN

William Howman of Harrietville was the holder of a run east of St Bernard as early as 1876. This would have been the top end of the Dargo High Plains. In 1883 Peter Howman of Eskdale shared Maddison's Sub-lease of Mt Bogong and in 1884 Peter Howman was on the Bogong High Plains and retained licences there continuously until 1924. Frank A. Howman shared one of the runs with him from 1919–1922.

HOWMAN'S HUT

BLAIRS

Thomas Blair was a ship's engineer who left his vessel in Adelaide and came overland to the Ballarat diggings. He then moved on to Wandiligong where he married. His four sons were William Francis (Frank), born at Freeburg in 1879, Jack, George and Thomas.

Frank sub-leased part of William Hollonds run in about 1900 and lived for a time in the Kiewa valley where Frank, Jack and George had properties. He returned to Freeburg in 1913 and in 1917 bought a second property at Freeburg. Dungey's Track, which had been used earlier was closed by fallen logs and Blair took his cattle up around Hotham and on to the High Plains. He obtained a lease in his own right in 1918.

Frank Blair at Saleyards, 1952.

Early Grazing

Following the re-opening of Dungey's Track in 1922, Tom and Frank Blair built Blair's Hut on the west Kiewa River. This hut was destroyed by fire in 1931 and a second one was built to replace it.

Frank and Tom packed in the first skiing party to visit the Bogong High Plains. Leaving Blair's home at Freeburg on July 22nd 1925, they rode 22 miles to Blair's Hut and used this as a base for their exploration.

Frank's son Ross, and grandson Max are carrying on the Blair tradition, which now encompasses 80 years of High Plain grazing.

Ross Blair, from an oil painting.

Frank Blair with daughter and friends at Blair's Hut.

Frank Blair on skis.   *Fireplace of Blair's Hut*

Blair's Hut under snow about 1928.

Bryce Blair, late 1950s.

LAWLERS

The Lawler family had a long association with grazing on the Bogongs. John snr. took out the first of four licences in 1897 and following his death in 1909, three licences were held in his wife Ellen's name until 1943.

John Edward, Michael, Victor, William and E.A.Lawler all held licences during this period.

Their cattle were brought from Freeburg along Dungey's Track and two of their huts were along the East Kiewa valley. The first and earliest hut was located near Dungey's Gap and the second was about six miles short of Blair's Hut.

Bob Croll in his "Along the Track", recalls meeting the builder in 1929 who claimed it was "Started one morning, and slept in that night". A slight exaggeration perhaps, but this hut of Lawlers is certainly not the most pretentious on the Plains.

A third Lawler's Hut was located on Mt Higginbotham, adjacent to 'Hotham Heights' at an altitude of 5,800 feet, thus sharing with Maddison's Hut on Mt Bogong, the distinction of being the highest cattlemen's hut in Victoria.

LAWLER'S HUT
Situated on Dungey's Track.

KELLY

Patrick J. Kelly of Omeo grazed the Bogongs illegally from the 1890s to 1908 and was (with his family) licenced between 1908 to the present time. Kelly built a hut in about 1900, possibly the fourth or fifth hut built on the High Plains, on the site of a previous hut which had been built in 1891 by Kyran Marum and Jack Platt.

The hut site is at 5,300 ft at the head of Wild Horse Creek and is within about ½ mile of Fitzgerald's Hut which was built a short time after Kelly's. The hut is delightfully situated, in a timbered glade at the very fringe of the High Plains.   South-eastward the snowgum forested spurs lead down to Woollybutts and finally on to "Shannonvale", while to the west are the broad expanses of the High Plains.

Sunshine and shadows on the snow-covered surroundings of Kelly's Hut.

Kelly's Hut in the summer of 1932

Another view of Kelly's Hut in the winter of 1928.

Osborne Young

Osborne Young was originally a horse breeder in Benambra and George Fitzgerald recalls droving for Young in 1882, when he took as many as one hundred and sixty head from Benambra to Sale, travelling via the Livingstone, Wentworth and Dargo Rivers to Dargo (the Cobungra stock route) and thence via Waterford and Cobannah. George also took Young's horses to sales at Wodonga.

Young took out his first High Plains licence in 1879 when he acquired the Bundaramunjie run which he held until 1889. Between 1886 and 1913, he also held three other runs on the Bogong High Plains.

Young's Hut was the third to be built on the Bogongs, following the Tawonga (1888) and Wallaces (1889). It was located about 8 miles from Mt Cope and 3½ miles from the site later to be occupied by Dibbins Hut, at an altitude of 5,500 feet. Construction was timber sides and shingle roof, later to be replaced with iron. The hut was burnt down in about 1930 or 1931, but was rebuilt a year later by the then holders of the run.

For a period about 1883, Osbourne Young was employed by Ensay Station to manage the cattle they ran on the Bogong High Plains.

Osbourne Young was a one time President of teh Omeo Shire Council, and as befits a horse breeder, was President of the Omeo Racing Club. His brother S.H.Young, also held a grazing licence on the High Plains for a brief period between 1887 and 1889.

Arthur Dibbins died on September 3rd, 1946, at the age of 76. This grand old man first visited the Bogong High Plains in 1884, when at the age of 14 he began riding to the area with cattlemen neighbours who grazed cattle there.

In the 1890s he began grazing his own cattle on the Plains and continued to do so until 1938, when his health failed and he was forced to retire.

Arthur Dibbins brought his cattle up from Harrietville via Dungey's Track and he built a log hut on the upper reaches of the Cobungra River, which carves a deep valley between Mt Loch and the Bogong High Plains.

The famous Dibbin's Hut, which is frequently referred to as "Creep Inn" because of its low door opening, and which survives to this day, replaced the first structure. "Creep Inn" was built in 1920.

Arthur Dibbins and J.Blair erected the first snow-pole line which ran out from Hotham, past Mt Loch to connect at Mt Jim, with what was once known as the "Glen Wills Poles".

OPPOSITE;

DIBBINS HUT   *Seen from its most photogenic angle, the substantial old bark-roofed, log structure, built in 1920 and photographed in 1933, still survives. An unusual feature is the interior chimney at the far end, which persuaded the builder to sheath the upper portion with corrugated iron, now rusted and in urgent need of repair.*

A winter skiing party of about 1928 welcomes the shelter provided by Dibbins Hut en route for the Bogong High Plains from Mt Hotham.

Frank contemplates the climb out of the Cobungra valley to the heights of Mt Loch. The seemingly ageless hut is here shown almost ten years after the winter photo above.

... at an altitude of about 4,400 ft on a small snow plain – short tufty snowgrass covered the ground, twisted snow-gums with their stiff leathery leaves formed a boundary. The open spaces were brilliant with wildflowers. The Trigger plant was the predominant flower. Wild asters, violets and several species of orchids were to be found and the boggy nature of much of the ground encourages many kinds of moss. Water collects readily here and the cattle know it. A silent suspicious mob came up to the waterhole. For a time they gazed at us, then moved slowly down the hillside, making their way through timber seemingly impossible for any horseman to penetrate.

R. H. CROLL

RYDERS

John Ryder, born 1799, and his wife Eleanor, migrated to Australia, with their family of four, John, Thomas, Thelma and Eleanor, in 1852 and first settled at Ocean Grove. They later moved to Tawonga, where both parents died in 1882 — John at the age of 83 and Eleanor at 73.

Son Thomas, a one-time mounted policeman in New Zealand, later set off to make his fortune with two racehorses. They were, however, slightly less fleet of foot than he would have wished, and Tom ultimately returned home carrying his swag! He lived to declare that although fortune had eluded him, he had spent a very happy, if unproductive life.

John jnr. married Elizabeth Higginson in 1857. Her family were early High Plains graziers, and like many others, it is said, without the formality of a licence. John became manager of Tawonga Station and then in 1869 he selected land in Tawonga, which property is still in the hands of the Ryder family. Along with most of his neighbors, John ran cattle on the High Plains, using Tawonga Hut and yards as a mustering and holding point. John died in 1913 and his two sons, William James and Walter carried on the grazing tradition.

John Ryder, who selected land in Tawonga in 1869.

William James Roper, his wife Esther and son Syd.

Walter Ryder who married Ada Sullivan. Their sons were Walter (Wally) and Victor.

William James' son Syd. first visited the High Plains as a boy, before World War I and later held a lease in the Mt Cope, Mt Jim, Rocky Valley region. He retired in the early 1970s. It is interesting to record that Syd believes that the Bogong Jack's Hut which was erected after World War I, was the first such hut to be built. He discounts the suggestion that there ever was an earlier hut of the same name, supposedly burnt down in 1914. The name for the 1920 - 1962 hut, he believes was bestowed upon it because the location and nearby creek bore the name 'Bogong Jack's'. The occupation of the site by the legendary John Paynter in the late 1850s could merely have been a camp, with tent. Older cattlemen all agree that the earliest stockmen on the Bogongs used tents and not huts — Tawonga and Wallaces' being the first to be constructed, many years after grazing commenced.

John and Elizabeth's second son, Walter married Ada Sullivan and their son Wally married Freda Treasure of Dargo, thus uniting two cattle families, each of whom have the unique distinction of belonging to that select band who have continuously grazed the mountain pastures for more that a

Syd Ryder, a superb horseman who rode as a Jockey in his youth.

hundred years. Together, they run cattle on both the Bogongs and the Dargo High Plains. Their son Harry, currently a vice-president of the Mountain Cattlemen's Association, is thus, a fifth generation Ryder in Tawonga. After the Maddisons vacated Mt Bogong, Wally ran cattle there for a period, but has now reverted to the Bogong High Plains. During his 66 years, Wally has been involved in numerous mountain rescues, but his most dramatic experience was surviving the 1939 bushfires by sheltering in

*Ross Blair of Bright and
Syd Ryder of Tawonga.*

Wally Ryder.

*Wally Ryder, Vic Maddison and Jack Hobbs (nephew
of Wally).*

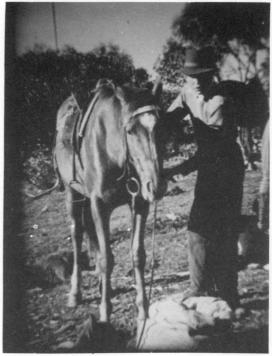

Wally Ryder leading a pack-horse (a fast disappearing sight).

Jack Hobbs, member of a prominent Tawonga mountain grazing family.

the stone Cleve Cole hut.   Across the High Plains, Bill Spargo, an old identity of the area who was involved in the construction of the original "Hotham Heights" in 1925 and later the development of his Red Robin gold mine, had prepared for the coming of the fires.

He sheltered in his iron hut after having dug a channel to divert a flow of water from the nearby stream, to flow through his hut.   Drenching himself and the hut interior as the fires raged, Bill survived.   And so, two lives were saved by the shelter afforded in these mountain huts — proof, surely that in emergencies created by bushfires or blizzards, strategically placed huts can be life savers.

Mrs Walter Ryder snr., nee Ada Sullivan, still enjoys the unmatched beauty of the Upper Kiewa Valley, at the age of 94 years.

The Ryders, along with most Tawonga cattlemen, shared the Tawonga Hut. The original Tawonga Hut is reported to have had an extremely short life. The story goes that a horse was tethered to a corner post!

The hut was quickly replaced with Tawonga Hut No. 2 (1888) and this structure served the Tawonga cattlemen until it expired from old age and was replaced with Tawonga Hut No. 3 in 1923. This had been a drought year on the low country and the cattlemen left their herds to graze the snow-

Bogong Jack's Hut built about 1920, which Syd Ryder believes was the first hut to be built here.

Heavy snow at the doorway to the "Maddison's Hut", built by Wally Ryder and Bill Hodgkinson to replace the original Maddison's. Burnt down in 1978.

The Tawonga Hut No. 3 — built to replace No. 2, in 1923.

plain until the first signs of a break in the weather. They left them just too long. The break came suddenly on May 7th, the evening of the muster, and extremely heavy snowfalls caught the cattlemen unprepared, trapping cattle and horses, in up to five feet of soft snow. Half the cattle were near the Tawonga Hut, but the remainder were some distance away. The stockmen enveavoured to clear paths to get the cattle out by the shortest means possible, but the herd, which instinctively follow the known tracks down from the mountains refused to be driven and floundered instead to greater peril in the mountains. Three thousand head perished.

Over on the Omeo side, George Fitzgerald and Bill Batty struggled until June 28th to save every beast in their mob.

Syd Ryder recalls that he spent the coldest four days of his life, trapped without food.

The Tawonga cattlemen have written their names into the history of mountain Cattle grazing, and amongst the best known and remembered are the Ropers, the Maddisons and the Ryders.

The old Tawonga Hut (number 2) which survived until 1923.

ENSAY (Numla Munjie) STATION
(their Bogong High Plains involvement)

The entire Bogong High Plains run of 90,000 acres was first licensed to Pierce, Jones and Williams in 1866–1868, who were speculators and who also acquired the Dargo High Plains lease of 121,000 acres for 1866–1867. They appear to have made little or no use of their holdings.

In 1875–1878 Malcolm McKenzie and in 1878–1883 Henry Campbell acquired in turn the entire run formerly registered to Pierce, Jones and Williams. McKenzie and Campbell were involved with Ensay Station as managing partners between the years 1873–1883, and the Bogong High Plains was operated as an outstation for summer grazing of Ensay cattle (but never for Ensay sheep). For a period Osbourne Young, a horse breeder from Omeo and a prominent grazier in his own right, managed the High Plains run for Ensay.

In 1887 the Bogong High Plains run was divided into 20 grazing blocks ranging in area from 640 acres to 8,800 acres and Thomas McKnight Hamilton, owner of Ensay acquired the largest (F Block), which was located around Mt Cope and Pretty Valley and was the best section of the Plains.

Thomas McKnight Hamilton, owner of Ensay Station and Licensee of the Bogong High Plains 1883–1913.

259

Receipts for 1883 grazing rights to Henry Campbell, managing partner of Ensay (1877—1883) for £27.10.0 and an undated, but presumably earlier one to Mr McKenzie, managing partner of Ensay (1873—1877) for £25.0.0 are reproduced opposite. Another interesting letter (reproduced) indicates that illegal grazing on the Bogongs took place (in this instance from the Tawonga side).

The golden years for Ensay may have been drawing to a close by 1890. The run had been considerably depleted by selection and the Bogong High Plains run reduced from 90,000 to 8,800 acres, although it is doubtful if the full potential of the Bogongs was ever utilised by Ensay.

Ensay finally relinquished their Bogong run in 1902.

This sketch, titled "Bogong Hut 1895" is reproduced from the sketch book of T.McK.Hamilton. Ensay's Bogong run at that time was the Pretty Valley and Mt Cope area, but the origin and whereabouts of this hut is not known.

Early Grazing

Bogong High Plain

90. 000 acres

Being the unoccupied and unal..
land in the County of Tambo
and the Omeo Run District and
formerly known as "Bogong High Plain
Run

leased to Mr. McKenzie

Rental £25 per Annum

Documents reproduced from the Ensay papers. McKenzie was managing partner of Ensay 1873–77 and Henry Campbell from 1877–83.

No. 13468

Revenue Office, Omeo

26 Jan.y 188.

RECEIVED from Henry Campbell

the sum of Twenty seven pounds sixteen shillings and

—— pence, as 12 Months Fee in advance, from

1 Jan.y 1883 for Grazing

a Bogong High Plains occupied under Sec. 45-47 of *The Land Act* 1869.

£ 27: 16: 0

Receiver of Revenue

Entd.

This Receipt to be produced on payment of next Fee.

Harrietville March 1st
1883.

H. & J. Campbell
Gentlemen

I received your letter and i do not
Remember the man that you allowed
to have cattle on the Bogong Plains
I received a letter from you asking
me if i could make the herd that
of them and i sent you a letter
to say that i could not as Mr Hetson
Manager told his men to drive of
Every thing that i put there and
the Refusal would not stand
there cattle i have put nothing up
"i drive the time you let you
there but i can give you
the men that
i this year

Mr John Walker 50 Head
cattle
Mr Dennis Freeman 80 Head
cattle
Mr Alfred Abrahams cattle 60 Head
Mr Barrett O Riley cattle 80 Head
W. Holland cattle 80 Head
Do Horses 30 Head
J Holland Horses 10 Head
Do cattle 80 Head
Mr Hetson cattle 200 Head
and Mr Hetsons Manager
Mr Markes Nobbs took one
Hundred Head of cattle to
Graze at ten shillings per
Head for the season from
Mr Arthur Woodside
and their cattle were all in

yours this year if it
was that year was out
Peter Howman
yours &c

The signature on the damaged letter is
believed to be Peter Howman.   Ed.

*A letter to Ensay in 1883 suggesting that a number of cattlemen were
grazing their herds on the Bogong High Plains, at that time held by
Henry Campbell for Ensay.*

262

Weston's Hut in its original form with paling sides, roof and chimney, photographed in early 1930s (above) and (below) looking much shabbier after roof and verandah were clad in old galvanized iron.

Over the years, a considerable number of cattlemen have shared the grazing on the Bogong High Plains, and a book could be devoted to this area — indeed, many of the long established families deserve a volume to themselves. Perhaps the Historical Societies of the surrounding areas may initiate the necessary research.

Space limitations prevent a more detailed coverage in this work, but mention should be made of names such as Ben Cooper of Tawonga, whose High Plains grazing extended over more than 50 years and whose memory is perpetuated by a plaque placed on the High Plains his cattle grazed; the Duanes, Patrick and Mathis were early cattlemen from the Tawonga side (1887 - 1919). The family had grazing interests in other districts and their run north of Mt Nelse was used for summer fattening. They are remembered by Duane's Creek, a tributary of the Big River, and the adjacent Duane's Spur, which runs down to the Big River, at a point where the T Spur leads up to Camp Valley. The Duanes built a hut on Duane's Spur, which, after being burnt, was replaced by Roper's, who acquired the lease after Duanes moved out in about 1919.

Westons of Porepunkah had grazed Mt Buffalo for over thirty years until the cancellation of licences there in 1922. Eric Weston took out a Bogong High Plains lease in 1929 and built a hut on the western end of the Plains, about 2 miles from Blair's, near a head of Niggerheads Creek, and due west of Mt Jim. Of paling construction (including roof), it enjoyed the luxury of a front verandah! The paling roof was later re-clad with galvanised iron.

Interior of McNamara's Hut. The hut was built in 1930s to replace Young's Hut, burnt in 1931. In recent years it has been upgraded by a Melbourne based Scout Group.

William Howman from Harrietville was running cattle on Mt St Bernard as early as 1876, and possible before, and Peter Howman from Eskdale was licensed for the High Plains in 1884. He partnered George Maddison on Mt Bogong and his name appears in Ensay Station correspondence in 1883, when he and George sub-leased Camp Valley. From Eskdale, his stock route came up the Granite Flat Spur and he had three huts along the way. Frank Howman shared Peter's High Plains lease from 1919 onwards.

Marcus Hobbs was another Tawonga man grazing with his neighbours from as early as 1883. He took out his first licence in 1887. Marcus's great-grandmother, Mrs Jane Hobbs, accompanied by her son James and his sister, sailed with Lieutenant Governor Collins for Port Phillip in the steam-ship "Ocean". They arrived in October 1803 and went to Sorrento to form the first settlement in the Port Phillip district. Governor Collins abandoned Sorrento as unsuitable in 1804 and left for the Derwent in Van Dieman's Land. James Hobbs sailed under Captain Bligh in the Royal Navy and in 1817 James was appointed to chart the Van Dieman's Land coast, which he did in two whaleboats.

James moved to Victoria in 1854 and his son settled in Dederang in 1873. James grand-son Marcus joined Alfred in 1875 and later moved to Mongan's Bridge near Tawonga. Marcus's son Ibbotson succeeded to the property.

William Johnston from 1908, and Chris Johnston from 1924, from Tongio had a forty year involvement with the eastern end of the Plains. Johnston's Hut was located east of Mt Nelse, about three miles from Kelly's and Fitzgerald's, and as it was at an altitude of 5,500 feet, it was a popular base for ski tourers. It was mysteriously burnt down a couple of years ago, but a Melbourne based ski group commenced re-building operations the following week-end!

Brumbies on the Bogong High Plains.

Bush Ballads

SWINDLER'S GAP

There's a valley in the ranges where the hills are always green,
    With Cobungra River winding like a living thing between,
'Tis the wildest spot in Gippsland and, though missing from the map,
    Yet it's known throughout Australia, far and wide, as "Swindlers' Gap"
It was early in the sixties, long before the diggers came,
    Long before Detective Dungey blazed the track that bears his name,
That this hollow formed the centre in a tale of love and crime,
    And a cattle stealer's daughter is the Princess of my rhyme.

She was Andy Brady's daughter. He was known among the bands
    As the prince of cattle stealers and a king at faking brands;
And 'twas said of Andy Brady, from the Centre to the sea,
    There was not another living knew the bush as well as he.
But, with all men's hands against him, he could never rest in peace
    And was hunted like a dingo by civilians and police
Save a band of lawless comrades — silent members in the game —
    Who pricked their ears like heelers if you whispered Brady's name.

Though the social system banned him as an outcast and exiled
    There was one who served him truly — 'Twas his one and only child
And her faithful, filial duty, in the face of flood and fire
    Leaves a haunting memory, somehow, that we cannot but admire.
She was bred on old Monaro, where the girls, for native grace,
    'Mong their fair Australian sisters, take with ease the pride of place
And, among the mountain beauties — in the show-ring or the ball —
    The cattle stealer's daughter was the fairest of them all.

Now, it chanced that Trooper Kelly had been sent to Cooma town
    With a Queensland native tracker, to hunt Andy Brady down;
And his Sergeant's last instructions to the point were brief and few —
    "May you capture Andy Brady and his daughter, Mary, too!"
But the wily bushman's daughter was a student of disguise
    And had learnt in early childhood to provide against surprise,
And to her the trim-built stranger on the shapely dappled grey
    Was an object of suspicion and a likely bird of prey.

So, she watched his movements closely and discovered that a trap
    Had been laid to catch her father far away in Swindlers' Gap;
And she made a vow to save him from a felon's fearful doom,
    For the knowledge of his danger filled her heart and soul with gloom,
In the silent hour of midnight she rode down the bridle track,
    Never dreaming, for a moment, she was shadowed by the black;
As the early morning sunbeams tipped the mountain peaks with gold,
    She paused to reconnoitre — and her blood ran very cold!

She had laughed at mounted troopers, but her rosy cheeks went pale
    When she saw the native tracker like a blood-hound on the trail,
And she urged the pony onward, through the wild and tangled brush —
    With his evil shadow following like a spirit of the bush.
When she reached the Snowy River, the brave heart within her sank,
    For the swollen mountain waters rolled in flood from bank to bank,
But she neither paused nor faltered — it was simply sink or float —
    And the sturdy mountain pony stemmed the torrent like a boat.

Then across the Pilot Ranges, as a swallow homeward flies,
    And away towards the Bogongs, where the Mitta takes its rise,
She rode ever to the sunset, not a sign to guide her flight,
    Save the mountain peaks by daylight and the Southern Cross by night.
Through the weary hours of travel she had seldom drawn the reins
    When, at last, appeared before her the great rolling, Fainter Plains;
And the rosy flush of morning tipped the topmost mountain cap,
    Then her pony's hoofs went ringing down the slopes of Swindlers' Gap.

There was stir and consternation in that lonely mountain camp,
    For his daughter's hurried visit fairly terrified the scamp!
So, he vowed to clear to Queensland — there to change his life and name —
    And he gave his child a promise to forsake the life of shame.
Then away rode Andy Brady from an evil past of crime,
    From his stronghold in the ranges, in the very nick of time;
For the trooper and the tracker, with their horses spent and blown,
    Had almost reached the hollow as their wary bird had flown.

And the trooper gazed in wonder on the dainty, daring girl
    Who had led him such a gallop. Well, his heart was in a whirl!
His captive captivated him with look and manner sweet
    And he vowed to lay his fortunes and his future at her feet.
Was there ever such a wooing in this queer old world of ours?
    For the maiden's heart, responsive, thrilled to love's seductive powers.
It was all so strangely novel — 'twas a case of love at sight —
    And the glory of her conquest filled her senses with delight.

So the trooper, with his captive, rode in haste to Cooma town
    And was joined in holy wedlock ere the second sun went down.
Then he straightway drove to Sydney with his bonny, blushing bride,
    Where he boldly faced the Sergeant and presented her with pride.
There was mutual satisfaction in the interview, 'twas plain,
    For he promised Andy Brady would not trouble them again.
He'd his daughter as a hostage, who was then his lawful wife —
    His orders were to take her, so he'd taken her for life!

There was kindly human nature 'neath the Sergeant's honest tan
    And, beneath the stern official, lay the father and the man.
He was quick to grasp the issue and the moment then was ripe,
    So he gave the bride a blessing and assured her spouse a stripe.
And we learn that Andy Brady wandered to the Queensland side
    Where the place and he were strangers and the tracks of life are wide
That he prospered in a district better honoured on the map
    Than the valley in the ranges which was known as "Swindlers' Gap".

The morals of the mountains have improved in tone since then,
    For the Gippsland boys are noted as a model type of men;
They have grown so shy of cleanskins, that they wouldn't steal a kiss —
    (We have this as a secret from a modest mountain miss.)
Father Time brings many changes on his sweeping, silent wings
    And, with Andy Brady's exit came an altered state of things
And the cleanskin swindle ended with a sharp and sudden snap,
    When the prince of cattle stealers bade "Farewell" to Swindlers' Gap.

Wm. Jas. Wye.

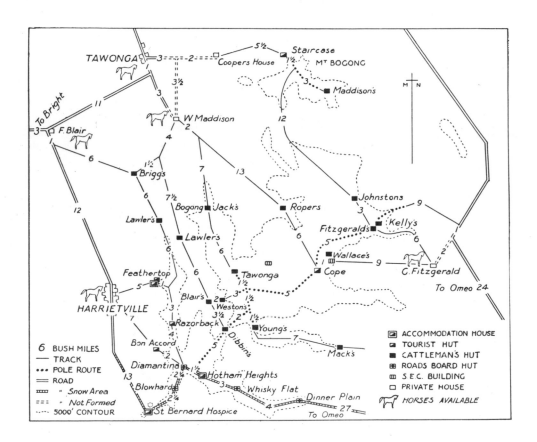

HUTS OF THE BOGONGS

This diagram, showing all huts on the Bogong High Plains and surrounding areas was prepared by Cleve Cole in the early 1930s. A number of the huts were owned by the Country Roads Board, Victorian Railways, Tourist Committees, Harrietville Progress Association, miners and others.

Many, however, were cattlemen's huts and only these have been described or illustrated in this book. Due acknowledgement is made to Cleve Cole, an old friend.

The Bogong High Plains

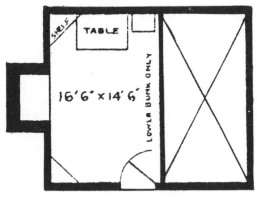

TAWONGA HUT

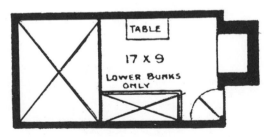

WALLACE'S HUT

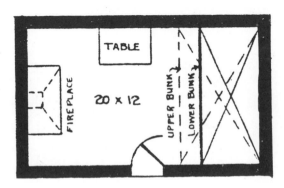

DIBBIN'S HUT

HUTS OF THE BOGONG HIGH PLAINS

The following Hut Plans and details were prepared by the late Cleve Cole in the early 1930s for the guidance of ski tourers of that era. The very few of these huts which are still standing have undergone structural changes and the details listed and now of historical interest only.

Situated on Bogong High Plains at the head of Tawonga Creek, a branch of the East Kiewa river, 18 miles from Tawonga and 6½ miles from Cope Hut, at an altitude of 5,380 feet. Constructed of split palings with iron roof and slab floor. A shelf bunk accommodates 8 people. Size 17 x 15 feet. In a heavy winter the hut may be snowed in, with only the chimney visible. The original Tawonga Hut was built in 1888 and was claimed to be the first cattlemen's hut to be built on the High Plains.

WALLACE'S HUT:
Situated 1 mile north east of Cope Hut at an altitude of 5,750 feet in delightful surroundings. Constructed of snowgum frame and slab sides with roof of mountain ash shingles, rough lined with malthoid. Stone lined fireplace. Bunk accommodation for 6 people. Size 17 x 9 feet, the hut is no longer weatherproof, having been built in 1889.

DIBBIN'S HUT:
Located in sheltered position on the Cobungra River, 8 miles from Cope Hut and 5 miles from Hotham Heights, at an altitude of 4,400 feet. Woollybutt log construction with bark roof and earth floor. The fireplace is inside the hut (no exterior chimney). A shelf bunk accommodated 5 people. Size 20 x 12 feet. This hut replaced an earlier one nearby. The low doorway earned it the title "Creep Inn".

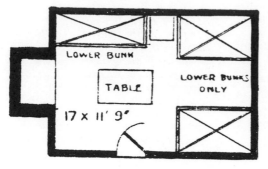

FITZGERALD'S HUT

FITZGERALD'S HUT:
Situated at the eastern end of the Bogong High Plains at an altitude of 5,500 feet, 5 miles from Cope hut and 6 miles from Shannonvale. Constructed of palings with shingle roof, floor and window, lined, table and bunk accommodation for 5 people. Size 17 x 12 feet. Water handy. Built 1903.

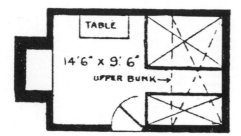

KELLY'S HUT

KELLY'S HUT:
Situated ¼ mile from Fitzgerald's Hut in a sheltered position among snowgums at an altitude of 5,470 feet. Constructed of palings for walls and roof, lined with hessian, slab floor and bunk accommodation for 6 people. Size 15 x 10 feet. Water handy. Built about 1900.

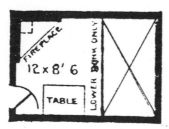

MADDISON'S HUT

MADDISON'S HUT:
Located on Mt Bogong in Camp Valley 3 miles from Summit Cairn at an altitude of 5,800 feet, this is the highest Cattleman's hut in Victoria. Constructed of snowgum logs with an iron roof and earth floor. Bunk accommodation for 3 people. Decidedly draughty, it has been christened "Aertex". Size 12 x 9 feet.

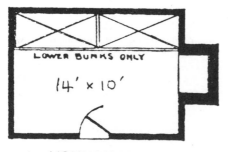

YOUNG'S HUT

YOUNG'S HUT:
Located on southern edge of the High Plains, 1½ miles from Pole 193 on the main route and along a line of unnumbered poles, 8 miles from Cope Hut and 3½ miles from Dibbin's. Altitude 5,500 feet. Timber sides, iron roof and accommodation for two.

The original hut was burnt in 1930 or 1931 and was rebuilt a year later.

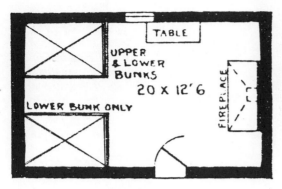

BLAIR'S HUT

BLAIR'S HUT:
Located on the West Kiewa River, east, south-east of Mt Feathertop, 3½ miles from Dibbin's Hut and 6 miles from Lawler's Hut, at an altitude of 3,650 feet, on the famous Dungey's Track. Constructed of woollybutt log walls, bark roof, window, earth floor. Bunk accommodation for 8 people. Size 20 x 12. This hut replaced an earlier one which was destroyed by fire in 1931.

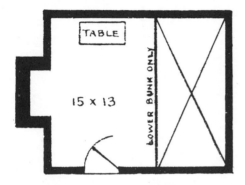

BOGONG JACK'S HUT

BOGONG JACK'S HUT:
Located in snowgums 1 mile north of Mt Fainter, 12¼ miles from Tawonga and 12¼ miles from Cope Hut, at an altitude of 5,000 feet. Constructed of woollybutt shingle sides, chimney and roof, with slab floor and a bunk for 8 people. Built by Mr Syd Ryder in 1919 after an earlier Bogong Jack's Hut was burnt down in 1914. Size 15 x 13 feet.

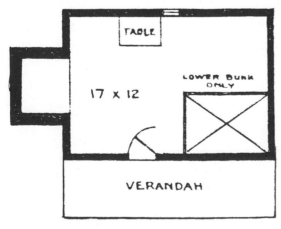

WESTONS HUT

WESTON'S HUT:
Located on western end of Bogong High Plains, 2 miles from Blair's Hut, at an altitude of 5,000 feet. Constructed of woollybutt split palings throughout with verandah, window, bunks for 4 people, earth floor. Size 17 x 12 feet. Built in 1932.

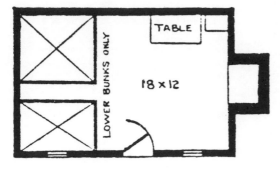

LAWLER'S HUT

LAWLER'S HUT:
Located on Mt Higginbotham, adjacent to Hotham Heights at an altitude of 5,800 feet. Construction is galvanised iron walls and roof, timber floor, 2 windows and shelf bunks for 5 people. Size 18 x 12 feet.

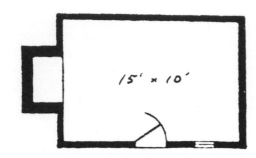

JOHNSTONE'S HUT

JOHNSTONE'S HUT:
Located east of Mt Nelse at an altitude of 5,500 feet, 3 miles from Fitzgerald's and Kelly's Huts. Constructed of paling sides and iron roof, earth floor and no bunks. Size 15 x 10.

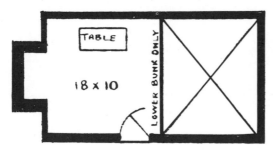

ROPER'S HUT

ROPER'S HUT:
Located in Rocky Valley at the headwaters of the East Kiewa river, 6 miles from Cope Hut and 19 miles from Tawonga at an altitude of 4,150 feet amongst woollybutts. Constructed of woollybutt slabs, shingle roof with earth floor. Shelf bunk for 5 people. Size 18 x 10 feet.

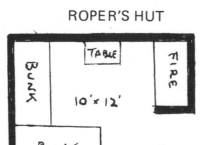

ROPER'S HUT

ROPER'S HUT (No.2):
Located in timber on Mountain Creek, 6 miles from Tawonga, 200 yards on south side of Mt Bogong track, at an altitude of 2,000 feet. Timber construction, iron roof, window, earth floor and shelf bunk for 4 people. Size 10 x 12 feet.

BRIGG'S HUT

BRIGG'S HUT:
Located on Snowy Creek, 10 miles from Bright, altitude 1,900 feet. Constructed of palings, with shingle roof. No bunks.

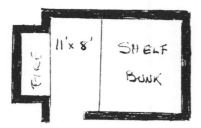

LAWLER'S HUT

LAWLER'S HUT:
Located on Dungey's Track, west branch of the Kiewa River, 19 miles from Bright and 6 miles from Blair's. Altitude 2,800 feet. Constructed of logs with iron roof, bunks for 4 people. Size 11 x 8 ft.

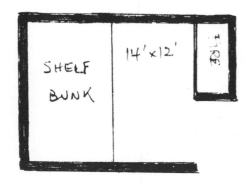

LAWLER'S HUT

LAWLER'S HUT:
Located at head of Snowy Creek, 16 miles from Bright, 6 miles from Brigg's Hut and 7 miles from Feathertop Bungalow. Altitude 4,500 ft. Constructed of logs with bark roof – shelf bunk accommodates 6 people.

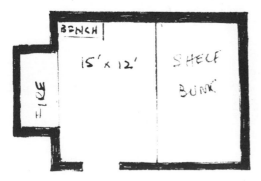

McNAMARA'S HUT

McNAMARA'S HUT:
Located on Dinner Plain, portion of the divide between Cobungra and Bundarra at 4,900 feet. 7 miles from Young's Hut. Timber floor and sides, iron roof. Double bunks.

The Bogong High Plains

THE FAINTER TRACK

This route to the Bogong High Plains commences at the village of Tawonga on the Kiewa River near the junction with Mountain Creek.

Three miles up the Kiewa Valley, the river is forded and a cattle track climbs the Fainter Spur which splits the East and West branches of the Kiewa river and leads in a further 6 miles to The Springs Saddle and to Bogong Jack's Hut (in ruins in 1962. Ed.) in a further 3. At both of these locations water is available. A mile past "Bogong Jack's", the track skirts the east side of Fainter North and in a further mile Mt Fainter is passed. Mt Fainter is a splendid viewpoint, close at hand across the West Keiwa Valley, the wedge shaped Mt Feathertop rises to 6,300 feet, while in the opposite direction, across the East Kiewa the bulk of Mt Bogong dominates the skyline.

Tawonga Hut, built in 1923 to replace an earlier hut on this site, is used by a group of Tawonga based cattlemen.

The track is now well above the timber line and ahead the Bogong High Plains unfold. Across the well watered Little Plain, the Tawonga Hut is reached at 18 miles from Tawonga.

The Fainter Spur is the one which stood out so prominently when Brown and Wells first saw it from Mt Nelse and gave them the key to the first route off the Bogongs to the North East.

The Tawonga — Mt Fainter track was originally cut by Jack Fitzgerald. It is the traditional route used by the Cattlemen of Tawonga.

DUNGEY'S TRACK

In the 1930s, some three or four miles from Bright along the Alpine road to Hotham was a sign which read "Dungey's Track". Tradition has it that the track was named after a Detective Dungey, who used the route in his constant search for cattle duffers last century.

The track left the Alpine road a mile past Germantown and followed the valley of Snowy Creek for some distance before climbing over Symond's Gap at seven miles and sidling numerous small heads of West Kiewa tributaries before dropping on to the West Kiewa near Bogong Jack's Creek, at Lawler's Hut, 19 miles from Bright. Passing Dungey's Gap to the right, the track follows the easy gradient of the West Kiewa valley with numerous crossings of the stream.

The original Dungey's Track followed Snowy Creek to its head and then over Dungey's Gap before dropping down to the West Kiewa.

The track leads on to Blair's Hut, 6 miles from Lawlers and 25 from Bright. From the head of the valley the track crosses the Cobungra Gap to reach Dibbin's Hut on the Cobungra River. This river is then followed to reach the Alpine road at Rundels. From Blair's Hut, a branch track leads to Weston's Hut and past it to reach the snow pole line between Mt Jim and Tawonga Hut.

From Dibbins, of course, a track leads back around Mt Loch to Hotham and in the opposite direction, climbs out of the valley on to the Plains not far from Young's Hut.

For a period the track was closed by fallen logs, and cattle had to be driven through Harrietville and around Hotham to the Plains. The track, however, was re-opened in 1922 and since that time has been in constant use.

Whether Detective Dungey ever caught his man is uncertain, but the track which bears his name is the main stock route for the cattlemen based in Bright. Today it is the way in and out for Westons, Briggs and Blairs and in earlier times it provided access for Dibbins.

FITZGERALD'S TRACK

My old Bogong High Plains map refers to Mt Nelson, 6269 ft., and George Fitzgerald declared that it was named after a mining prospector of that name. Maybe he changed it by Deed Poll, for today we know this great peak as Mt Nelse.

Fitzgerald's cattle graze the southern slopes, as they have for almost a hundred years, unless they get the urge to wander elsewhere, and Fitzgerald's (and Kelly's) huts are about four miles south east of the summit of Nelse.

Fitzgerald's Track leads out from here to the "Shangri La" that is 'Shannon Vale', and then to the Glen Wills Omeo road.

The huts (Fitzgerald's and Kelly's) are located in a snowgum wooded glade that is on the eastern extremity of the Bogong High Plains. From here (eastwards) a well defined timbered spur winds down, with Middle Creek to the south, once threading an avenue (long since burnt), known as 'The Lanes' and in six miles drops in to the Fitzgerald home property and then in a further two miles, out to the road.

It is a conventional spur route, short and well graded, affording reasonable shelter along the way.

George Fitzgerald must have known every tree on the spur, for he rode up and down to attend seventy annual musters on the High Plains.

ROPER'S TRACK

The Ropers were grazing the High Plains from at least the 1890s and after Fred Roper was granted his first licence in 1908, he commissioned John Crossthwaite, member of a pioneer Dederang family, and an accomplished surveyor to mark out a track from Tawonga to Rocky Valley.

Leaving Mountain Creek valley about three miles from Tawonga, Fred Roper cut the track, which wound around the heads of Bogong Creek tributaries and over Bogong Creek saddle and on to Timm's Spur. The track skirted Timm's Lookout, to reach the Ropers' hut on Falls Creek in Rocky Valley, about 1½ miles due south of Spion Kopje, at a height of 4,150 feet and a distance of nineteen miles from Tawonga.

Later, when Ropers built a new hut on the site of the old Duane's hut, only a slight deviation was required to reach the new site.

BON ACCORD TRACK

From Harrietville, a track up the east branch of the Ovens River led in about four miles to the foot of Bon Accord Spur and a sharp climb of another four miles along the spur reached the Razorback (between Feathertop and Hotham), a mile or so short of Mt Hotham.

This track led cattle on to the Hotham - Loch snowplains and it was also used by Blairs and others, who climbed up out of the Cobungra during the period, prior to 1922, when Dungey's Track was closed by fallen logs.

MADDISON'S TRACK

George Maddison had pioneered a route on to Mt Bogong by, or earlier than 1883, when, with Peter Howman of Eskdale, he sub-leased the Mt Bogong run from Ensay Station. Maddison's property was on the east bank of the Kiewa river, just across the stream at the end of the Kiewa Valley road at Tawonga South. He was almost at the foot of the Fainter Spur which led up to the High Plains, but it was the impressive bulk of Mt Bogong, eight miles to the east that attracted him. A mile and a half across the flats from his home, Mountain Creek joined the Kiewa River, and his route to Bogong followed the valley until at about six miles, Staircase Spur led up to the summit of Mt Bogong. Mountain Creek required only about seven crossings (how different from the Howqua track to Mt Howitt with twenty-eight, and the Avon river way to Mt Wellington with about forty).

The Staircase Spur, however, as its name implies provided tougher going with its steep climbs to each 'step' and its sharp drops to the valleys on either side. From Mountain Creek (2,000 ft.) the site of the eventual Bivouac Hut (4,900 ft.) was reached in about two miles, and from here the way became steeper and more rugged. Cliff faces to the north-western approach made it necessary to skirt around the summit of Bogong on the north-east side and join the snow plains east of the top at an altitude of about 6,000 feet, a mile and a half from Bivouac Hut site. In about three and a half miles the track had climbed 4,000 feet!

The going was now easier with snow-plains leading down all the way to Camp Valley, 2½ miles to the south-east, the location in which Maddison built his hut at 5,700 feet. An area of about 1000 acres (1½ miles by 1 mile) was eventually fenced, and the Falls at the head of nearby Camp Creek, were named Howmans.

HOWMAN'S TRACKS

Howman used a track which left Mountain Creek about a mile downstream from the Staircase Spur turnoff, followed a low spur which led to the head of Trapper's Creek and after meandering down the valley finally reached a spur that split the two heads of Snowy Creek and reached the road just south of Granite Flat, some 12 - 14 miles from the commencement at Mountain Creek.

Later Howman brought cattle up the Granite Flat Spur, from his Howman's Hollow Hut. Eskdale Spur, between Staircase and Granite Flat spurs was also used.

But, by whichever route the cattle travelled, there was no diminishing the fact that from a starting point of 2,000 - 2,500 feet, there was an inescapable climb to 6,000, and if the cattle throve in the brisk air and the lush pastures of Bogong's summer 'springtime climate', then they had really earned it.

These are the recognised routes by which the stock are taken in to the snow-plain pastures in November, and brought out in April. Dick Johnson, in his "Alps at the Crossroads", briefly describes the summer grazing, as follows:

> Each year the cows and their new calves are led to the leasehold up established tracks by a few old stagers trained to the routes. On the high plains the calves toughen and strengthen on the natural fodder and in the bracing climate, and the herd is prevented from straying excessively by its need for salt in which the alpine environment is generally lacking. The regular salting of the herds provides a reason and a means for keeping the cattle under control and a method of reconcentrating their numbers from time to time. The muster is held at the end of the season.
>
> On the date selected cattlemen gather at break of day and begin to round the cattle to three mustering points — Pretty Valley, Mt Jim and the Bucketty Plain. When the muster is completed each mob is concentrated by rounding the cattle into a tighter and tighter circle until the mob is moving in a slow wheel on the mustering flat. At this stage, in a display of expert horsemanship, riders begin at the periphery of the mob, moving counter to it and gradually cutting out a selected individual, walking it sideways away from the others. The process is repeated innumerable times until each cattlemen has sorted his stock from the herd, when he leads them to their familiar track down the mountain and turns them towards their home pastures.

When the muster of the autumn of 1980 was completed and the mobs 'cut out' by their respective owners, 4,200 head set out along their various routes to lowland pastures or the mountain cattle sales.

Fitzgerald's and Kelly's cattle headed down Fitzy's Track to Omeo, Pat Sykes and Faithful brothers took the Buckety road to Omeo and the Cobungra cattle went in the same direction. Jack Maddison and Ian Roper drove their mobs around the back of Nelse into Mountain Creek, while Wally Ryder, Bill Hicks and Jack Cooper went down the Fainter Spur to Tawonga. Charlie MacNamara went out across Dinner Plain leaving Eric Weston, Ron Briggs and Blairs to head down the West Kiewa, the traditional Dungey's Track route to Bright.

SNOW POLES

Few people in Victoria realise the extent of our snow fields and the consequent necessity to provide reliable indications of the location of tracks when the winter has covered them with a blanket of snow, maybe several feet thick. The skier, the cattlemen, and all who must needs frequent the higher places of the State have good reason to bless the snow pole, sticking up above the mantle of white when the absence of trees makes blazing impracticable and the presence of fog makes recognition impossible.

The snow poles on the Bogong High Plains are almost entirely old snowgum posts from eight to ten feet high and about three chains apart.

R.G.HEMMY 1950

Stores packed ready for loading a pack-horse team.   A one-time common sight outside Wraith's Store.

WRAITH'S STORE
On a recent visit to Harrietville I noticed that Wraith's Store had disappeared.   Henry Wraith took over the store from a Mr Mitchell in 1869 and his son Frank carried it on until recent times.

R.G.HEMMY 1963

No story of the Bogongs would be complete without mention of Wraith's Store.   Henry Wraith took over the store from a Mr Mitchell in 1869 and it remained in the family for ninety years.   Frank Wraith succeeded his father and still later Frank's son Victor assisted in the management.

The Gows, who had run cattle and operated Gow's Hotel and Store on the Dargo High Plains joined with Frank Wraith to form a company Wraith and Gow, and this company, managed by Frank's youngest son Carl, operated as storekeepers and cattle graziers, taking over the Gow's licence on the Dargo High Plains and wintering their cattle at Harrietville, Myrtleford and at Everton.   The Everton property "The Grange" which had at one time belonged to Cobb & Co, was then a staging point for change over of horses.

The Gow's Dargo leases were acquired by the Treasures about 1950 and the store closed later in the 1950s.

279

George Silas "Dad" Fitzgerald.

Fitzgeralds of "Shannon Vale"

GEORGE SILAS FITZGERALD, of 'Shannonvale', was in his eighty-seventh year when he recounted the following details of his life to W.F.'Bill' Waters in 1954. He was still hale, hearty and full of vigor. Known variously as George, 'Dad, Fitz or Fitzy, he had a cheery laugh and a sense of humor and had a host of friends steadily accumulated over the years.

In the mountains and hill towns of the Omeo country, he was well and favourably known and had been a good friend of bushwalkers, Rover Scouts and skiers, and on many occasions packed food in for them or accompanied them on their mountain wanderings. 'Bill' Waters first met George and his brother Tom in 1924, and in his annual visits to Melbourne, George (or as we Rovers always referred to him, 'Dad') regularly visited the Waters home.

"Shannon Vale" the home of George Fitzgerald.

Fitzgerald's Hut on snow covered Bogong High Plains.

Looking towards the Bogong High Plains from "Shannon Vale", near Omeo.

George ('Dad') Fitzgerald tells his own story:

"I was born on the 9th of May 1867, at Omeo, on the banks of Livingstone Creek. My father, Edward D'Arcy Fitzgerald, an American citizen, was born in Iowa, U.S.A., in 1828, from whence he came to Australia with one of the gold rushes, and landed at Twofold Bay. He eventually settled in Omeo in February 1853 on the Dry Hill above the Livingstone Creek. He lived till the advanced age of 87 years.

My mother Mary Gallagher, was born in Dublin, Ireland and landed at Port Albert in 1853, from whence she moved to Omeo, where she met and married my father.

After rearing a family of six boys and two girls, who attended school in Omeo, she lived till the ripe old age of 84 years.

My father was an alluvial miner on the Livingstone, where he worked a claim for twenty-five years, eventually selling out to take up a farm in the Omeo district.

In 1861, my father bought 160 acres of what is now known as 'Shannonvale', a name I gave to the property many years ago, after a station in New South Wales. The property had been leased from the Crown by William Charles Jack, who died without making a will, with the result that the lease was forfeited and then my father took over the place.

Messrs W.J.C.Pendergast, G.S.Fitzgerald, J.S. Holston and H.Witham. Pioneers of the Omeo District. There must be something in the Omeo air which promotes longevity. There are few places of its size that can boast of so many pioneers in the octogenarian class.

When I went to 'Shannonvale' first, I lived in a log hut and later decided to build a house.

My brother Jack and I were the first men to take a bullock waggon into 'Shannonvale' from Omeo. We packed the first plough and a set of harrows in pieces, and the only thing I haven't packed is a piano.

The road was first built by me in 1900 as a waggon track from 'Shannonvale' to Glen Wills.

My wife, Margaret Shanahan, was born in 1870 at Gordon, and passed away on the 22nd March, 1920. We reared three sons and two daughters at 'Shannonvale' and now Brendan, my youngest son and his wife and family are with me there. In 1936, son Tom played an active part in the rescue of Mick Hull and Cleve Cole from Big River, after they came down from Mt Bogong's snows.

"Dad" Fitzgerald shows the way to two walkers.

George Fitzgerald and two faithful companions.

FITZGERALD'S HUT
Packed by 'Dad' Fitzgerald, a 'Skyline' party outside Fitzy's hut in summer 1928. Note the hut is in its original form, with shingle roof.

In 1888 I took a contract to grub box trees on the new road to Doctor's Flat from Ensay and got enough out of the contract to have a holiday in Melbourne where I saw Carbine defeated in the Victoria Derby. In 1890 I worked for 7/- a day for six days a week on the new Tambo Valley road.

Locally-made butter in those days was worth 10d. a lb., and eggs 6d. a dozen; flour was £10 a bag of 200 lbs., carted by pack-horses and bullock teams from Bairnsdale. The first butter at Omeo cost 5/- a lb., and came, salted in kegs, by packhorses from Dargo. The first ton of potatoes to arrive from Dargo by packhorses cost £50 a ton, packed in by Dinny Connolly of Dargo Flat.

The Jim and Jack Creek, which feeds the Livingstone, and Mt Jim and Jack (afterwards Mt Cope), on the High Plains, were named after Jim Brown and Jack Wells, who were the first men to cross the Bogong High Plains from Tawonga to Omeo in 1852. Mt Jack was afterwards named Mt Cope, after Judge Cope, and Mt Higinbotham was named after Mr Justice Higinbotham of Melbourne.

Mt Nelson took its name from a mining prospector called Nelson; Marum's Point after Keiran Marum, a manager for Mrs Huggins' family, of Tawonga; and Hollond's Knob, after Bill Hollonds, of Tawonga; while Mt McKay was called after a cattleman named Jim McKay.

The Watchbed, at the head of Rocky Valley, was so named because a man running horses from Tawonga lost a gold watch. His horse fell with him, and must have put its hoof on the watch and buried it, as it was never found.

One year later another 'Skyline' tour visited the hut but the roof was then covered with corrugated iron. The shingles had survived for 25 years.

Spion Kop I named after the battle of the Boer War. Mt Wills was named after Wills, of the Burke and Wills expedition.

The Tawonga Hut was the first hut built on the Bogong High Plains, then Wallace's, then Young's, then Kelly's, and then my hut which was erected in 1903. Kelly's hut was built by Huggins, of Tawonga.

When I was fifteen, I used to drove horses, as many as one hundred and sixty, for Osborn Young, a horse breeder, from Benambra to Sale, travelling via the Livingstone, the Wentworth, and the Dargo Rivers, to Dargo, and thence via Waterford and Cobannah. I used to get an allowance of 30/- for eight days for hotel meals and accommodation. When the Sale market declined, I took ninety horses for Young to Wodonga.

The first cattle to go to Cobungra Station were driven there by Neddie Gray, from Wangaratta. He started out with eleven hundred head, and lost one hundred between Peechelba and Cobungra, and met a blackfellow who put him on to the Cobungra country. The blacks called the area Kabungara. Cobungara is now owned by the Norton brothers.

I have always kept open-house for cattlemen, hikers and skiers; and visitors of all sorts have been made welcome. I used to take the Melbourne Women's Walking Club skiing on the High Plains, and the annual party became known as Fitzgerald's Circus. The girls used skis, but I always walked through the snow. I always gave them a good dinner and a big plum pudding on the night they arrived. I have taken Railway Skyline tour parties across the High Plains with 72 riding hacks and 23 pack-horses, and trail

FITZGERALD'S HUT
'Dad' Fitzgerald, veteran high plains cattleman of "Shannon Vale", at doorway of his hut, built in 1903. The original shingle roof was replaced with galvanised iron in autumn 1928. (Photo 1937)

riding parties with Roy Gollan as manager on one occasion and W.T. McConnell on another. I have packed Rover Scout parties annually up to Cope Hut, and later to their own chalet at Middle Creek since 1932.

In 1896 my brother Jack and I erected a line of snow poles from Rocky Valley to Tawonga Hut. Many miners then working at Glen Wills had their homes in Harrietville, and the Mines Department put in the track to enable them to travel between the two in safety. A man named Joseph Fitzmayer was the Mining Track Inspector in those days, and I met him in Omeo with packhorses to take him out to inspect the track.

The weather on the High Plains can be very varied, sometimes sunny and warm, and then bitterly cold, foggy and snowing heavily. The winters now are not as heavy as they used to be. The biggest blizzard on the High Plains occurred in February 1903. The late Sir Thomas Blamey's father had 4,000 sheep in Rocky Valley, and next morning after the storm, they skinned 1300 dead. In the same year a big mob of cattle was brought from Tawonga to the top of Mt. Fainter and turned adrift. Next morning, after a storm, 30 calves were dead.

In 1923, there was a big break in the weather about 1st May.[*] There were 600 head of cattle below Mt. Nelson, and on the first day of the muster we got 500. We shifted the rest, and about the 10th May, Bill Batty and I went back and saw 16 in a moss bed. We spent a day trying to get them out of the snow, and had covered about 100 yards when they started charging us.

[*] It was May 7th. Ed.

We got on top of the snow, lit a fire and lay down beside it for the night, without food or blankets, and the next day moved the mob about a mile and spent another night by a fire without bedding or food. Next day, we went back for shovels and dug a long trench in the snow for a mile. The cattle followed out along the trench. Eventually we got them all out by the 28th June, without losing one.

I was mustering late one autumn about seven years ago. Snow had fallen and thick fog came down when I was on Mt. Nelson - so thick the dog couldn't bark in it. I dug a hole in the snow behind some rocks, and held my horse by the bridle until daylight, and that was the longest night I ever put in!

I have been present at seventy annual cattle musters on the High Plains, with one break, and have never had a serious accident off a horse in the bush. In 1930, I had a dangerous accident when I was thrown out of a car. A man named Duffin was driving me home when the car turned over some miles from Omeo, and Duffin was killed. I rolled down eighty feet into the Livingstone, and pulled myself out of the water. I lay there till daylight, with my feet and legs frozen to the waist. In the morning I crawled up to the road, when a man came along with a horse and dray. He had a bike in the dray. He got me into the dray to hold the horse, and biked to phone the Omeo doctor and the police, who both came out and took me to the Omeo hospital, where I took two months to recover. On account of that accident, I missed the only muster on the High Plains for seventy years.

I have had a lot of fun in my life, and if I had my time over, I would do the same with it."

"Shannon Vale" is occupied today by Brendan Fitzpatrick, son of George, and Fitzgerald cattle still graze the eastern end of the Bogong High Plains, and Fitzy's Hut, built in 1903 and re-roofed in 1928 is still in use.

Tom Fitzgerald and Bill Batty, two Bogong cattlemen who were leaders in the search party that rescued Cleve Cole, Mick Hull and Howard Michell in the winter of 1936.

Snow at "Shannonvale".

Cobungra Station

EARLY HISTORY records that in 1841, two stockmen, Jem Brown and Jack Wells held the original Cobungra lease of 150,000 acres. This run included all Hotham and part of the Bogong High Plains and had its southern boundary close to the Jim (Jem) and Jack Creek. A second source suggests that Wells Brothers were the original leaseholders. Those claims would appear to conflict with the 'Discovery of the Bogong High Plains' by Stella Carr on page 221 , in which its is recorded that Brown and Wells accompanied Gray to Cobungra in 1851, having been guided by an aboriginal. Cobungra was deserted on their arrival, but Gray was of the opinion that others had been there before him.

On June 14th George Gray successfully tendered for the fourteen year lease of 32,000 acres with a carrying capacity of 640 head of cattle. The terms of the lease were £10.2.0 and £2.10.0 for every thousand sheep or equivalent in cattle above 4,000 sheep. Gray who died in 1854, apparently extended his lease for on 30th May 1859 the run was subdivided into Cobungra and Bynomungee, and on 2nd November that year Cobungra was transferred to James Parslow (who it is understood was related to Wells) and John Meighan. On 8th October 1868 Parslow and Joseph Rawson were in control of the station.

The Parslow homestead was on the western half of the run on the banks of the Victoria River, later the site of the Cobungra Hotel.

Several small stations were in existence for a few years, but little is known of their history. Cassilis Station, Bundarah Station, etc., were amongst them, but were never very extensive and were obliterated by free selection.

The run was again subdivided into Cobungra East and Cobungra West on September 18th 1871. Rawson taking the East and Parslow the West. The following transfers then eventuated – Cobungra East – September 18th

1871 Frederick William Dreverman; January 5th 1878 Hans Maas and Claus Maas; December 16th 1878 Hans Maas and Richard King of Omeo; August 14th 1884 William and Walter Coughland of Omeo. Cobungra West — April 25th 1884 James Parslow and Richard King. Several changes occurred until Richard Riggall purchased Cobungra about 1898. He also took over Fred Box's adjoining property and hotel. He had a new brick home built before moving in and he then lived here with his wife Ellen and the family which grew to seven sons.

In 1919 Richard died as the result of a tragic accident. A mob of cattle broke away one evening and Dick, galloping after them in the darkness, rode into a wire line, which caught him across the mouth and lower jaw. Badly injured, he was rushed to hospital, but died a short time later.

The trustees decided that the property should be sold by tender, and along with others Richard's son Alan tendered for the property.

His tender was the highest, but due to an oversight in the trustee's office, it was not passed on to the trustee and Naughtons became the successful tenderers.

The Cobungra cattle were not part of the sale and Richard's son Alan, who was born at Cobungra, recalls driving the station mob down the regular route to their final destination at Bairnsdale saleyards.

Naughtons, who had never seen Cobungra, tendered only because they had seen Cobungra cattle, the sight of which convinced them that the property was a very rich one. Naughtons expanded the station to almost its original size by purchasing the neighbouring properties.

The disastrous bush fires of 1939 caused the germination of seed which eventually turned the greatest part of the relatively open grazing country into thick forest thereby considerably reducing its value. As a result, Ed. Naughton, in 1960, sold out to the present owners, Cobungra Pty Ltd. This deal entailed the transfer of approximately 17,000 acres of freehold, 68,000 acres of leasehold and 2,400 head of cattle.

Annual pasture improvement, rabbit control, etc. have enabled the present owners to turn off between 700 and 1,900 head of stock annually. Cobungra cattle have always been noted for their quality. Even the freak storm of June 22nd 1949 which enveloped Omeo in the heaviest snow within living memory (the drifts averaged three feet and sometimes six feet) caused only minor loss. Most of the cattle came out of the experience in good condition.

Cobungra, also, was once noted for its horses which were sold chiefly as remounts for the Indian Army. Sometimes as many as 300 foals were running on the station.

The terrible fires of 1939 took their dreadful toll of Cobungra. The residents took refuge in the Livingstone Creek; however, a stockman named Richards and his dog were incinerated when the flames overtook them near Bright. Thousands of head of station stock were destroyed and the homestead was reduced to ashes.

The first Cobungra home which one finds mentioned is that which Parslow built on the bank of the Victoria River on the western half of the station. Claud Maas on the eastern half had a slab and shingle roof home. Frederick Box established his hotel on the Victoria River side.

The second homestead which replaced that destroyed by the 1939 fires, was partly built of bricks made and burnt on the site. The rear portion and some of the outbuildings were of timber, quantities of which came from the old Box Hotel. An existing hayshed covers the site but a few of the original steps can be seen. The present 40 square homestead built in 1961 replaces a home destroyed by fire which originated in a kerosine refrigerator. Of thick walled adobe construction, it was designed by Alistair Knox, famous for his mud brick and is in fact the forerunner of the present return to favour of that style. Its wide eaved verandahs are paved with local stone.

DROVING

During the years prior to the advent of motor transport, stock from Cobungra (and from other stations) were driven annually along the 38 miles of winding mountain track through forests of red gum and messmate to D'argo, on to Stratford to the saleyards of A. McLean and Co., and Theo B. Little at Maffra on the Gippsland plains.

Deep winter snow on Mt Birregun made it necessary for the drive to start usually in the autumn. Cattle are not taken if snow is covering the mountain. Stockmen on the Cobungra Station would spend perhaps up to a month preparing for the trip, mustering, culling, etc. before putting a mob ranging in size from 300 to 500 head of Hereford cattle on the road.

Cattle in the highlands love the taste of salt, although the salt is not really necessary for the health of the animals. The reaction of the animals to the cry of s-a-l-t is exciting to witness. The nearest animals bellow their acceptance and pleasure and come pounding down the hillsides. Bellows from the nearest animals echo back into the hills and are answered by those further afield until the message reaches into the outer limits of the station. Some of the animals are so far back into the hills, they may take a week or more to reach the salt.

Feeding of salt is mostly routine and the benefits are two-fold; mustering is made easier and it quietens the cattle. Mountain bred cattle are unused to yards, gates, dogs and humans with the accompanying smells, sounds and sights, are nervous, suspicious and frightened when first acquainted by them. Beasts yarded for the first time can become quite maddened with fear; hence the cry of s-a-l-t is frequently heard by the cattle and they come readily to accept the tasty portion.

Further preparations for the drive to the sales included the yarding and shoeing of the extra horses needed. Horses are always cold shod and those used for the drive had to be experienced, sure footed and sturdy. Drovers rode their own horses and as many as ten drovers were needed for the journey. Extra stock horses were required as well as five or six pack horses. Horses were not injured very often, but accidents did happen. The extra stock horses allowed a change of mount when the drover's usual mount became tired.

Pack horses just had to be reliable and experienced, after all they were not led as a rule and they carried the provisions and supplies. They followed along with the cavalcade judging the width of their packs with skill and patience, negotiating the distance between the rocks and trees. The packs placed on horses needed to be very secure and well balanced and required all the skill and experience of the drover, as a badly balanced pack could easily push a horse over the edge of the track and result in the death of the horse and loss of the pack. Ropes and halters were usually greenhide and made by the stockmen.

Food prepared for the trips was simple - flour, baking powder for Johnny cakes and damper, fresh and salted meat, tea, sugar and treacle were the main fare. A couple of dogs accompanied each drover and killers were included in the mob to feed the dogs.

To protect the men from the intense cold of the mountain nights, drovers donned the famous Tasmanian Bluey made from wool and shower proof. Also the equally famous Thomas Evans oiled coat, long, wide shouldered, light weight and rain proof. Thick grey woollen blankets were carried and sometimes waist coats of tanned animal skins were worn. Leggings for protection of the drovers' legs in the rough bush terrain were also worn.

In the period of this story there were no huts and conveniences at the stopping places, but later huts were built where dry wood and some comfort for the men and dogs was available.

When all was prepared for the drive, the holding paddock gates were opened in the early hours of dawn and to the accompaniment of the bellowing cattle, the shouts and whip cracking of the stockmen and the barking of dogs, the cavalcade moved off on the eight day journey that was hard on both man and beast.

Good drovers always made camp before dark, never be caught making camp in the dark was number one rule of droving; so always a dawn start and camp before dark. Usually the drovers and their dogs bedded down between logs using whatever they could arrange near the camp fire. A tent fly or tent was sometimes used.

If it so happened that a mob had to be taken through short handed, the drovers were often forced to drop some cattle on the way. Such was the hospitality of the bush in those days that adjacent land holders would muster and hold those cattle until they could be picked up the following year.

The first two days journey was south then south-westerly from Cobungra's southern paddocks to the site of the Dog's Grave, a distance of twelve or thirteen miles between the Dinner Plain and Jim and Jack Creek. At the end of this and the next stretch, the stock were held in holding paddocks. Therefore accommodation paddocks were used. The second day the mob travelled to Matheison's Flats on the Dargo River south west of Mt Birregun.

The skill and patience of the drover was severely tested on the third day's journey to Phelan's at Dargo. The first ten miles of the sixteen mile walk was along a bridle track approximately four and a half feet wide. In places the drop was sheer to the river some 1,000 feet below. This track had to be seen to be believed. As one drover said - "The cattle only went over once."

It was single file for the men and the cattle and trouble occurred when an aggressive beast turned to horn into the animal closely pressed behind. Unless the aggressor could be stopped quickly, one or more beasts would be forced over the side hurtling to the river below. In order to prevent trouble, the drovers endeavoured to split the mob evenly between them and with the aid of their intelligent dogs keep the animals on the move until they reached the next small river flat.

John Sadlier writing in the 1850s of his first ride in the area, probably on a horse not used to the terrain said - "The view down into those awful depths at one's feet, range rising upon range, striped with snow even at this late season (February) took one's breath awy."

"Fearsome also for man and beast was the deep descent to the River Dargo below. The track was too steep for rider to remain in the saddle yet it had the appearance of having been much used. It was only by hanging on to the reins that we could get the horses to follow and then the fear that should the horses not be able to check their descent, we and the horses would be over the side."

He continued - "Ascending from the river towards Cobungra, the road was very much the same with this difference. The horses went first and we hung on to their tails. We reached the top in a series of short scrambles, horses and men stopping every few yards to recover their wind. Few men would care to undertake alone the journey described." This was the same route taken by the Cobungra drovers and in the same year.

The fourth day, the mob grazed along to Traill's or Long's at Waterford and at the end of the fifth day camp was made at Bulgoback Hotel. The sixth stage was an extremely long one which included travel along the Insolvent Track (originally Anderson's Track) from Lee's Junction on the Dargo Road to Stockdale, the site of the night's camp.

John Sadlier's comment on the Insolvent Track - "I took what was called the Insolvent Track, I found it a most abominable one over broken and stony hills at every step."

The seventh stage brought the mob to Stratford. On the eighth day it reached Maffra. It is believed that the last time this arduous drive was undertaken was in 1932.

The Insolvent Track was opened up in 1881 at a cost of £1,500 and it's formation was the main reason why Dargo joined the Avon Shire. The road was kept free of fallen timber by Richard Lee. Some said the track was so called by out of luck diggers who wished to avoid the storekeepers at Iguana Creek to whom they owed money. Another version has it that the contractor working on the track went insolvent.

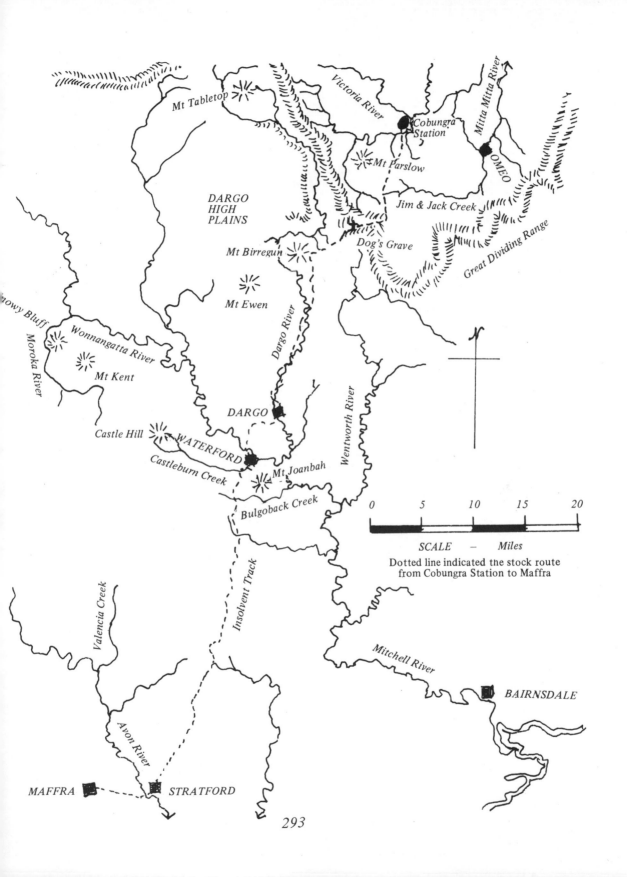

Mt Tabletop

Victoria River

Mitta Mitta River

Cobungra
Station

OMEO

Mt Parslow

DARGO
HIGH
PLAINS

Jim & Jack Creek

Mt Birregun

Dog's Grave

Great Dividing Range

Mt Ewen

Dargo River

Snowy Bluff

Wonnangatta River

Moroka River

Mt Kent

Wentworth River

N

DARGO

Castle Hill

WATERFORD

Castleburn Creek

Mt Joanbah

Bulgoback Creek

0   5   10   15   20

SCALE   —   Miles

Dotted line indicated the stock route
from Cobungra Station to Maffra

Valencia Creek

Insolvent Track

Mitchell River

BAIRNSDALE

Avon River

MAFFRA

STRATFORD

293

Upper Buckland

*A*N AMERICAN, James Morgan came to Australia during the gold rushes and after prospecting his way up the Upper Buckland valley he eventually settled on the upper reaches. He erected a fine timber home 23 miles from Porepunkah and raised a family, established a plantation of trees, many native to his homeland, and bred cattle. It was a fine property until bushfires reduced the entire holding to ashes.

Much later, the Beveridge Brothers, Jack and Sid, bushmen and cattlemen took over the property, erected a timber house and ran cattle on the Upper Buckland and the Barry Mountains between Mts Selwyn and Murray. The 1939 bushfires swept through the area and again the property was devastated.

Jack and Sid returned after the fires, built a hut on the Upper Buckland flats and another one, a tiny log structure in the central saddle between the two peaks of Mt Selwyn. They used a third hut, tucked away in a gully in the shadow of Mt Murray and thus had their roughly triangular shaped run serviced with a hut on each corner.

Access to their run was normally via the Buckland Valley road from near Porepunkah, but an alternative pack route led in from Harrietville, across a 4000 ft grassy saddle on the Ovens—Buckland divide, to drop down through a grove of snow gums until the Beveridge flats came into view. A third track leaves the valley below the old Buckland Cemetery where the pioneers James Morgan and his wife, Alec Goldie and others lie buried. Then near Brookside, a hamlet on Devil's Creek, it leads back over the hills to Wandiligong.

> *BEVERIDGE HUT*
> *Tall gums and wattles screen the steep flanking spurs and form a leafy canopy over mossy green banks almost devoid of scrub. The Beveridge Hut makes an excellent starting point for the final assault on the Barrys.*

> CLYDE GRANT 1949

Beveridge's Hut and Flats, Upper Buckland Valley.

A gravestone in the Goldie family plot at the Buckland Cemetery. Goldie, a pioneer cattleman, discovered the Goldie's Spur route from the Buckland valley to Mt Buffalo

The Upper Buckland Valley.

Bogong Jack's Hut, believed by many to have been used by the cattle duffer, was, in fact built after World War I.

"Bogong" Jack

A NEBULOUS, WILL O' THE WISP CHARACTER who appeared and disappeared at infrequent intervals in the pubs and saleyards of the towns surrounding the alpine regions of North Eastern Victoria in the 1850s is remembered under the name of Bogong Jack, and remembered mainly because a mountain hut, located on the Fainter Spur, which splits the headwaters of the Kiewa River, bore his name.

Bogong Jack's Hut was situated mid-way along the 24-mile cattle route between Maddison's and Wallaces' Hut and was believed to have withstood the ravages of time for almost a century. Unless it had been there to shelter mountain cattlemen and bush-walkers and have its name recorded on their maps, there is little reason to suppose that the man whose pseudonym it bore would be remembered today.

However, Bogong Jack's Hut that bushwalkers of the 1920s, 1930s and later knew was actually built after the 1914-18 War to replace an earlier hut on the same site, which had been destroyed by fire in 1914. Mr Syd Ryder, a well known cattleman of the area, was a member of the construction team and split the roof shingles and chimney palings from Woollybutt timber obtained in the valley below the hutsite. Bogong Jack had departed the scene some sixty years before the hut which bore his name was built! However, maybe Bogong Jack had sometime used the original cattlemen's hut, but there is no evidence and little logic to suppose that he built it.

For a cattle duffer seeking seclusion for his supposedly mysterious comings and goings with stolen cattle, across the Victorian Alps, would he have erected his hide-away home in as prominent position as the Fainter Spur, on a direct route from the Kiewa valley to the Bogong High Plains?

Little is known, but much has been written about the man whose only positive record is contained in police reports of the time, in which documents he is named as John Payne, alias John Paynter. Stories passed down from pioneer cattle families of the Omeo district suggest that John Payne, an Englishman with a good education arrived at Port Albert from Melbourne in the early 1850s and became a drover. Employed by Mr Edward Crooke, whose properties in the years between 1841 and 1859 included *Hinno Mungy, Benambra, Holey Plains, Bindi, Tongeomungie* and *Lucknow,* totalled 101,300 acres and were spread from present day Benambra, through Omeo and the head of the Tambo River to Rosedale and Bairnsdale. Payne, we are told, made droving trips with the EC branded cattle between Crookes various properties and Port Albert, using a track followed by bullock teams that brought supplies from the port to the inland cattle stations and the goldmines. Payne, most likely, also drove cattle for slaughter at the Omeo goldfields.

He worked with other drovers and soon learned to match their ability in bushcraft and horsemanship. Between them, they devised a means, perhaps not so uncommon at that time, of increasing their earnings. The isolation and extent of the cattle runs and the presence of 'clean-skins' running with the older EC branded cattle afforded opportunities for the drovers to by-pass the head station with its book-keeper and tally sheets, with a portion of the mobs they mustered for droving to their ultimate destinations. The un-tallied ECs and the cleanskins could then be disposed of in other markets. The year was 1856.

Whether discovery or fear of discovery of their nefarious activities prompted them to forsake their droving employment is purely a matter of conjecture, but as indicated later, Mr Edward Crooke had his suspicions.

Stories indicate that the drovers widened the area and scope of their activities by pioneering routes from Gippsland across the alps into north eastern Victoria and after stealing cattle in Gippsland, drove them to the headwaters of the Dargo River and from here drop down over the divide into the Buckland, Buffalo and King river valleys, to reach the lucerative markets at Wangaratta, the goldfields of Beechworth and the Buckland Valley, areas containing , at that time, upwards of 30,000 meat hungry miners, where butchers were not over inquisitive about brands or the origins of the cattle. Eric Harding, in his book 'Bogong Jack' would have us believe that the gang built a hut near the head of the Dargo River, as a headquarters and staging point for their journeys to and from the North East and Gippsland, but there is no evidence to suggest that such a hut ever existed.

Additional routes open to the gang were the Ovens Valley which could be entered a few miles above the Dargo headwaters and which led to the gold fields at Morse's Creek and Growler's Creek (now Bright and Wandiligong), and the one which has been the main reason for Bogong Jack's name being remembered - the way across the Bogong High Plains (pioneered only a few years previously by George Gray's stockmen, Brown and Wells), to the Fainter Spur and thence to the Kiewa Valley. It was on the Fainter Spur that the two huts, which between them stood in good condition for almost a hundred years, serving the needs of cattlemen and bush-walker, were built. The second hut certainly and the first one probably bore the name Bogong Jack's.

Lifting cattle from the Gippsland runs and droving them to a holding area, they had a number of possible routes into the North-East and it has been suggested that in preference to making the return trips empty handed, they stole North Eastern cattle for sale in Gippsland! There is reason to believe, also that they engaged in legitimate dealing - buying and selling in the market towns as a cover for their less commendable activities. They could then openly frequent the local pubs and saleyards and listen for talk of possible police suspicion and activity.

The story goes that the gang turned to the more profitable vocation of horse stealing, following the same pattern of selecting well-bred stock from Gippsland runs for sale in the North East, and vice versa. Horse stealing, however, was considered a much more serious crime than cattle duffing, many people considered that until a station owner had branded his clean-skins, they were running "free". However, the continuing reports of losses to horse thieves spurred the police to action and eventually suspicion fell on John Payne and his friends.

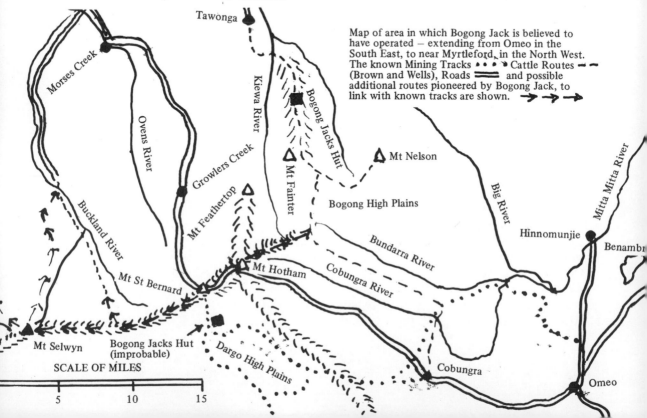

Map of area in which Bogong Jack is believed to have operated — extending from Omeo in the South East, to near Myrtleford, in the North West. The known Mining Tracks • • • Cattle Routes — — (Brown and Wells), Roads ═══ and possible additional routes pioneered by Bogong Jack, to link with known tracks are shown. → → →

A Livingstone Creek Police Station report of the 12th October, 1858 now in the Archives of LaTrobe Library tells that Constable Fane of that station followed John Payne for more than a month through Pendergast's Station, Benambra, across Gibbo Creek, Wheelers River, Whiteheads', Wilsons' and Days' stations to Table Top, Wagga Wagga, Albury, and back via the Mitta Mitta, a ride of about 700 miles, but a fruitless one, for no information of value was obtained.

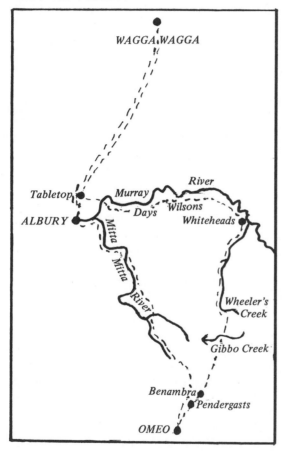

It was not long, however, before John Payne again attracted police attention. Early Gippsland records show that on 3rd January, 1859, a gold escort with 1500 ounces of gold left Omeo for Sale, en route to Melbourne. The party consisted of Cornelius Green, a gold buyer of Omeo, Miss Mutter, to whom the buyer was engaged to be married, and Constable Greene, a police escort. Before leaving, Cornelius Green was visited by two friends, Chamberlain, who was a butcher in Omeo, and an undesirable named Armstrong, who was a deserter from the 40th Regiment. They stayed the night, and Cornelius, who was on good terms with Chamberlain requested Armstrong, an expert with guns, to clean and load his revolver.

Next day, as the escort party of three was coming down Omeo Gap, Chamberlain, Armstrong and a lad named Penny, who was a servant to Cornelius Green, met and pleasantly greeted the party. That evening the entire party stopped at the Old Tambo Inn of Alan Burns, at Tongio, and the next morning set off for Mr Dicken's store at Swift's Creek, after they had been joined by the storekeeper. The pack-horse which was carrying the gold belonged to Mr Dickers and was now nearing its home.

When the party was about a mile from Dicken's store, two shots rang out from behind trees, and Cornelius Green, the buyer, was wounded in the neck and fell from his horse. Further firing continued and Constable Greene, wounded in both arms, fell from his horse, but managed to retain hold of the reins, remounted and galloped back to the Tambo Hotel to seek assistance. Dickens, wounded in the back, dragged and carried the fainting Miss Mutter to the creek, and safety. There they saw John Paynter holding three horses. In the confusion, the pack-horse with the gold galloped on to its stable, and the outlaws lost the prize.

As the wounded Cornelius Green lay on the ground, he recognised Chamberlain approaching, and despite his pitiful pleadings, he was brutally killed when his skull was crushed by blows from a tomahawk. Later, Green's revolver, which his 'friends' had earlier cleaned and loaded, was found nearby. It had been loaded with dummy cartridges!

Site of hold-up of gold escort, January 1859.

A day or so later, Tom Toke, a storekeeper on the Gibb River about 30 miles from Omeo brought in a letter from the wanted men for John Paynter, demanding money to assist in their escape into New South Wales. Paynter read the letter and handed it back to Toke, saying he would have nothing to do with it, and telling Toke to take it to the police.

Toke returned to his store and sent a native boy with a message telling the police the wanted men were in his area. Chamberlain and Armstrong left the district but were followed and eventually apprehended by the police.

Chamberlain and Armstrong, charged with murder, were tried in Melbourne and on June 30th 1859, were found 'Not Guilty'. Paynter and Penny who had been apprehended and charged as accessories, were released following the acquittal of Chamberlain and Armstrong. A public outcry ensued, however, and Chamberlain and Armstrong were then charged with

BOGONG JACK'S HUT
The last of a probable three huts on this site, midway between Tawonga
and Cope Hut, along the Fainter Spur. A 1937 photo shows the hut
with a dusting of early winter snow.

shooting at the police with intent to kill. They were found guilty and condemned to death. They were executed on 12th July, 1859.

Public opinion in looking for a motive apart from the gold, was that Chamberlain, who was much attached to Miss Mutter, acted out of sheer jealousy of Green.

John Paynter had once again escaped without a conviction against his name!

A few months later, in September, Paynter was back in the Beechworth area. The Police Gazette No 26, dated 3rd November, 1859 carried the following: "A Warrant for the arrest of John Payne, alias Paynter, has been issued at Beechworth in which he is charged with stealing a brown filly, the property of Robert Gregory , Allen's Flat, Yackandandah, on 15th September last. Description of Payne, age about 30 years, 6 ft. high, fresh complexion, dark hair, rather thin on top of head, a large aqualine nose, stoops slightly, but is otherwise a well made man and a butcher by trade. The filly was seen in Payne's possession on the road to Omeo with JC newly branded on near shoulder." A description of the filly followed. It is noteworthy that the warrant contained the only description of Payne we have and also listed his trade as that of 'butcher'. It is interesting to note that there is a butcher's shop in Omeo, still bearing the name Payne on the window.

John Payne was arrested in Omeo on 15th November 1859 and the following report of his apprehension was despatched to Melbourne by Police Inspector Hill:

301

BOGONG JACK'S HUT
In excellent condition when photographed by Cleve Cole in about 1935.

John Payne alias Paynter charged with horse stealing at Yackandandah in September last was this day apprehended here and remanded to Beechworth to be further dealt with. Stolen horse has not been recovered and has probably been disposed of by him at Snowy Creek or some other place on the Omeo route as he did not make his appearance here with the animal. I have communicated with Supt. Boothby on this subject.

(Sgd.) Henry Hill,
Inspector.

The *Beechworth Constitution* of 7th December 1859 reported that in the Beechworth Court that day John Paynter faced a charge of horse stealing. As the prosecution were unable to produce either the witness or the horse, the Magistrate dismissed the charge.

Discretion, from this point onwards, appears to have been the better part of valour, for John Payne, alias Paynter received no further police mention. He was believed to have retired to his hut on the Fainter Spur.

It is fitting that this will o' the wisp figure who appeared in the Gippsland district without any antecedents, punctuated his allegedly nefarious activities with comings and goings across hitherto largely unexplored and untravelled spurs and valleys of Victoria's alpine regions, most likely pioneering some routes from Gippsland to the North East, should have the curtain lowered in a manner as uncertain and mysterious as any of his former exploits had been.

A stockman riding the Fainter Spur stopped one evening at Bogong Jack's hut and shared the night with an uncommunicative occupant, who merely gave his name as 'John'. The stockman had never met John Payne, but he believed that his companion at the hut fitted Payne's description.

The late Walter Maddison, veteran cattleman of Tawonga, has stated that the stockman was John Eyers from Tawonga. However, the late Mrs W. A. Pendergast, a member of Victoria's oldest surviving mountain cattle family, was equally certain that the travellers name was Paddy Hekir of Omeo. She quoted as her authority two Omeo identities, centenarians Michael McNamera and James Madden, who each recalled their respective fathers giving this information to them when they were boys!

A descendant of John Eyre, currently living in the Kiewa valley, recalls that the family believes that John Eyre spent the winter in company with Bogong Jack, living in the hut and spending the days prospecting for gold. John Eyre may well have returned to the Kiewa valley before Bogong Jack's disappearance and Paddy Hekir may have been the last solitary traveller to have spent a night with Jack.

So, was it John Eyers of Tawonga or was it Paddy Hekir who was Bogong Jack's last known companion? Last known companion, because after the visitor's night at the hut, John Payne was never seen again. Nor was his body ever discovered. He had disappeared as effectively as on many previous occasions he had when mountain mists had descended blotting from sight the mysterious horseman and the cattle he was droving. But this time, he was not to re-appear. Rumors persisted. Had he met with an accident in the bush and died a lonely death? Had he been murdered at his bush hut and his body hidden by someone in search of possible savings he had hidden in the hut. Or, had John Payne, alias Paynter, alias Bogong Jack, unquestionably a fine horseman, a capable bushman, simply decided it was time to pack his saddle bag, mount his horse, cast one backward glance at the mountain country that he had made his own - and ride away, to seek 'fresh fields and pastures new' in a part of the country where he was unknown.

Bogong Jack's Huts are no more. The first survived for more than fifty years before fire claimed it, and the second for forty odd years until it was allowed to disintergrate into a heap of ruins in the early 1960s, but the name of Bogong Jack has survived only because it was associated with two mountain shelters that he never build and never owned. The police records quoted are the only written evidence of John Payne's presence in the district All else is based on snatches of folk lore and the almost legendary reminiscences of the early residents. Edward Crooke's descendants, still living in the area, recall that John Payne was suspected of stealing cattle from the Crooke properties. Edward Crooke was known to the Pendergasts. They purchased his Benambra Station in 1858 and it is largely Pendergast family recollections supported by the memories of Walter Maddison and others that provide what little is known of a drover turned cattle duffer, a 'bushranger' without a single police conviction against his name, a horseman, bushman, explorer who left no records of his exploits. But almost as effectively as the written word, a lonely mountain hut which bore his name invested the memory of Bogong Jack with a charisma that will live on.

The linking of the name of John Payne with that of Bogong Jack, which connection Eric Harding believed to have been missing came from the Pendergast family. Mrs W.A.Pendergast, again relying on the memories of Michael McNamera and James Madden, asserted that at the time of his escapades, John Payne was also known as Bogong Jack. This fact was also known to W. F. (Bill) Waters, doyen bushwalker and friend of the Pendergasts, in the late 1920s and 30s.

Amongst the reminiscences of Mrs Jane Vince Pendergast, is the story of several residents who quietly mustered in Murphy's Forest, a number of cows with unbranded calves, belonging to other residents. They intended to put their own brands on the calves that night in moonlight, but when they returned with all necessary branding irons, etc., they found the calves had already been freshly branded! They had been forestalled by a smarter gang.

John Paynter, who lived at the Limestone at the time, had an excellent supply of branding numbers and letters, and was an adept at changing the brands of stolen cattle. Also, she claims, he could alter the complete appearance of a horse with the use of dyes and bleaches. For these horses he found a ready sale in Gippsland and elsewhere.

Bogong Jack

THE BOGONG SPRINGS

They named the spot "The Bogong Springs" the bushman's crown of praise,
    A name that back to memory brings the cattle duffing days,
The name recalls a welcome stage along the bridle track,
    Where fate has written on the page the name of "Bogong Jack".
They nestle in the "Fainter Range" beneath the Great Divide,
    Amidst a silence lone and strange down on the "Kiewa" side,
And trickling from the mountain's heart in limpid, silver streams,
    Leap through the ti-trees with a dart into a vale of dreams.

Where Nature prodigal of mood bestowed her favours there,
    For native beauty wild and rude runs riot everywhere,
A lonely land where tracks but lead to end in converts wide,
    A spot wherein the "Fates" decreed a hunted thing to hide.
'Twas there the cattle stealers met away back in the past,
    'Ere law and order wove the net that landed them at last,
The social outcast of the land the harrassed human hare,
    Fled to these haunts when shunned and banned and found a refuge there.

The leader of the lawless gang the arch knave of the pack,
    Whose misdeeds through the ranges rang was hailed as "Bogong Jack".
To none was told his history, none knew his rightful name,
    While shrouded too in mystery from where and whence he came,
Yet well 'twas known about their Chief as though 'twas carved in stone,
    His prowess as a daring thief was to the bush winds thrown,
Was there some deed devoid of clue, some theft of special brand,
    The troopers as by instinct knew and regognised the hand.

They followed him by day and night from down at "Twofold Bay",
    And vowed to shoot him down on sight up "Kosciusko" way,
While oft from "Monaro" side he rode with bated breath,
    In many a reckless midnight ride while hand in hand with death,
The troopers oft times called a halt and groaned in their defeat,
    The trackers found themselves at fault and owned to being beat,
For they who hoped the prize to claim and victory seemed so near,
    From out the far off ranges came a wild derisive cheer.

But cunning though the wild dog be and light of foot and fast,
    The law of life ordains that he shall meet his match at last,
And since 'twas war unto the knife since fate her web had spun,
    There came a time in "Bogong's" life when law and order won,
'Tis told of how he fought and ran upon that fateful day,
    Then stood outwitted man to man a dingo brought to bay,
And thus he bade a long farewell to "Bogong's" purling streams,
    That maybe in his prison cell ran rippling through his dreams.

A hunted man will rove the earth unto its furthest plane,
*   And flee the land that gave him birth but to return again,*
Then pity such however wild for sad indeed his lot,
*   When from his country's laws exiled and by his friends forgot,*
And so it was with "Bogong Jack" when freed from prison bars,
*   He sought again the mountain track the silver streams and stars,*
Where there at least with saving grace to face the worst alone,
*   He found at last a resting place unhonoured and unknown.*

By W. Wye.

BOGONG JACK'S HUT
The ruins of the 1919 built hut, in 1962.   An earlier Bogong Jack's
was burnt in 1914.

A small creek flowing past the hut at the Limestone is still known as Paynter's Creek, and about a mile downstream there is a small river flat, where the rotting posts and rails of a strong yard have almost disappeared; the name of Paynter's yard still clings.

Among the many uncertainties that surround the life and times of Bogong Jack, one thing is certain. We shall never know.

The Barkly-
Macalister

LICOLA, little more than a spot on the map, was a key junction for early cattlemen droving their mobs into the mountains. Strategically placed at the confluence of Target Creek and the Macalister River, the cattle routes here diverged to Glencairn, to Tamboritha and the Bennison Plains, and to the Wellington River track (Riggall route) to Mt Wellington.

A simplification of the map shows a horseshoe or inverted J shaped mountain range commencing at Mt Selma and leading via Mts Skene, MacDonald and Clear to Mt Howitt (a section of the Great Divide). From Mt Howitt, the right hand side of the horseshoe runs across Howitt, Snowy and Bennison Plains (why not High Plains?) to Mts Reynard and Tamboritha. Within the horseshoe the Macalister River and its main tributaries the Barkly and Caledonia flow down from the periphery with the confluence of all three a little above Licola.

Along the Great Divide from Mts Selma to Clear there are numerous small snowplains, the largest being Connor's Plain and the flat-topped Summit area of Skene and these areas have been grazed by cattle belonging to Mitchell and Hoskin (from the Jamieson side) and the Rumpff brothers from Seaton.

Within the horseshoe, much of the grazing was on grassy forested areas as well as the Glencairn and Barkly river flats. Prominent names among the pioneer families were Fullarton, Sweetapple and Williamson.

The way to Tamboritha from Licola was up the Wellington River and Dinner Creek to Bennison Spur and Tamboritha Saddle. This was the gateway to the finest stretch of snow plains in the State, extending northward across the lush Bennison and Snowy Plains and broken only by a short narrow spur (The Bastard's Neck) before continuing on to Howitt Plains.

Lands Department records indicate that the first holder of the Glencairn run was Caleb Anderson, 22nd August, 1866, although nothing more than this brief entry is known of him. Another early holder was Edward Riggall of Glenfalloch, in 1878.

Another source suggests that Glencairn, another run, Ficary and Mt Wellington were all taken up in 1857. However some of these early dates are difficult to confirm and the run holders did not register.

FULLARTON

Robert Fullarton, (great grandfather of Norman Chester) and his brother David took up land after being recommended by Malcolm Macfarlane. Robert selected Glenmaggie and David chose Glencairn.

Glencairn, on a creek of the same name, is a lush river flat that is believed to have been on the original course of the Macalister River. Geographically it became the half-way stage between Crooked River and Matlock diggings and David Fullarton grew vegetables and fattened pigs for bacon, which he packed on horse teams across to Woods Point for sale to the miners.

He left the junction of Glencairn Creek and the Barkly River and then climbed out along a spur which bears his name, to reach the main divide. His track climbed through a barrier of rocky outcrops, through the "Toll Gate" and over Spring Hill to Mts Skene and Singleton before reaching Matlock and Woods Point. The route became part of the Moroka Track which linked the Jordan and Crooked River diggings.

Fullarton provided travellers going to and from the diggings with an overnight refuge and he made a charge of 5/- a feed for horses. They were supplied with "chaff" which was hand cut on a chopping block, using a broad axe!

Fullarton is credited with having introduced pigs to Gippsland — to the regret of a certain pack-horse. The story goes that Fullarton's pack-horse was loaded with a huge sow securely strapped in a wooden box on one side and a second box carried the litter on the other. Fullarton underestimated the time required for the overloaded pack-horse to cover the distance to Heyfield and he was forced to camp half-way on the first night. Fullarton, alone, was unable to unload and re-load the sow, so the unfortunate packhorse was obliged to spend the night, standing tethered to a tree.

The old iron hut at Licolo, of unknown origin, was used by cattlemen who passed that way en route to Glencairn or the Bennison Plains.

The old Moroka track showing two blazes made by the McMillan Expedition. 1927 photo.

Robert Fullarton's original bark roofed house at Glenmaggie. Reproduced from an oil painting in the possession of his great-grandson Norman Chester.

All that remains to mark the site of David Fullarton's hut near the foot of Fullarton's Spur.

SWEETAPPLE

William Henry Sweetapple selected property in the valley in the 1870s and had two sons, Charlie and William, by his first wife. His second wife, Stephanie, a French girl, was a governess. She had no children and died on 23rd February, 1902, at the age of 72 years.

Sweetapple began grazing cattle on the Bull Plain run in 1879 and 101 years later his great-grandson Ron (Ike) Sweetapple still carries on the family tradition.

Sweetapple was also the registered leaseholder of the Dargo High Plains in 1870, but he relinquished this in favour of Glencairn.

Charlie and his wife Wilhelmina ("Minnie") were well known for their hospitality to bushwalkers of the 1920s. Mrs Sweetapple was a cat-lover and "Bill" Waters once counted twenty-six of her felines. Doubtless there were a few more that escaped his notice.

Charlie's two sons, Bert and Harry were the third generation and they ran up to 13,000 wethers on the Bull Plain Paddock area and the Sheepyard which lay between the Barkly and the Macalister on a spur running down from the Nobs. As mentioned above, Ron (Charlie's son) maintains the sheep and cattle property in the verdant valley could be anybody's idea of "Shangri La". In about 1942-3 George Barraclough and Ron Sweetapple took over the Connors Plains, Spring Hill run from George Gregory. Barraclough had the Jamieson side almost down to Jamieson and Sweetapple the Barkly fall.

The original Sweetapple home at Glencairn.

Charlie and Minnie Sweetapple (seated)
with their sons Bert and Charlie (standing).

William Sweetapple (son of William Henry).

Barkly River crossing.   Charlie (son of
William Henry) on white horse.

Harry Sweetapple, son of Charlie and uncle
of Ron (Ike).

HOSKIN

George Hoskin and his brother Robert, from Jamieson, took over a small selection and isolated homestead on Mitchell's Creek, a tributary of the Jamieson River, from an earlier settler, Mitchell, in the early 1900s.

The property was accessible, only by pack-horse, along the old mining track up the Jamieson, and was located about 20 miles from Jamieson township. The brothers operated the property as a small mixed farm. They also grazed cattle in the forest country around the homestead, to the heads of the Jamieson, and on snow leases from the head of Sunday Spur to Mt Skene and beyond to Connors Plain and Spring Hill.

They build several huts and in each instance they selected the wettest possible location, believing, quite correctly, that such spots would be safest in the event of bushfires. One hut, in a gully just off Sunday Spur, and about half way down, was difficult to find, and few bushwalkers were aware of its existence. A second hut was located near the junction of Middle Ridge

312

and the Divide, that was later to become known as Rumpff's Saddle. Like their other huts, it was a log cabin with bark roof and was already in ruins when Eddie and I passed that way in 1936.

Further along, at Frogs' Hollow, where Mt Skene joins the Divide, Hoskins built a third hut., and on this one the bark roof had been replaced with iron before 1936. It was the smallest hut in which I have slept, the shelf bunk occupying the full width and two thirds of the length of the floor space.. With a later change in run holders, the latter two huts became known as Rumpff's.

George Hoskin accompanied Cleve Cole to the Frogs' Hollow Hut in the Winter of 1935, when Cleve did a reconnaisance of Mt Skene's skiing potential. Today, the hut, over 60 years old, is still standing but is in need of some structural repairs. The other old Hoskin huts are beyond repair.

George was noted for his habit of riding up to the head of Sunday Spur, and then, after removing the bridle., turning his mount loose to find its own way home. The small rocks which covered the ground around Skene were hard on mounted horses feet, and George believed that with the assistance of dogs, he could drive his cattle as well on foot!

The home at Mitchell's Creek, with its pine trees and apple orchard, was vacated in about 1913, when the Hoskins moved down to Jamieson to live. They entered into a cattle dealing partnership with Richard Dale, a keen cattle dealer, and used the old homestead only as a base from which to control their cattle grazing.

Hoskin relinquished most of the runs in 1929, when they were taken over by the Rumpff brothers.

George Hoskin outside Rumpff's hut near Mt Skene. George had accompanied Cleve Cole to the hut in 1935 when Cleve became the first to ski on Mt Skene.

The old Hoskin homestead on Mitchell's Creek, 20 miles by pack-track from Jamieson.

RUMPFFS

The Rumpffs worked out of Seaton, where Rumpff's Hotel was a landmark. They originally used 16 horse pack teams to transport stores into the goldfields. The severe winters never deterred them and it was not uncommon for Joe Rumpff to arrive in Walhalla with hands frozen, unable to unbuckle the straps on his pack-team.

On a prospecting trip they camped near Mt Skene and saw some of Hoskin's cattle which were grazing there. They remarked on their splendid condition and when Hoskin retired in 1929 Arthur Henry Anton, Richard Juer ("Joe") and Alfred James August Rumpff of Seaton who had taken out the Spring Hill lease on 1921, took over the remaining Hoskin holdings across Connors Plains and Mt Skene. They relinquished their runs in the 1940s. Fred and Eric Grimes from Heyfield had run cattle in part of the area before the Rumpffs took over.

Amongst cattlemen, whose care of their dogs is legendary, the Rumpffs stood out. They always fed their dogs before they ate themselves, and if food was running short, the Rumpff dogs got full rations. But, they were noted for travelling fast with their cattle. They would drive a mob from

Glenmaggie to Skene in 2 days (50 miles) and were known to bring cattle down from Skene to Gleesons Bridge (45 miles and usually a two day trip for them) in one day! With George Barraclough they drove from Primrose Gap to Rosedale (53 miles) in 2 days, from Seaton to Primrose Gap (40 miles) in one day and one day from Primrose Gap to Mt Skene (23 miles). With Ron "Ike" Sweetapple they rode from Primrose Gap and then returned with cattle the same day (46 miles)!

When snowbound in the Skene Hut for 2–3 weeks they lived on a bag of flour. It was their habit to carry a leg or shoulder of bacon into the bush, hanging it in a tree and using it as required. In the 1950s Art, unaware that the curing process had been altered, took the customary bacon and almost died as a result of food poisoning. He wrote to the bacon company and received the reply "We cure bacon for eating not keeping!"

The Rumpff's Hut at Riggalls Gap (Primrose Gap) was accidentally burnt down by George Gregory in 1938 and the resulting bushfire, although not serious, cleared the bush and was the means of saving the area from the holocaust of 1939.

With the approach of the 1939 fires police asked George Barraclough to go up to Glencairn and assist in bringing Mrs Sweetapple out to safety. Mrs Sweetapple, however, was convinced that the safest place was in the Glencairn valley and she refused to leave. Her assessment of the situation proved correct. The clearing done by the 1938 fire left little to sustain the 1939 blaze and the Glencairn valley suffered little damage.

On their retirement, the Rumpffs' runs were taken over by Ernie Hugg.

Rumpff's Hut (originally Hoskins) near the junction of Middle Ridge and the Great Divide (in ruins in the 1930s).

315

Eddie at Rumpff's Middle Ridge hut when we passed on our way to Skene in 1936.

Rumpff's Hut at Frog's Hollow, just off the Divide at the foot of Mt Skene.

Two views of Rumpff's Hut at Frog's Hollow.   The hut is still standing, although in need of repair.

GREGORYS

George Gregory was one of the younger generation of cattlemen in the mid 30s. He was born at Gaffney's Creek and had spent the first thirty years of his life in the high country of northern Gippsland. We first met him at Christmas '36, about 180 miles out from Harrietville and after a sweltering day's trudge up the dusty Licola-Glencairn track, throats parched, he greeted us at his home.

Glencairn, on Glencairn Creek, a tributary of the Barclay was little more than a name on the map in those days and its inhabitants were the pioneer Sweetapple family, the Higgins, Williamsons and Gregorys.

George met us at the door. "It's been a dry summer", he apologised. "We're almost out of water, the creek's stopped running. Will you settle for a beer?" George's beer, however didn't have the familiar label. He produced four bottles of varying shapes, corks securely held with string over and around the neck of the

George Gregory

bottle. It was our introduction to George Gregory's special — home brew ginger beer, prepared from George's ginger-beer plant culture.

"You've got to be quick", said George, handing us enamel mugs. "Cut the string" - and his cork hit the ceiling, half the ginger beer followed it and quickly upending the bottle, George managed to get the remainder of the contents into his mug. "Try it", he said, and we did, with no better success. George had perfected, without realising it, the perfect, economical hand-size fire extinguisher.

Glencairn is situated some 50 miles from the railhead at Heyfield and the nearest supplies, in a valley surrounded by great mountains - Skene, McDonald, Shillinglaw, The Crinoline, Wellington, and Gregory's cattle grazed the poorly grassed approaches to Mt McDonald and the small river flats along the Barclay, as well as such locations as he could find further afield. For a period he held the Connors Plains — Spring Hill run.

But George knew the country far beyond his leases and packed in fishermen and bushwalking parties to remote sites. A day's ride to Woods Point, across a rugged trail that crossed the Great Divide was not unusual for this horseman, who had also grazed a few cattle as far afield as Matlock.

With his young wife, herself a splendid horsewoman and three young children (who later accounted for 60 per cent of the local school enrolment), George lived in a small home that I believe he built himself. Two rooms and a kitchen, sapling frame, clad in bush materials, lined with hessian to which was applied annually a fresh wall-papering of newspapers. After the dry summer heat had tightened and cracked the corners and George's 'brew' had left a few stains, it was time for re-papering in the Fall. Year by year, the walls acquired added layers and stiffening.

On one occasion George was driving Mrs Sweetapple to Licola. As the pony was straining at a shallow ford at Glencairn Creek (one of half a dozen crossings) the harness broke, the shafts tipped upwards, the gig tilted back and Mrs Sweetapple and George were deposited in the water.

George's meagre holding did not yield him the prosperity he deserved, and some years later he left the valley. Not, however, before he had made many friends among the fishermen and bushwalkers who passed his way.

Car Reeves bought the Gregory property and later his son-in-law Bob Elliot lived there.

George Gregory, regrettably, was run down and killed by a car, when walking home along the road one evening.

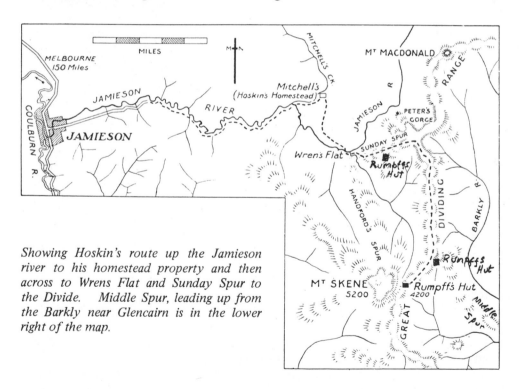

Showing Hoskin's route up the Jamieson river to his homestead property and then across to Wrens Flat and Sunday Spur to the Divide. Middle Spur, leading up from the Barkly near Glencairn is in the lower right of the map.

Norman Chester

NORMAN CHESTER

Norman Chester, of Heyfield, joined the firm of Shaw Logan, stock and station agents, in 1918 and obtained his auctioneer's licence in July 1922. He is still actively engaged in the business (now Dalgety Ltd) and his 58 years service makes him the longest licence holder in the records of the Institute.

Norman's maternal grandmother married Robert Fullarton who selected Glenmaggie on the recommendation of Malcolm Macfarlane. He first went into the bush, as a boy, with his father, Harry Chester.

The old log hut on Tamboritha was standing then, and Norman recalls camping in it in 1914. Harry Chester was a partner with Michael Higgins snr. in the Tamboritha run about 1910.

Norman too up a lease of country beyond Glencairn and running up to Mt Clear, with his cousin Merton, in the Depression years of 1928-29. Later he took a half share with Jimmy Kelly in the Holmes Plain run and he acquired the whole run following Jimmy's death.

Mick Higgins snr. left his freehold 640 acre Bennison Plains paddock to his four sons. Tom sold his share to Patrick, who later sold the half holding to Norman Chester. Today, Norman shares ownership with Kevin Higgins (¼) and the Higgins family (¼).

Dick Chester, one of Norm's three sons, manages the mountain runs and his two brothers are following their father's chosen profession as auctioneers one in Victoria and the other in New South Wales.

Norman Chester is "Mr Cattleman" in the Heyfield district, the most knowledgaeable and respected member of the cattle industry.

MOUNTAIN ASH HUT

Norman Chester's Hut on Mountain Ash Spur, Barkly River area.

GEORGE BARRACLOUGH

George Barraclough, who had formerly been a rabbit trapper, settled near Primrose Gap on the Licola - Glencairn road in 1938. Primrose Gap had earlier been known as Riggall's Gap, but its original name was Primrose Gap, so named after a flower that abounded there. It was not a primrose but had a similar appearance! From his home property George commenced running a few cattle and in 1942 -43, as mentioned earlier, he joined with Ron Sweetapple in taking over the Rumpffs' runs when they finally moved out.

George's access route to his runs was up the Middle Spur to the head of Sunday Spur and across the Barkly and up Fullarton's Spur to Connor's Plain and Spring Hill. These were summer routes only, as the winter flow of the Barkly made crossings dangerous.

George married in 1948 and he passed his great interest in local history to his daughter Linda and his son Ralph. The Hunters in 1841 failed in an attempt to find a way from their run on the Delatite into Gippsland. In 1844 they tried again and successfully reached Gippsland going by way of the Howqua, Mitchell's Creek, Sunday Spur, the Divide past Skene and across the Barkly to the site of Glencairn and past the present day Licola.

They had found a route, but did not select land along the way. Possibly Maurice Meyrick who held Glenfalloch B in 1846 and Tabberabbera in 1847 was the first settler in the area George Barraclough held a century later. But he was not to hold it for long. Maurice Meyrick was drowned in the Thompson River at Heyfield in 1848.

George Barraclough had a keen interest in this area in which he lived for forty years. He died of a heart attack in early 1980, and although his family have moved away, they too, retain a keen interest in the area in which they were born.

THE OLD POST YARD (above) on the Licola road is believed to date back to Maurice Meyrick. Variously believed to have been a stockyard as a defence against natives, or a sheep yard for protection against dindos, it is constructed of logs simply standing upright on the ground. Divided into two sections, it contains no shelter hut nor fireplace.

TABBERABBERA

(Left) We enter the extensive clearings of Tabberabbera and perceive the scattered abodes of the Webbsdale family, who comprise the community. Tabberabbera was first selected in 1847 by Maurice Meyrick. The name Tabberabbera appears on the earliest maps, but its origin is uncertain.
                                    C.W.GRANT 1963

Illustrated is the old Harrison homestead.

The Bennison Plains

RICHARD BENNISON, after whom the Bennison Plains were named, arrived from Van Dieman's Land some time before 1846. He occupied land known as "Bennison Farm" just north of Port Albert. At the Alberton Court House on 18th April, he acquired the licence of the Port Albert Inn from W.B.Howden.

This Inn was frequently used by shippers of cattle from Maffra and Sale districts who found the accommodation to be first rate. Mr Bennison sold the Inn to John Gellion on the 4th September, 1857. He moved to Sale where he had the licence for the "Carrier's Arms" in Foster Street.

In 1859 he built the Club Hotel in Foster Street, and on the 11th November of that year announced that he and a partner, Mr Douglas, would run a four-horse coach from Sale to Port Albert.

It is believed that Mr Bennison held a grazing lease on Mt Wellington from 1860 – 1869. An entry in the Receipt and Pay Office records on the 12th January, 1864, reads – R.Bennison, Mt Wellington, half year's rent £25.

He also held the Bennison Plains lease from 1861 – 1868. The Bennison-Snowy Plains are situated some 40 miles to the north of Heyfield, lying in the shadows of Mts Arbuckle, Tamboritha and Reynard.

The plains themselves, roughly 150 square miles in area, and 4,000 feet above sea level, with the higher points such as Mt Reynard reaching to 5,500 feet.

Cattle have been grazing on these plains and mountain slopes since about 1860, perhaps before. Malcolm McFarlane, the first occupier of "Glenfalloch" station from 1847 – 1868, Edward Riggall who purchased "Glenfalloch" from him, and Angus Shaw from Glenmaggie, all ran cattle at varying times in the area. Local landmarks such as McFarlane's Creek, Shaw's Creek, and Riggall's Spur are named after these early cattlemen.

Holme's Plain is named after two English gentlemen, successful miners before turning to cattle, Jimmy and Constantine, who apparently lived at Stratford and had the Eagle Vale run, registered to Constantine Shira Holmes 1869 — 1908 and to James Holmes 1908 — 1913. According to Kenneth Cox, author of "Angus McMillan, Pathfinder", Eagle Vale was the site of McMillan's former property. The Holmes brothers, with stockman Culhane, drove cattle up through the Crooked River, Wonnangatta and Moroka, to the plains. Constantine Holmes was an Avon Shire Councillor from 1893 — 1899, and a leading member of the local race club. The Holmes brothers had a hut situated over near Shaw's Creek, at the north-eastern portion of Holme's Plain, not far from the present Kelly's hut. This hut was in ruins in the 1920s, but some of the rock foundations of the chimney can still be seen today.

The old stockyard on Holmes' Plain.

HIGGINS

Michael Higgins Snr., from Crooked River took up the Bennison Plains run together with a 640 acre freehold in the mid 1890s, probably after the Holme brothers vacated it, and was assisted in the management of his run by son Patrick.

The old Tamboritha log hut was built by Mick Higgins Snr., who used it until it was burnt down.

A second Higgins' hut was also accidentally burnt in 1933. Rex Miller rode out one morning for Wonnangatta, and on his return the hut was gone! The present Higgins hut, is thus the third.

Following the death of Mrs Higgins, Jack, one of her four sons was reared by the Bryces at Wonnangatta.

The old log hut on Tamboritha, built by Mick Higgins, was possibly the finest log hut built anywhere on the High Plains. It was accidentally burnt, probably in the early 1920s.

TAMBORITHA HUT

A few miles upstream through snowgums – some of them lovely trees, others wierd and grotesque – is another little plain dappled with alpine daisies, buttercups and clover, and surrounded with sheltering timber. On one side is a well-built cattleman's hut. The temptation to laze away the afternoon cannot be overcome and so we stay.

J.SANSOM 1936

A group of cattlemen (unidentified) outside the old Tamboritha Hut. The bark roof is well past its prime.

A family wedding group which includes Mick Higgins jnr. (top left), Mick Higgins snr. (front left), Mary Higgins (nee Kelly), extreme left, and Mrs Peggy Higgins on extreme right.

Two views of the second Higgins Hut on Bennison Plains (burnt in 1933). Log construction with iron roof.

The third Higgins Hut on the Bennison Plains. Clad in iron, it is a little less picturesque than the earlier two.

Harry and Roy, with Kevin and Mick Higgins, at Higgins' Hut, in January 1937.

KELLY'S HUT

The Eagle Vale or Plains run was held for a while by J. Norton. However, after the end of the First World War, and with the introduction of the Soldier Settlement Scheme, Jimmy Kelly, a young returned serviceman, was granted the lease.

When Jimmy Kelly obtained the Holmes Plain lease in November 1920, he shared a hut with other cattlemen, McMichael, Higgins and Garvey. John McMichael was at early settler at Licola, with a property near Stony Creek Bridge. He had three sons, Billy who built McMichael's Hut, Alf and Arthur. All are now deceased. Pat Garvey, Jimmy Kelly's uncle, ran cattle in the Wellington area. Denny Connolly, whose name appears frequently, was a son of Denny Connolly Snr. who originally owned Connolly's Hotel at Dargo. This hostelry was the one acquired by Oliver Smith after he vacated Wonnagatta Station.

Jim Kelly outside Kelly's Hut on Holmes Plain, 1942.

Denny Connolly's old hotel at Dargo which was taken over by Oliver Smith after he left Wonnangatta Station.

The story is told of Denny Connolly Jnr., who was a fine bushman and a great rider, that on one occasion he accepted a ride on a buckjumper at Wirth's Circus. Ignoring the customary practice of riding for fifteen seconds and then dismounting (in order not to 'tame' a buckjumper), Denny rode his mount to a standstill and then shouted to the attendants "Bring me my bloody spurs, and I'll really make him buck".

After the hut (Higgins') was burnt down in 1933, Jimmy Kelly decided to build his own hut, the one now on Holmes' Plain. In the autumn of 1933, Denny Connolly and Charlie Howlett dismantled a two rail fence that ran from the site of the present hut down to Shaw's Creek. The slab type rails from the fence were used in the construction of the new hut which Connolly and Howlett built in January and February 1934. Most of the timber for the frame came from ti-tree cut near the present-day rails into McMichael's paddock.

Kevin Higgins, of "Glencourt", Glenmaggie, as a young lad gathered all the stone for the hut and dragged it to the site with a sledge and horse. He vividly recalls how he and Jimmy Kelly packed in on horses, the iron for the roof, hand saws, nails, axes and other necessary material to build the hut.

Some years later Jimmy Kelly and Dick Chester built a chaff and saddle shed extension for use as a store room.

This hut, along with all other cattlemen's huts, has been a welcome shelter to many an appreciative bushwalker and cattlemen over its 45 years of existence. One particularly grateful party, the author and two companions, reached the hut at dusk on a June day of 1936, during a winter crossing from Glenmaggie to Merrijig, by way of Mt Wellington and Mt Howitt!

Kelly's Hut on Holmes' Plain, photographed during a mid-winter trip in 1936.

Outside McMichael's Hut - Clarrie Gell, Eric Cumming and Fred Fitzpatrick.

This group includes (second from left to right) Norman Chester, Jack Kelly, Denny Connolly and Eric Cumming at Guy's Snowy Plains Hut, 1946 - 47.

The number of cattle grazing on these runs is strictly controlled by the Soil Conservation Authority. Since 1974 each run has been allocated a maximum stocking rate that cannot be exceeded. In adverse seasons, this stocking rate is reduced to suit the conditions. Stock in a normal season are allowed entry in the second week of November, and generally, must be out by early May. Cattle run on these leases are mainly dry cattle, bullocks, steers and speyed heifers, with some breeding cows.

The mobs are walked from Glenmaggie and Licola, two days to Licola and another two days from there to the plains. The last day of the trip can be most frustrating, cattle already tired are loth to "walk out", parts of the Bennison Spur being steep and rocky. Many a new chum has finally succumbed to bursts of profanity during the slow climb to the top.

After spending the summer in the mountains, the cattle are sold at the annual snow lease special held at Heyfield. This sale attracts fatteners from all over Victoria, there being few other sales that can supply bullocks and steers of such good quality and age.

Prior to 1963 when the Forestry road was officially opened, everything had to be taken to the plains by pack-horse. Careful planning and packing was a necessity, and a good, quiet pack-horse invaluable.

The sight of a wildly bucking pack-horse desperately endeavouring to unload his pack may have been spectacular at the time, but it didn't do much for the eggs, flour, sugar, tea and other essentials he was carrying.

During March, cattle are mustered from the runs, taken to the yards at Holme's Plain, and drafted into their various owners' earmarks.

MOROKA HUT

The typical cattlemen's log hut at
Moroka was built by Bill Gillio and
Andy Estoppey in 1946, helped by
the late Eric Bateson and Arch Timbs,
who had just returned from the war.
Bill Gillio was a renowned bushman,
a First World War soldier, and a great
axeman, and the Moroka Hut is a
monument to his skill.

*Bill Gillio leading pack-horse
over Mt Stirling in 1935.*

Andy Estoppey of "Bonnie Doon", Briagolong, at 83 years could be the
oldest cattleman still tending cattle and riding the bush, running cattle in
Moroka and Freestone Creek. For well over 60 years he has worked with
cattle in the mountains, with the Treasures of Dargo and Millers of
Wellington.

Remains can still be seen of the "Old Horse Yards" of mortised posts and
split rails on the Moroka flats. These were built by John Hubbard, who lived
at Crooked River - Wonnangatta Junction. He bred and ran horses on
Moroka and Mt Wellington. Wild horses which descended from Hubbards are
still seen in this area. He was known to trade horses in the mining days.

At present Jack Guy and D. Freeman run cattle on the Moroka country,
while Bob Dunsmuir and Kevin Higgins are in the Mt Wellington area.

MOROKA HUT
Andy Estoppey looks on while Jack Treasure splits firewood.

McNamaras

Michael Francis McNamara

*D*ENNIS McNAMARA came from Ireland and was one of the earliest settlers in Melbourne. He had five sons — Dennis, the eldest, who broke his neck and died at the age of sixteen after diving into the Yarra River and striking his head on a sandbank; Patrick, who remained in Melbourne; Jack, who settled in Cedgewa; Tom, who went to Cobungra and ran cattle on Dinner Plain with his brother Michael Francis. Michael Francis was born in Bourke Street, Melbourne in 1839. As a boy, he grazed the family cows at the top of Bourke Street, in the area now occupied by Parliament House.

Some would be inclined to say that the McNamaras made better use of the site than is now the case! Michael moved to the north-east to live in Wangaratta and there he became acquainted with the Gray family at "Pelican Ponds", before they sent cattle in 1851 to pioneer cattle grazing on the Bogong High Plains, from the Cobungra Station. Michael Francis probably met Hannah Gray while in Wangaratta.

Leaving this town he operated a butcher's shop in Omeo, then at Dargo and at the gold diggings at Jericho and the Jordan. He also worked as a horse-breaker and wandered as far as the Blue Mountains. Returning to Omeo, he selected land at Cobungra and married Ned Gray's daughter, Hannah. It was from here that he joined with his brother Tom in sending cattle up to graze on the Bogong High Plains.

Michael Francis and Hannah had five sons — Patrick, Michael, Charlie, George and Ned, and Charlie's three sons were Jack, Patrick and Charlic.

Charlie, whose paternal grandfather was Dennis McNamara and whose maternal grandfather was Ned Gray, is continuing an unbroken family connection with Bogong High Plains grazing that stretches back almost 130 years. Only the Pendergasts of Omeo can claim a longer continuous occupancy of Victorian Alpine Country. Charlie is grazing the same country that his grandfather ran — Bucketty and Dinner Plain to the head of Bundarrah, a holding of some 19000 acres and in addition he shares 6500 acres with Cobungra Station.

It is erroneously stated (on pages 264—270) that Young's Hut was burnt in 1930 or 1931, but prior to this the S.E.C. transported and erected a pre-fabricated hut for use by their surveyors doing preliminary work on the Kiewa Hydro Electric Scheme. When the S.E.C. no longer required the hut, Charlie and Naughton of Cobungra bought it for £16 and they still use it.

McNamara has a second hut on Dinner Plain and a third on Bucketty Plain. The interior of this hut is illustrated on page 264.

Pinnibar–Gibbo

*T*HE BOWEN MOUNTAINS, with a spur commencing at Mt Tambo and running north-east across Mt Leinster and Mt Misery splits the Tambo River and then the Limestone heads of the Murray on the eastern fall and Leinster and Benambra Creeks on the western side before reaching Mt Gibbo. From Gibbo the divide swings around to Mt Pinnibar before continuing north towards Corryong with Wheelers Creek (which becomes Nariel Creek and then Corryong Creek) on the west and Thougla Creek on the east.

Mostly the ridge is between 4000 and 4500 feet with Gibbo rising to 5750 feet and the twin peaks of Pinnibar reaching 5100 and 5200 respectively, before dropping away as it approaches Corryong.

The area around Gibbo and Pinnibar was not used for summer grazing until just before the turn of the century, although it was well known to the earliest settlers. Charles Wheeler settled at Nariel in January 1842, and found his way up Nariel Creek to the upper section which bears his name. He was, however, more concerned with possum hunting than cattle grazing.

From the Omeo Plains, Stirling's map of 1880 (refer endpapers) showed a track running around Macfarlane's Lookout then heading up Benambra Creek, skirting the heads of Gibbo River, around Mt Gibbo and then dropping down to Tom Groggin. So, although known, the grazing potential was ignored until 1899

THE GIBSONS

John Gibson came from the Orkney Isles and settled first at Orbost. He had five sons — John, David, Joseph, William and James.

James came to Corryong in 1899 and settled at upper Thougla. A spur from near his property led up on to Pinnibar in about fifteen miles with Gibbo about four miles further on. Here was summer grazing for his cattle and Joseph Gibson took out the first grazing licence for the area in 1899. He died in 1919 and his son Joseph acquired the run and has held it since. Today Joseph's sons Lachlan and John assist their father. The 29,000 acres run has thus been held by the Gibsons for eighty-one years.

Ranging through well defined areas of Woollybutt, peppermint and snow-gum the forest grazing is mostly open country without scrub and with small snow-plains on Gibbo and Pinnibar. The cattle are provided with salt troughs and these provide focal points for mustering. The Gibsons had huts at Thougla, Surveyors Creek, Pinnibar and Wheeler's Creek at Horseshoe Bend (below the snow-line).

The Gibsons have always run Herefords and favour those of darker configuration, these being less susceptible to "pink-eye", an affliction which has affected some of the lighter coloured cattle in the district.

Their leases adjoin Tom Groggin and they were run neighbours of John Pierce of "Greg Greg" when John Riley managed his run.

Trout were first released in the streams in the 1912–1915 period and quickly multiplied. Then cormorants discovered the fish and provided keen competition for the fishermen who came to try their luck.

Joseph Gibson occasionally rides across to Benambra and has done the trip in a single day. However, he says, if he stops to do a bit of fishing on the way, it is a two day trip!

Timber millers have pushed their logging roads into the area and they are cutting the stands of fine timber. The Gibsons, however, having grazed the area for over 80 years hope the leases will be unaffected and allow them to continue running their Herefords in what has always been "Gibson country".

"In Memory of the Man from Snowy River"
Jack Riley's grave and headstone in the
Corryong Cemetery.

Around the Camp Fire

Campfire near Cobbler Stockyard at Christmas 1935.

*A*BUSH PUB is as good a place as any to hear the local gossip, meet the identities and occasionally pick up a good yarn. The "Star" at Harrietville was no exception. On my first visit, Alex and Bill, a couple of veteran drovers had just got back from a week on the road with a mob of cattle. After their customary few beers, Alex said to the barman, "W'jer 'appen to 'ave a niner? Me 'n Bill 's gunner 'ave a party ternite." The answer being in the affirmative, Alex and Bill accompanied the barman down to the cellar and struggled back, managing the nine gallon keg between them. Safely trundled out through the swing doors and out into Alex's gig, Bill followed the barman back into the hotel to settle the account. As he turned to leave, the barman called, "Hey! What about the glasses?" Bill paused, stroked his chin and said, "Glasses?" "Yeah", answered the barman, "nine gallons, you'll need a few glasses". "Give us two", said old Bill. "Two!" queried the barman. "Aw well", said old Bill, "better make it three - just in case we break one!"

We were back at the "Star" a few Christmases later. Train to Wangaratta and a slow bus to Harrietville dropped us there at around midnight, not the best hour to pitch a tent, so we sought beds for the night. It was in the days of six o'clock closing and the barman was doing his best to empty the bar. "Time, gentlemen, PLEASE!" he was pleading. Some character answered, "Ten to twelve!" but the barman was not amused.

We made our request for three beds and were pointed in the direction of one of several cabins in the hotel yard. We entered the nominated one and by the feeble light of a match discovered that an inebriated gentleman, fully clothed, including overcoat and muddy boots had prior occupancy of one bed. We politely informed the barman. "Bloody hell!" he muttered and moved decisively towards the cabin. Confirming our story, he produced a key, locked the door from the outside and said, "He got in for nothing, but it will cost him the price of a 3-bed cabin to get out in the morning. Unless he kicks the door down, and then it'll cost him PLENTY!"

We got another cabin.

We had arrived at dusk at a cattlemen's hut, while on a trip across the Bogong High Plains. Dinner was cooked in the failing daylight and eaten by candlelight. My companions, inquisitively searching the hut's shelves discovered a treasure - a glass jar containing honey - left behind by earlier visitors. Bread toasted over the log fire and a liberal spread of honey made a memorable supper.

Next morning, at breakfast, my companions enquired the whereabouts of the honey. "It was empty", I prevaricated. "I threw it out." I was eyed with suspicion, but the explanation was accepted, with, I believe, some reservation. I had achieved a degree of diplomacy beyond my years, for how else does one explain that the honey, so enjoyed the evening before, had contained the corpse of a mouse?

.   .   .   .   .

It is unwise to rely on left-overs in huts to augment your meagre food supply. Jimmy, on his first long trip in our company, was intrigued with the dampers which it was our custom to cook in the hot ashes every evening. At Greymare's Hut, midway through our trip, Jimmy excitedly announced his discovery of a sizeable bag of flour and believing he had learnt the art, set about making the King size of all dampers. A camp oven in the hut was two-thirds filled with Jimmy's dough and duly buried in a huge heap of glowing ashes. After a suitable interval, the damper was pronounced 'done' and Jimmy carried it to safety, to await cooling and the morrow.

Next morning an excited J. attempted to cut his damper, first with a knife and then with a tomahawk. To no avail. The flour had been 'plain' and it requires self-raising, or the addition of baking powder for successful damper cooking! In disgust, Jimmy rolled his damper down the slope in front of the hut. It careered on its way, gathering momentum, until finally it made contact with a protruding boulder and shattered. And so did the boulder!

The following story is attributed to a north-eastern stockman, but it was re-told by a newspaperman, so its accuracy may be suspect. A small hound of uncertain parentage, bearing the name "Mr. Chips", lived on a country property. His favourite sport, almost amounting to a passion, was chasing possums. Now, it happened that on this property lived a King-sized bushy tail possum, who on the day in question was ambling sedately across the grass from one tree to another. Houn'dog sprang into action, covered the distance between his starting point and old bushy-tail at top speed and sank his teeth into old man possum's tail. Possum shifted into top, leapt for the nearest tree, scrambled up the trunk, out and along a branch and stopped only a foot or so short of its wavering end. He was, of course, in his element, some forty feet above the ground. Mr Chips was still grimly hanging on, his teeth firmly grasping the bushy tail. He then chanced to look down, saw the ground a great distance below, and paniced and let out the doggy equivilent of "HELLLLP!". To do which, of course, he opened his mouth and promptly plumeted earthwards.

Onlookers are reported to have heard the old bushy-tail call out, "Good-bye, Mr Chips". The little hound hit the ground with a sickening thud, lay there for some time, and then limped unsteadily back to his kennel.

The moral, of course, is "If you're in trouble, keep your mouth shut!"

Alan vouches for this story, but knowing Alan . . . !

He was camping one evening an the bank of a creek that adjoined a dairy farm. The sturdy lady of the property was bringing the cows in for milking, but one decided to pause when mid-way across the creek. No amount of pleading, threatening or bombardment with clods of earth had the desired effect and finally madam hitched her skirt above her ample knees and shod in gum-boots, waded into the stream, pausing only long enough to pluck a very prickly branch of blackberry from the bushes lining the creek. Cow, unperturbed, stood placidly in mid-stream, chewing the cud, until madam swooped, lifted the cow's tail and applied the prickly branch with all the force she could muster. The cow, emulating her illustrious and legendery ancestor who had jumped over the moon, leapt from the water, scrambled up the steep bank and made a new track through a dense clump of blackberries. Not, however, before she had left behind a bow wave of sufficient dimension to capsize madam in mid-stream!

The late W. F. "Bill" Waters, doyen of bushwalkers, knew and was respected by most of the mountain cattlemen of his time. In the late '20s he took a small party into the high country east of Benambra and "Big Jack" Pendergast went along with a couple of pack-horses. (Never, never take pack horses without their cattleman owner - they have an uncanny knack of departing in the night and forelegs securely hobbled, kangaroo hopping half-way home before dawn!). One day, a pea-soup fog descended on the party as they slowly made their way forward. "Big Jack" proceeded cautiously, peering ahead for landmarks, while Bill, true to his Rover Scout training was consulting his map and compass at frequent intervals. "Big Jack", like most cattlemen had no time for such refinements as maps or compasses and was unimpressed. (An irreverent bushwalker once declared, when safely out of Bill Gillio's hearing, that "He wouldn't need a map, he's got his pony and dog to lead him home safely, if he gets 'bushed'.)

Somewhat amused at Bill's reliance of map and compass, "Big Jack" swung round in the saddle, looked straight at Bill Waters and asked, "Where's Kosci, Bill?" Treating the matter seriously, Bill oriented his map and compass, deliberated for a moment and then extended his arm, indicating the direction of the mountain. "Big Jack" spat with unerring accuracy at a spot on the ground and said, "If that's where Kosci is, we're bloody well lost".

In the years that followed, I was with Bill on many trips and at some unexpected time on almost every trip, some wag was sure to ask, "Where's Kosci, Bill?". The old master was never allowed to forget that you can't point the way to a bushman.

.   .   .   .   .

Snakes, when met along the track, are seldom the subject of amusement - at least until afterwards. A few years after the turn of the century, my mother and two of her sisters were making their way sedately along a country road, not far from *Pelican Ponds,* Gray's old station, from whence came the first cattle to graze the Bogong High Plains.

The three sisters were trotting along serenely in a gig, when the pony, more observant than they, espied a snake on the road ahead, shied, swerved to one side, avoided the snake himself, but ran over it with the near side wheel. The snake, caught temporarily by spoke and rim was thrown high into the air and landed, wriggling frantically, in the apron of the gig. The three young ladies immediately 'bailed out' and the pony emulated Paleface Adios, as he headed for the horizon!

.   .   .   .   .

Coming down off Mt Buller, via Little Buller and a spur calculated to lead us to the Howqua River and Fry's (not a recommended route, however desperate the situation) we slithered over loose scree and steep rocky slopes until we reached a small tributary of the Howqua. The day was hot and the banks almost impassable with thick scrub, so we elected to wade down-stream. Happily we splashed our way, almost knee-deep in the cool water. Then, without any warning, Eddie, who was leading, made one giagintic leap that landed him on the left bank. Slightly bemused, I enquired of him, "What was that for, what happened?" "Stevo," he replied, "I saw a bloody snake swimming upstream, and you didn't!"

.   .   .   .   .

An hour later we were at Frys' and we called in to find Fred and Steve busy in a harness shed. Steve was sitting on a stool, a whisky bottle, emptied to the half-way mark at his elbow, his face twisted in agony, bemoaning the torture he was enduring from an impacted wisdom tooth. The imperturbable Fred, was nonchantly repairing some harness straps, completely indifferent to Steve's plight.

As we entered, Fred nodded a greeting (he never wasted words) and Steve, rising from his stool reached up for a rusted and blackened pair of farrier's pliers that were hanging on a nail. He held them in the direction of Eddie and pleaded for the offending tooth to be pulled out. Eddie paled at the thought. He was not lacking in courage, having on a previous trip, stood while a cattleman plying a 12 foot stockwhip, flicked half a cigarette from between his lips, without removing half his nose. But this time, Eddie demurred at the suggestion of entering the dentistry profession with such equipment. Steve pleaded, but in vain. As we swung our packs to our shoulders to proceed on our way, Steve wailed, "What am I going to do? What am I bloody well going to do?" Eddie, never at a loss for an answer, replied, "Keep sippin' the whisky, Steve. Keep sippin' the whisky."

. . . . . .

Next afternoon, we reached Mansfield, then a cattle town - the infant timber industry had not made any significant impact . As was mandatory for bushwalkers, we made our first call at the "Delatite". A fortnight's 'growth', dirty clothes and sweat-stained bodies could wait, but the dust had to be cleared from our throats. "When did you blokes get in?" the barman somewhat unnecessarily enquired. Eddie solemnly checked his watch and answered "Thirty four seconds ago - three beers please." "Then you missed the fun on New Year's Day?" asked the barman, putting three glasses before us. Eddie swallowed his beer before replying, "What happened?" and the barman's tale unfolded.

It appeared that on New Year's Eve - the year was 1938 - a few of the 'boys', in an endeavour to liven up the festivities a little, waited for the inhabitants to head homewards, then visited the Shire Sanitary Depot, some distance out of town, harnessed themselves up to the 4-wheel waggon, already loaded with empties in preparation for next nights 'collection', and silently hauled the vehicle back into town. They parked it outside the front door of the "Delatite". As an added touch they attached to the side, the hotel's sign which announced, "Under R.A.C.V. patronage."

The odoriferous waggon attracted attention of the hotel's patrons early next morning. Some Shire councillors, however, were 'not amused' and they requested the local Police Sergeant to apprehend the offenders. Sarj, himself was amused at the prank, but Justice must appear to be done. Donning his tunic and cap, he set off in quest of one or more of the practical jokers.

In the Mansfield of 1938, it did not require the deductive powers of a Sexton Blake to guess who at least one or two of the suspects might be. The identity of must of the likely 'boys' was fairly predictable. A couple of streets from the station, Sarj spotted one of the hapless youths, who on seeing the Law approaching, made a belated effort to hurry on his way.

Sarj inserted two fingers of his left hand between his teeth and gave an old fashioned whistle. Aforesaid youth halted and looked over his shoulder to see Sarj's right hand extended and his index finger beckoning him. "G' day, Sarj, 'ow yer goin'? "I'm still chuckling over the practical joke of leaving the 'honey cart' in the main street, last night", replied the Sergeant. "Bloody good fun, everybody's amused" he continued. The youth, somewhat reassured, smiled. "Now", said the Sergeant in a friendly tone, "please tell me, WHO BLOODY WELL DID IT? YOU AND WHO ELSE?"

There was no escape, and the offenders were duly named. "Six of you, eh!" said Sarj. "Well I don't intend to make a big deal out of it, but you do understand that I must read you all a lecture. Slap your wrists and tell you not to do it again. So, make sure you are all at the Station at 2 o'clock sharp. 2 o'clock sharp, mind you, or I'll have to come and get you."

Chuckling to himself, Sarj hurried back to the "Delatite" for a well deserved glass, and to send a message over the Bush Telegraph, that means of communication whose speed and efficiency has never been equalled by Telecom.

Sharp at 2 o'clock, a knock on the Sergeant's door announced the appearance of six rather sheepish 'boys'. "Bloody good stunt you pulled last night, fellows", smiled the Sergeant. "How far did you have to drag the cart?" "About two miles", was the reply. "Two miles, eh!" said Sarj. "Well get over there and PULL THE BLOODY THING BACK".

Shepherded to the main street by the Sergeant, the dejected youths were dismayed to find approximately half the populace in attendance (the Bush Telegraph had done its job) and to the rousing cheers of the onlookers, they trundled the cart back to whence it came.

Almost forty years later I happened to call in at the "Delatite" and recounted the story to an obviously disbelieving young barman. Then, glancing up the bar to an 'old-timer' he asked, "Jack, you were here before the War, do you recall the incident?" "Bloody oath, I do", replied Jack, "I had to help pull the cart!"

. . . . .

Cattlemen are generally more than a match for inquisitive 'new-chum' bushwalkers. 'Dad' Fitzgerald was no exception. "How many cattle would there be in that mob over there?" he was once asked. "A hundred and nine-teen" he quickly replied. "A hundred and nineteen?" queried the astonished new-chum. "How can you count them so quickly?" "A trick the old man once taught me", replied 'Dad' Fitzgerald. "Just count the legs and divide by four!"

Signposts

Snowpole on the Bogong High Plains - invaluable in winter.   *(right)*

The Kelly Tree in the Tolmies - re-cut after the original was burnt.

Stanley's Name Tree on the King-Howqua Divide, 1896 *(centre right)*

Two trees on the way to Mt Wellington.   The carvings are credited to John Wilson, a bushman-journalist-historian of the Avon Shire, who disappeared mysteriously in 1954. *(bottom left and right)*.

INDEX

Mt Torbreck 150, 152
Mt Trooper 37
Mt Typo 90
Mt Typo Cattle Station 91, 142
Mt Useful 187
Mt Wellington 81, 90, 167, 168, 170,
172–177, 179, 182, 184, 185, 187,
188, 189, 191, 193, 277, 307, 318,
322, 328, 329, 332
Mt Whitelaw 147
Mt Whitelaw Hut 147, 149
Mt Wills 284
Mt Yorke Station 229, 239
Mueller, Baron von 143, 163, 222,
223, 224, 227
Muir, W 229, 239
Mullindolingong 229, 238
Murendal River 3
Murphy's Forest 8, 304
Murray River 1, 223, 225, 334
Mustering 196–201
Mustering Flat 147, 149
Mutter, Miss 299, 300, 301
Myrtleford 58, 60, 66, 91, 279

Mc

MacAllister, Matthew 1
Macalister, Lachlan 2, 5, 10, 11
Macalister River 85, 131, 167, 168,
172, 173, 187, 188, 307, 308, 310
Macalister Springs 131
McConnell, W.T. 285
MacCrae, John 226
McCullock, C.C. 12
Macfarlane, Ellen, 170; James 1, 2,
5, 9, 14, 20, 167, 168; Malcolm
167, 168, 308, 320, 322; Violet
169
Macfarlane's Creek 167, 322; Flat 1,
2, 3, 39, 45, 167; Hut 167;
Lookout 20, 334; Saddle 167;
Track 168
McGrath, Thomas 167
McGuffie, Jas 29, 33
McIlroy, Joe 137
MacIntosh, Flora 168
McKay, Jim 283
Mackay, Matthew 48
McKellar's Crossing 47, 51
McKenzie, Colin 12; Hector 27, 30,
37, 39, 42, 44, 49; Malcolm 12
McKenzie, Malcolm K. 229, 259.
260, 261
McKerrall, Detective 72, 73
Mackillop, George 2
McKillop's Bridge 51
McLean, A and Co. 49, 290
Macleod, Arch 5, 11; John Campbell
11; Norman Patrick 11
McMichael, Alf 328; Arthur 328;
John 328; William 328
McMichael's Hut 328, 330
McMillan, Angus 1, 2, 3, 5, 7, 10, 11,
68, 168, 309, 323
McMillan's Lookout 7
McMillan's Smoke House 59

McNamara, Charlie 126, 129, 264,
278, 333; Dennis Snr. 333; Dennis
Jnr. 333; Edward 226, 333;
George 333; Jack 333; Michael
Francis 333; Patrick 226, 333
McNamara Huts 273
McRae, John 212, 215, 216, 217,
218
McVeighs 147

N

Nariel Creek 334
National Parks Association 149
National Trust Classification 237
Native Cat 3
Native Dog 3, 28
Naughton's 289, 333
Navigation Creek 7, 175
Neilson, John 126
Nesbitt, Thomas 60
Newman 152
Newry 173
Nicholas 152, 159; Henry Thomas
158, 160; Les 158, 159, 160
Nicholas Huts 160
Niggerheads 222, 264
Nigothoruk Creek 190
Nine Mile 3, 4
Nixon, Hugh 68
"Noon's" 109, 123
Norris, Harry 137
North Wellington River 167
Norton Brothers 284
Norton, J. 328
Nunniong 12
Nunniong Hut 21
Nunniong Mt. 9
Numla Mungie (Ensay) 2, 5, 10, 11,
12

O

O'Brien, Annie 170
O'Brien, Harry 137
O'Connell Centenary Hotel 48
O'Keefe, Jim 42
Old Wangaratta Bridge 222
Omeo 1–5, 8, 9, 13, 16, 20, 24, 28,
78, 94, 124, 126, 127, 129, 168,
214, 221–224, 226, 237, 258, 259,
278, 280–283, 285, 286, 297, 301,
303
Omeo A (Homeo) 5, 6, 14, 16
Omeo B Station (Omio) (Mt Pleasant
Station) 1, 5, 6, 14, 33, 46, 49, 167,
299
Omeo Plains 7
Omeo Gold Rush 4, 7; Shire Council
127; Telegraph 9
Orbost 334
O'Riley, Barnett 262
O'Rourkes 27, 30, 31, 32, 33, 36,
40–44, 46, 47, 49
O'Rourke, Andrew (death of) 31;
Christopher 33; Edward 33; Eliza
31; Elizabeth Anne 34; David 33;
James 31, 48

Ovens River 163, 227, 276
"Overlander" 225

P

Painter Creek Hut 21
Paradise Plains 152, 153
Parker's Corner 147, 149
Parslow, James 288, 289; Miss 16
Paterson, "Banjo" 76, 94, 96, 169
Payne, John (See John Paynter and
Bogong Jack)
Paynter, John (See Bogong Jack)
Pearson, William 168
Peck, Harry 169
"Pelican Ponds" 221, 333, 339
Pendergasts 4, 14, 15, 33, 45, 303,
304, 333; "Big Jack" 18, 19, 20,
26, 338, 339; C.H.V. 6, 15, 17, 18;
Cornelius 15, 18; James 14, 15, 16,
17, 20, 21, 23, 24; Jane Vince 7,
304; John 2, 5, 6, 14, 15, 16, 17,
20; Louis 18; Patrick 18; Thomas
2, 5, 14, 15, 16; William 2, 5, 6, 14,
15, 16, 17, 20; W.J.C. 282; Mrs
W.A. 303, 304
Pendergast's Hut 21
"Penders Court" 8, 14, 16, 20
Pender, "Straightly" 4
Penny 300
Peterson 229
Phelan's 292
Phillips, Arthur 66, 69, 70, 73, 133
Pierce, John 95, 97, 335
Pierce Jones and Williams 229, 259
Pilot, The 20
Pinch River 3, 4, 19, 27, 54, 55
Platt, Jack 247
Playground, The 3, 45
Plummer, William 117
Poley Range 152
Porepunkah 164, 294
Port Albert 6, 34, 48, 322
Port Albert Inn 322
Post Yard 321
Pretty Valley 12, 222, 237, 260, 278
Primrose Gap (Riggall's Gap) 315,
321
Purgatory Spur 173, 174

R

Ram's Head Range 203
Randell, Margaret 79
Range, Gibbo 221, 222
Rawson 94
Rawson, Charlie 147, 148, 151;
George 147, 148, 150; Harry 147,
151; Harry Jnr. 148
Rawson, Joseph 288
Rawson's Hut 148, 151
Razorback (Buller area) 140
Razorback (Feathertop–Hotham)
222, 276
Razorback (Mt Wellington) 173, 177
Razorback (Snowy River area) 54
Razorback Hut (Delatite area) 144